Word PAINTING

A Guide to Writing More Descriptively

REBECCA McCLANAHAN

WRITER'S DIGEST BOOKS
CINCINNATI, OHIO

Word Painting: A Guide to Writing More Descriptively. Copyright © 1999 by Rebecca McClanahan. Printed and bound in the United States of America. All rights reserved. No part of this book may be reproduced in any form or by any electronic or mechanical means including information storage and retrieval systems without permission in writing from the publisher, except by a reviewer, who may quote brief passages in a review. Published by Writer's Digest Books, an imprint of F&W Publications, Inc., 1507 Dana Avenue, Cincinnati, Ohio 45207. (800) 289-0963. First edition.

Other fine Writer's Digest Books are available from your local bookstore or direct from the publisher.

Visit our Web site at www.writersdigest.com for information on more resources for writers. To receive a free biweekly E-mail newsletter delivering tips and updates about writing and about Writer's Digest products, send an E-mail with "Subscribe Newsletter" in the body of the message to newsletter-request@writersdigest.com, or register directly at our Web site at www.writersdigest.com.

03   02   01   00   99   5   4   3   2

Library of Congress Cataloging-in-Publication Data

McClanahan, Rebecca
   Word painting : a guide to writing more descriptively / by Rebecca McClanahan.
     p.   cm.
   Includes bibliographical references and index.
   ISBN 0-89879-861-2
   1. English language—Rhetoric. 2. Description (Rhetoric) 3. Creative writing.
   I. Title.
PE1427.M38   1999
808'.042—dc21   98-48002
                                                                         CIP

Editor: David Borcherding
Production editor: Michelle Howry
Designer: Brian Roeth
Production coordinator: John Peavler
Cover illustration by Edouard Manet (1832-1883), "Claude Monet and His Wife in the Floating Studio." Neue Pinakothek, Munich, Germany.

For my father,
who showed me the holiness of detail,

and my mother,
whose all-accepting eye takes in the big picture

ACKNOWLEDGMENTS

Jack Heffron invited me to write this book, then guided my early vision and revision. David Borcherding suggested the book's title and advised me on matters of content. My critique group—Gail Peck, Diana Pinckney and Dede Wilson—encouraged me along the way. Deno Trakas and Dede Wilson read the completed manuscript and offered sound advice. And my husband, Donald Devet, provided coffee, wine, humor and an attentive ear.

I am grateful.

CONTENTS

INTRODUCTION

When the editors of Writer's Digest Books approached me about writing a book on description, I responded the way I respond to all new challenges: *Yes. No. Well, I'll think about it.* *Yes* is the child in me, taking my seat on the roller coaster that will whiplash me into the tunnel, up the rickety mountain, around the next exhilarating loop. *No* is the adult, walking away from the ticket booth: What if the car derails? Who's driving this train, anyway? Does my insurance cover roller coasters? Most writers, I suspect, hear both these voices, often simultaneously, each time they put pen to paper. And I suspect that every book is a duet of opposing voices attempting some semblance of harmony.

Finally, *I'll think about it* won out. When I thought about it, I realized I was being offered the chance to combine three of my primary passions: writing, reading, and teaching.

As a writer, I know the daily struggle of describing the world around me and the world that dwells only in my head; my recycling bin holds evidence of that struggle. I also know the occasional click of the lock, the satisfaction of words slipping into place, and those few unspoiled seconds when the images in the developing tray coalesce. Yes, there's the barn in all its rotting splendor. There's the lumpy boy slicking back his cowlick and approaching the long-legged girl.

As a reader, I know which descriptions move me to laughter, terror or unwept tears. I can point to those I wish I had written. Wait, I say, running alongside you with a book in my hand: Listen to this one. You've got to hear this!

And as a teacher, I've sat up nights—for nearly thirty years now—charting paths to lead my students from there to here, and back again. It's one thing to recognize an effective description; quite another, to guide someone to write one.

Since *Word Painting* grew from these three passions, it combines direct instruction with personal reflections on the reading and writing process. I set forth basic guidelines for effective description and suggest specific writing exercises. (Some exercises are embedded within the text; others appear at chapter ends.) Along the way, I point out some of my favorite descriptive passages from novels, stories, essays and poems, suggesting ways to use these passages as models for our own writing. And occasionally I take you behind the scenes of this writer's ongoing journey to describe what she sees, hears, tastes, smells, touches and imagines.

The book is organized around three main concepts: *eye, word* and *story*. After establishing what we mean by *description* and summarizing the elements of effective description, I move directly into a discussion of the writer as the beholding eye— and, in turn, the beholding ear, mouth, nose and hand. Like painters, writers are the receptors of sensations from the real world and the world of the imagination, and effective description demands that we sharpen our instruments of perception. So in the first few chapters, I suggest practical ways to increase our attention to the real world: note-taking, journal-writing, sketching, research, eye-search and I-search. I also discuss techniques for engaging the eye of the imagination and discovering what the inner eye sees.

As I move from *eye* to *word*, I consider how to render our subjects clearly, accurately and imaginatively. Though engaging the senses is an important component of word painting, it takes us only so far; we must also describe those sensory images in a fresh way. This involves not only avoiding clichés, but also engaging the eye of the imagination through action-based description and effective figures of speech. In addition, fresh description requires attention to the musical qualities of language. The *word* sections of the book deal with forming descriptions that are accurate, sensory, imaginative and musical.

Finally, moving from *eye* and *word* into *story*, I explore how description contributes to the overall story, poem or nonfiction piece. How do we spot and evoke the revealing detail, spatially organize our descriptions, and weave description into the narrative arc? How do we use description to develop believable characters and settings, establish point of view, modulate tension and move the plot along? How can description reveal our story's theme and suggest the prevailing tone, mood or feeling? These are the concerns that dominate the *story* sections of the book.

I am grateful to every writer whose descriptions have challenged me to see the world in new ways, and to every writing teacher who encouraged me—and those who did not. I am grateful also to the thousands of students with whom I've worked, the five-year-olds and the eighty-five-year-olds, the beginners and the experts, and most of all, the continuers. And to readers like you, who with every page you turn in this book, complete the painting I've begun.

WHAT IS DESCRIPTION?

If I were fully conscious of my surroundings at this moment, I would describe the light through the miniblinds, the way it searches out the apples in the glass bowl, buffing them to an unnatural sheen. I bought them for their fragrance, not their freshness, so even if you were to close your eyes, you'd know you were in the presence of apples. You would smell the heavy softening, the sweet rotting where apple ends and cider begins.

Or I would tell you how the sofa cushion feels beneath my bare neck—rough and scratchy, a bit lumpy. A few minutes ago, before I lay down, I pounded the cushion with my fist to loosen the foam stuffing, and now it's fighting back. If I were noticing such things right now, I might even describe the pinprick tingling in my toes (a result of my feet being slung over the sofa back) and the stupefying sensation of willing the toes to move, as if they belonged to a stranger.

If you were sitting in the chair beside me, you'd probably notice the sounds filling the open window—the pneumatic wheeze as a bus rounds the corner, a jay's raspy squawk, the rhythmic clackclackclack of a roller skater counting each sidewalk seam. You might look in my direction, start to speak, then, noticing the open book in my hands, think better of it. Think better of stirring a reader from the world of her book. I might bolt, like anyone shaken too suddenly from a dream.

The place I've entered is what John Gardner, in his classic book *The Art of Fiction*, calls the fictional dream. Because the writer has done her job, the world of the book I am reading has become, for the moment at least, more real than the world at my elbow. Books this good should carry a warning: *Your quiche might burn, your child escape his playpen, the morning glory vine strangle your roses, and you'll never know.*

As a reader lost in a fictional dream, it's not my job to worry how the writer accomplishes her task. My job is to turn the pages, to enter the dream and remain there until someone, or something, wakes me. Most often that something is the work that awaits me at my desk. The words I've not yet written lure me, like silver trout flashing their fins. If only I could net them. If only I could create the kind of dream a reader would willingly enter.

Fiction writers aren't the only ones who create this dream. Poets do it too, and essayists and memoirists and biographers and travel writers and nature writers and journalists and letter writers. Even, at times, business writers and those who draft advertising copy—once I nearly drowned in a catalog description of a blue gauze dress. Diarists, perhaps because they are freed from the demands of an audience, create some of the most memorable dreams. My great-aunt Bessie's diary of 1897 is filled with vivid passages. Turning the pages, I dwell in a world I never knew, a world that becomes, in that moment, more real than the one I inhabit:

> This morning everything was ridged with frost, the sky cloudless except for a few fleecy ones in the east and the sun shining on the frost-beauty.

A few days later she writes:

> The mice and the moles have gone into cahoots. Yes, sir. Teamed up. I caught a—well, a something—in the trap in the bedroom, he had a mole head, a lovely mole jacket and mouse feet. What do they call a cross such as that?

Months passed, and one morning Bessie found that a haystack had tumbled onto the sheep.

> We slung hay high, wide and fancy for a while. It wedged against the fence so we couldn't use forks to any advantage, just pull with our hands and how the sweat did pour but we got the poor things out alive, my old Pet among them.

What lures me into Aunt Bessie's world is, in part, the power of her descriptions. This is no small gift, no mere ornamental flourish. Description is not, as one of my students once called it, "all that flowery stuff." Or, if description *is* the flowering, it is also the root and stem of effective writing. Every form creates its own challenges and provides its own props to the writer. The novelist has at his disposal the elements of plot and character; the poet, rhythms and rhymes; the nonfiction writer, arsenals of information. Almost all writers, however, employ description and can benefit from increasing their descriptive powers.

The afternoon sun has moved. Now it stripes the wall rather than the shiny apples. My toes have stopped tingling. I close the book, grab an apple from the bowl and walk across the living room, down the fourteen smoothly varnished steps that lead into my study. I'm fully awake now. No longer a reader adrift in the fictional dream, I've washed ashore, stunned and reeling. I blink my eyes. Yes, it's all coming back now. The oak desk, the ink-splotted blotter, the window, the empty page. My ballpoint pen is cocked and loaded. I pick it up and begin.

WHAT IS DESCRIPTION?

What do we mean by *description*? Perhaps no word is more commonly used in discussions of reading and writing. As writers, we struggle over descriptive passages. As readers, we close the cover on books that fail to accurately describe our world or the world of the imagination. As teachers or editors, we write in the margin "I can't visualize the character. Can you *describe* him?" or "I'm just not situated in the barbershop. Maybe if you *described* it more clearly . . .'' But what do we really mean? What are we asking for?

In the fields of science, linguistics, grammar and mathematics, description concerns itself with the study of things *as they exist,* with bringing forth the attributes of subjects rather than simply explaining or labeling them. In literature, description refers to the language used to bring these attributes to the reader's mind. Description is an attempt to present as directly as possible the qualities of a person, place, object or event. When we describe, we make impressions, attempting through language to represent reality. Description is, in effect, *word painting.*

Theoretically speaking, description is one-third of the story-telling tripod. Exposition and narration are the other legs on which a story stands. Exposition supplies background information while narration supplies the story line, the telling of events, leaving description to paint the story's word pictures.

These are helpful concepts in theory. The problem is, no story exists in theory. It lives and breathes only in practice, as it unfolds on the page. In the real world of the story, description cannot be totally separated from exposition and narration. Sometimes description supplies information. Sometimes it moves the plot along. Although a theorist may assert that exposition, narration and description are discrete elements, a practicing writer knows that they form a trinity, an inseparable union of three-in-one.

Perhaps the best way to fully define description is by considering what it is *not:*

- Description is not, as we've already pointed out, "all that flowery stuff." It isn't mere embellishment, something we stitch to the top of our writing to make it more presentable.
- Description isn't optional. The success of all fiction, and most poetry and nonfiction, depends in part on description's image-making power.
- Description doesn't always mean detailing how something *looks.* One of the best descriptions I've ever read was written by a blind child. Evocative and memorable description is rooted not only in visual detail but in the smells, tastes,

textures and sounds of our world.
- Description doesn't begin on the page. It begins in the eye and ear and mouth and nose and hand of the beholder. To write good description, we must look long, hard and honestly at our world. Careful and imaginative observation may well be the most essential task of any writer.
- Description is not a way to hide from the truth. The world isn't always pretty, and describing our world honestly sometimes requires facing difficult, even ugly, subjects.
- Writing descriptively doesn't always mean writing gracefully. Description won't necessarily make our writing more refined, lyrical or poetic. Some descriptions demand uneven syntax and plainspoken, blunt prose. Jagged, even. Fragments too. Slice of chin. Buzz saw.
- Description doesn't always require a bigger vocabulary. *House* is probably a better choice than *domicile*, a *horse* is easier to visualize than an *equine mammal*, and *red blood* is brighter than *the sanguine flow of bodily fluids*.
- Writing descriptively doesn't necessitate writing more. Description isn't a steroid, something to make our language bigger and stronger, nor is it an additive promising more miles to the fictional gallon. Sometimes writing descriptively means writing less. Our three-hundred-word description of the wedding cake might need to lose two hundred words; it may need to disappear altogether.
- Description rarely stands alone. Most description exists as part of a larger poem, essay or story, seamlessly intertwined with other literary elements. Description isn't something we simply insert, block style, into passages of narration or exposition. Yes, sometimes we write passages of description. But the term passage suggests a channel, a movement from one place to another; it implies that we're going somewhere. That *somewhere* is the story.

WHAT MAKES DESCRIPTION EFFECTIVE?

For as long as writers and speakers have been shaping discourse, the question of what makes for good description has been debated. In Book III of *The Rhetoric of Aristotle*, penned more than two thousand years ago, Aristotle discusses several techniques for calling forth the qualities of an object or a scene. Although his suggestions are aimed primarily at orators of persuasive rhetoric, they apply to writers as well. Aristotle's treatise is not an exhaustive one, nor should it be swallowed whole, like a pill, in an attempt to cure our descriptive ills. But it does provide a starting point for identifying the qualities of descriptive writing while also suggesting ways to expand our repertoire of techniques.

First, good description is carefully worded. When our aim is conciseness, says Aristotle, naming a subject directly and precisely is the most effective route. It follows that we must know the correct terms for the objects, people, places and events we describe. Although description begins with an accurate naming of our subject, it also refers to precision of image. We must go beyond the correct name for something, selecting the word that will call forth the particular image, emotion or attitude our story requires. To accomplish this, we must use language that is, to quote Aristotle, "appropriate in sound and in sense." Good description goes beyond accuracy and precision to include the musical qualities of language. The sounds of our words and the cadences of our sentences must reinforce the content of our description.

Second, good description is sensory, making the audience or reader, as Aristotle suggests, "see things." Good description, like most powerful things in the world—a salty kiss, a dancer's leap, the fine brown hairs on a lover's arms—accomplishes more than we are consciously aware of. We may not notice its power until our blood begins to simmer or cool, the Windsor knot in our stomach tightens, our breath shifts to quick hard pants. This is due, in part, to description's root in the physical world. Good description almost always employs specific, concrete detail so the reader can "see" what is being described, or experience it through one of the other senses.

These sense impressions are enhanced, explains Aristotle, by "using expressions that represent things as in a state of activity," our third test for description. It is not enough simply to engage the senses. We must also represent the fictional dream through word pictures—and, wherever possible, these should be *moving* pictures. (Moving pictures are especially important in fiction, where a descriptive passage must push the plot along or nudge a character from here to there.) Good description can create the illusion of movement and vitality, bringing even a static object to life.

Fourth, good description often employs metaphor or other figurative language. Though we usually think of metaphor and simile in terms of poetry, Aristotle argues that the use of figurative language is at least as important in prose, since prose writers have fewer of the poet's other tools available to them—rhyme, meter and established poetic forms. Description that employs figurative language, he says, can lend "metaphorical life to lifeless objects."

Unfortunately, description might contain all these elements and still not be effective. Description must be judged not only for its intrinsic value but also for how it serves the larger story, poem or nonfiction piece. A five-hundred-word description of a deserted barn might ruin the suspense of one story yet supply a breathtaking climax for another. A description employing metaphor might be the perfect choice in one poem while cluttering the lyrical clarity of another. Simply by reading an isolated passage of description, we can conclude it is, say, lyrical or dramatic or physically revolting or sexually stimulating. But we cannot conclude it is *effective* until we see how it affects the total piece of writing.

These guidelines are intended only as starting places for expanding the ways we think about descriptive writing, not as rules to be blindly followed. If we confine ourselves to a few tried-and-true rules for description, our writing will never break free from mediocrity, never create the kind of literature that, to paraphrase Emily Dickinson, can blow the top of a reader's head off. And if we think of description only as a tool to accomplish some literary task, we are cutting ourselves off from all the other ways description can serve us, our readers, and the work itself.

THE REWARDS OF DESCRIPTION

In exchange for your careful attention to its needs, description promises many rewards:

- Descriptive passages create the illusion of reality, inviting the reader to move in, unpack his bags and settle in for a spell. They provide verisimilitude, what John Gardner calls the "proofs" that support and sustain your fictional dream.
- Description composed of sensory detail penetrates layers of consciousness, engaging your reader emotionally as well as intellectually.
- Carefully selected descriptive details can establish your characters and settings quickly and efficiently.
- As a framing device, description establishes the narrator's, or character's, point of view. Shifts in the description frame (or eye) can signal shifts in point of view or a significant change in the character.
- Well-placed descriptive passages can move your story along, shape the narrative line and unfold the plot.
- Descriptive passages can act as gear shifts, changing the pace of your story—speeding it up or slowing it down, thus increasing the story's tension.
- Description can serve as a transitional device, a way of linking scenes or changing time and place.
- Description can orchestrate the dance between scene and summary.
- Description can serve as a unifying thematic device, what Stanley Kunitz calls the "constellation of images" that appears and reappears in a literary work, suggesting the idea or feeling that lives beneath the story line.
- Description can provide the palette for gradations in mood and tone. Dip your brush in one description and the sky darkens; in another, and the sun breaks through.
- The language of your descriptions, its rhythms and sounds, can provide the equivalent of a musical score for the fictional dream, a subliminal music that plays beneath the story line.

AN INVITATION

The dictionary on my desk suggests three definitions for *describe*:

To transmit a mental image or impression
To trace or draw the figure of; to outline
To give a verbal account of; to tell about in detail

Considering each definition in turn, we can map our journey to more descriptive writing. "Mental image or impression" suggests *seeing*. "Outline" or "figure" suggests a representation, the image made *word*. "Account" or "telling" suggests a *story* to be transmitted.

To discover and describe images, we must engage our senses. Simply put, we must look, listen, taste, smell and touch the real world or the world of the imagination. We must also find the words that will represent this world, or, as is sometimes the case, allow the words to find us. Finally, we must consider how our descriptions are shaping the larger world of the story, poem, essay or whatever form our fictional dream has taken.

By suggesting this three-part model, I'm not implying that creating descriptions is a simple, three-step procedure. The creative process is hardly ever linear. It loops back upon itself like a snake devouring its own tail. For some writers story comes first; as the telling progresses, descriptions emerge. For other writers a physical, sensory detail is the starting point. Still others, particularly poets, find within the words themselves—the sounds and rhythms and shapes—the route to description. The order in which these processes occur is not important. What *is* important is that somewhere along the way we give full attention to each of these matters: eye, word and story.

CHAPTER TWO

THE EYE OF
THE BEHOLDER

W hile giving birth to her second child, my sister con-
tracted a bacterial infection that blinded her. At the
time, we didn't know the blindness would be tempo-
rary. The family wept, we walked the halls of Intensive Care, we
muttered the strange dialect people mutter at such times—half
curse, half prayer. We made promises we'd never keep. I offered
up (to God, the universe or anyone who might be listening)
my own eyes in exchange for my sister's. After all, she was a
photographer, though a lapsed one. I was a writer. What did I
need with eyes?

When my sister finally woke to light, she could not stop blinking, could not stop staring—at the hospital bed, the ceiling, her
new son, the back of her own hand. "Bring me my camera,"
she said. That was ten years ago. Today her walls are filled with
pictures her eyes have taken. She claims the world is brighter
than it used to be, the outlines more defined.

Amazing grace, it appears, is bestowed not on the perpetually
sighted but on those who "once were blind but now can see."
Just as youth is wasted on the young, eyes are wasted on those
of us who see. Or think we see. The problem with eyes is that
we get used to having them. We get used to seeing our same
old world in the same old way. Marriages end every day because
of this. On those evenings when I need to fall in love with my
life again, I step out the door, down the front steps, and past
the iron gate that surrounds our townhouse. For emphasis, I

slam the gate and listen for the clang that reverberates, traveling down each iron post.

I'm outside my life now, a visitor at the gate. I close my eyes long enough to erase the accustomed scene the Dorothy in me has yawned away. Then I take a deep breath, open my eyes, and I'm not in Kansas anymore. The lights are on (all things become more beautiful when lit from within) and there's a man standing at the second-floor window, holding a cat in his arms. What a handsome man, I think. Wouldn't it be nice to live in that house?

Description begins in the beholder's eye, and it requires *attention*. If we look closely enough and stay in the moment long enough, we may be granted new eyes. Or ears. On his album *Noel*, Paul Stookey (of the Peter, Paul and Mary trio) talks about his process of writing songs. "Sometimes," he says, "if you sit in one place long enough, you get used. You become the instrument for what it is that wants to be said."

Gee, you might be thinking. *If it's that easy, I should have finished a dozen novels by now.* And I'd nod right along with you, wondering why the hundreds of hours I've recently logged on the sofa haven't translated into a new book of poems.

What we've been doing, of course, has nothing to do with attention. An attendant is one who is present at an event, who waits expectantly. Attention is a servant's word; it requires work, concentration and patience at the task. Most of us simply don't stay in one place long enough to be used. I'm that way about the Magic Eye, that maze of lines and shapes that appears each Sunday in my local newspaper. I tried it a few times, but it just made me dizzy. My husband loves the Magic Eye. He steadies the paper in his hands, brings it to his nose, moves it forward slowly, stares straight ahead, blinks, screws up his forehead, stares again, until a light snaps on in his eyes, his forehead relaxes, a smile appears and I know I've once again missed the show. He saw it and I didn't. He saw it because he opened his eyes, he kept looking, and he expected to be surprised.

A few years ago I heard a radio interview with a scientist, a comet-hunter who admitted he had stayed a total of nine hundred hours at the eyepiece before he saw his first comet. His advice to novice hunters?

1. Stay at the eyepiece and keep looking.
2. Watch the sky every day.
3. Study as many established comets as you can so you'll know what one looks like when it appears.
4. Be patient. The do-or-die approach rarely works

The comet-hunter's advice could easily apply to those of us attempting to write more descriptively. In order to describe— the world at our elbow or the one that dwells within our imagination—we must first open our eyes. We must stay at the eyepiece. Depending on your writing process and style, the eyepiece could be the physical world, or it could be the world of the inner eye, the world of dreams and illusions. Or you might be a writer for whom the words themselves—their sounds, rhythms and shapes—create the world of the story or poem. No matter what your eyepiece is, put your writer's eye to it as often as possible, waiting for the forms to emerge, to change patterns and reconfigure themselves.

In the meantime, read the best literature you can find, particularly literature rich in detail, so you'll be able to recognize an effective description when one appears in your work. I say *when,* not *if,* for the comet *will* appear. The universe is stacked in favor of possibility. If we are patient enough, if we don't force the process but rather remain open to discovery, one day, probably when we least expect it, a comet will show itself. We'll know it by its earthborne dust, its solid head and the fiery tail that ignites the sky in front of our eyes.

THE NAKED EYE

Good description begins with observation. The most common things can yield startling surprises when we give our attention to them. Look at what Audre Lorde does with two ordinary household objects, the mortar and pestle her mother used for grinding spices:

The mortar was of a foreign fragrant wood, too dark for cherry and too red for walnut. To my child eyes, the outside was carved in an intricate and most enticing manner. There were rounded plums and oval indeterminate fruit, some long and fluted like a banana, others ovular and end-swollen like a ripe alligator pear. In between these were smaller rounded shapes like cherries, lying in batches against and around each other . . .

The pestle was long and tapering, fashioned from the same mysterious rose-deep wood, and fitted into the hand almost casually, familiarly. The actual shape reminded me of a summer crook-necked squash uncurled and slightly twisted. . . . Long use and years of impact and grinding within the bowl's worn hollow had softened the very surface of the wooden pestle, until a thin layer of split fibers coated the rounded end like a layer of velvet. A layer of the same velvety mashed wood lined the bottom inside the sloping bowl.

—from *Zami: A New Spelling of My Name*

To train your naked eye to see more intently, try this exercise in observation. Choose an ordinary object in your home. It might be something you use every day—a comb, a blanket, a salad bowl. Or it might be an object that's been around forever but is seldom used—your mother's wedding pearls, a hammer hanging on a pegboard, the avocado-green fondue pot from your first marriage. Place the object in the center of a bare table; if the object is too large or heavy to move, station yourself in front of it.

Set a timer for ten minutes and don't move until the time is up. During these ten minutes, your only job is to study the object. Stare at it. Notice every detail—its color, shape, each part that contributes to the whole. Don't allow yourself to be distracted from the task at hand. If a memory floats to the surface, something you associate with the object, try to bring yourself back to your physical examination of the object. (There will be time for memories later.) For now, focus all your attention on the object itself. You might wish to pick it up, turn it around or upside-down. Notice its heft, its texture. How does it feel in your hand, against your face? How does it smell?

When the timer goes off, begin writing a description of the object. Report what your eyes have seen and your hands have felt. Use sensory details that the reader will be able to imagine— colors, shapes, smells, textures. Concrete nouns will anchor your description. Use only those adjectives that call forth the qualities of the object; avoid adjectives that label or explain. Words like *lovely, old, wonderful, noteworthy* or *remarkable* are explanatory labels; they do not suggest sense impressions. Adjectives like *bug-eyed, curly, bumpy, frayed* or *moss-covered*, on the other hand, are descriptive. Although Lorde's description contains some labeling adjectives (*intricate, enticing*), most of her details are sensory and concrete, allowing us to experience the mortar and pestle as physical objects rather than as disembodied ideas.

After you've described the object's qualities in concrete, sensory terms, you may wish to explore qualities only your *imaginative* eye can see. During your ten minutes of observation, did your mind wander? Did the object remind you of something else? Did you recall a memory associated with the object? Continue your description with details your imaginative eye noticed. Lorde does this in a subsequent part of this same passage, describing how the mortar made her feel "secure and somehow full; as if it conjured up from all the many different flavors pounded into the inside wall, visions of delicious feasts both once enjoyed and still to come."

The naked eye provides us with sensory, concrete experiences. The imaginative eye opens up other worlds.

THE EYE OF IMAGINATION

"Sometimes the soul takes pictures of things it has wished for but never seen," wrote the poet Anne Sexton. Like the soul in Sexton's quote, the imaginative eye can photograph things we've never seen, and these imagined pictures are as important to the writer as the actual pictures that register with the naked eye. We can fill hundreds of notebooks with precise, accurate, realistic depictions of objects, people and events without once writing an authentic description. Effective description occurs only when the naked eye merges with the imaginative eye. As Eudora Welty phrased it, "fiction's whole world is human nature. . . . But the imagination is the only thing that can find out anything about it and the only way you can see."

But how, exactly, does the imagination teach us to see? Like *description, imagination* is a term tossed around casually in literary circles. We accept it the way we accept air into our lungs, with little thought of its molecular structure. According to my junior high school English teacher, imagination was what my writing lacked. She preferred "creative" writers like Joel Aspinall, the boy who sat in front of me and stared out the window a lot. Joel wrote stories about three-eyed aliens sprouting from daisy petals and jabbering a kind of truncated pig latin. My poem about my mother repotting a geranium was returned to me with a pale check mark and the teacher's suggestion that I beef up my description with more adjectives and similes, or, better yet, read one of Joel's stories to get my creative juices stirring.

Although this experience did not stop me from writing poems about my mother, it did stop me from showing them to English teachers. Imagination, it appeared, consisted in making things up, which didn't include writing about the things of my everyday world—the things I saw, heard, touched, smelled and tasted. I concluded that I'd never be a creative writer; I'd just write poems instead. I liked the way I felt when I was writing, the places my mind traveled. When I was writing about my mother repotting the geranium, I could almost smell the rich, moist compost and feel the grainy dirt in my hand. After several lines I began to see my mother brushing back a strand of her thick black hair with the edge of the trowel, though I'd never actually seen her do this. Or had I? It was hard to remember every detail. It was October, after all, when I wrote the poem, and she'd repotted the geranium the previous July.

It would be many years before I understood that I'd been writing imaginatively all along. Although I hadn't set out to invent anything, to make something appear out of thin air like a magician's dove, I was nevertheless writing from the eye of the imagination. I was doing what the poet Stanley Plumly talks about in his essay "Words on Birdsong": "Poets cannot make things up. Poets make things *from*—from memory; from matter that cannot be changed, only transformed; from the rock of fact that may disappear . . . but cannot be made, out of hand, to evaporate."

These are comforting words to those of us who fear we lack imagination because we're unable to "make things up." Rather than spend time and energy trying to invent something imaginary, we can focus on reseeing our old world through the imaginative eye. This eye is known by many aliases, among them *the mind's eye, the child's eye, the dream eye, the eye of memory, the eye in the back of your head.*

THE EYE OF MEMORY

"Any writer has more to thank memory for than most anything," Eudora Welty once told an interviewer. She wasn't referring to instant recall. Memory is not the same as recalling information. A writer whose mind is a computer stuffed with random, meticulously recalled details may have trouble selecting which ones to use. Seen this way, a bad memory can be an asset to a writer. If you have a mind like a sieve, be grateful. A sieve filters, strains and selects; though much falls through the meshwork, some remains. Memory is an act of meaning-making. It collects the disparate pieces of our lives and distills them. For writers, what we forget is as important as what we recall.

Welty also wasn't referring to memory in terms of writing about the past. What we remember can just as well be used in writing about the present or the future. We store up the sights, smells, textures and sounds of our lives, and draw upon those experiences as we write. This doesn't mean merely transcribing the raw material of past experience—is such an act possible?—but transforming that raw material into a new shape.

Life continually provides us with raw material for our writing. Henry James calls this material—the fact, event or memory that is given to us—the "donnée." But the donnée is only one component in the making of a story, poem or essay. More important is how we organize and describe the raw material, how we marry experience to imagination. This may require letting go of what we've been given. We may need to release fact-for-fact's sake in exchange for fact-for-art's sake.

One way to reshape the donnée is to take an event from your life—your first home run, the birth of your child, the death of your father—and loan the entire experience to one of your characters. If you really want to engage the imaginative eye, loan the memory to a character very different from you. If you're a redhead, make the character a brunette; if you're a tall, shy man, give your experience to a short, vivacious woman. Hand over the event, no strings attached, and see what your character does with it. Describe the event from your character's point of view, perhaps even in his own words. Don't worry about losing the emotional impact of the event. If the event was emotionally moving for you, chances are the emotion will transfer to your character.

Another way to reshape the donnée is to take two events, years apart, and place them in the same story or poem to see how they interact. For instance, describe a childhood scene between one of your characters—call her Ellen—and her mother. Maybe the mother is brushing Ellen's hair before a mirror or pulling a splinter from Ellen's thumb. Stop the description before it's completed, inserting a description of another scene between Ellen and her mother, a scene many years removed from her childhood. Maybe the two of them are shopping for a wedding gown, or Ellen is visiting her mother in the nursing home after her stroke. The interaction between the two events will force you to describe the scenes in new ways. In the interplay between the two moments, your imaginative eye will take over, navigating the space between the two experiences.

Another way to engage your imaginative eye is to describe two or more versions of the same event—say, your sister's version and your husband's—and place them in the same piece. I used this method in the opening of "The Tale," an essay about the day my grandmother amputated a dying dog's leg in an attempt to save him:

There were as many versions of the tale as there were tellers. Grandma's neighbor, Mrs. Sisson, made it autumn. She said she was walking back from the milking barn when she saw a black horse leaping a bale of rolled hay with my grandmother on his back, clinging to his mane. Uncle Leland remembered it as April, the last gray patches of snow melting by the mailbox. Great Aunt Bessie, Grandma's sister, recited it reverently as if it were a Bible story, focusing on the wound itself, the miracle of the quick healing . . .

Describing each character's memory of the event allowed me to engage my imaginative eye. Once I left the bare facts, which varied from teller to teller, I was able to find the larger emotional truth beneath the event.

This does not mean that I lied about the facts. When we write nonfiction we relinquish our right to change what happened to suit our imagined version. The creative part of nonfiction lies elsewhere, in the way our imaginative eye views the factual world—selecting details, combining and recombining information, and reshaping experience. Artful arrangement of information was one of the cornerstones of the "new journalism" of Wolfe and Capote, and remains an important component of creative nonfiction. Facts, information and real-life events do not have to be presented dryly, like encyclopedia entries. They can emerge wrapped in the skin of story, or shaped like prayers, lists, recipes, letters, confessionals, dialogues or diaries. When the eye of the imagination is engaged, it illuminates the artful possibilities hidden within actual events. From the hard rock of fact, stone by stone the writer builds a castle.

Engaging the imaginative eye is hard work, especially when we find ourselves trapped within one version of an event, one way of describing the world of our story. Sometimes we don't want the imaginative eye to intrude on our memories. But intrude it must, if anything new is to be born. One of our duties as writers is to become surprised, to land in a different place from where we planned—a more difficult, provocative place. If we wish to engage the eye of memory, we must be willing to transform, reshape, even discard the donnée for the sake of the story.

THE GROWING EYE, THE THIRD EYE, INSIGHT

In 1988 scientists recorded the first sighting of what they termed "deep light," a mysterious light that emanated from the ocean floor. The discovery of this light, which was too faint to be perceived by the human eye and could be accessed only through the use of a special camera, seemed to suggest that undersea objects produced their own radiance independent of the sun.

Had the poet Gerard Manley Hopkins been alive at the time, he would not have been surprised by the discovery. Hopkins, like many other artists and mystics, believed that nature's expressive forms are molded by spiritual power, and he spent much of his life articulating the belief that each object in nature contains what he named "inscape." Inscape can be explained—and I am simplifying here—as the shape within the shape, a kind of glowing from within. It's a radiance that emanates from even the most common forms, a radiance that is visible only to the eye of the imagination.

Sister Wendy Beckett, the nun who wrote *Sister Wendy's Story of Painting*, a book based on the PBS series she hosts, spent twenty-seven years in chosen seclusion. Although she is no longer an isolate, she continues to practice silence and prayer seven hours a day. Much of this time is devoted to simply *viewing* art, usually postcard reproductions she keeps in her room. *Viewing*, however, does not begin to describe her process, which she calls "quiet attention" or "looking with awe and wonder." She says that if she looks long enough and hard enough at a painting—even one she doesn't like at all—it begins to take on a life of its own and she is able to see why it's considered a great work of art. I imagine what she's seeing with her imaginative eye is something akin to Hopkins's "inscape."

Hopkins called this eye the "growing eye" because it expands as it learns to participate emotionally and spiritually with the object itself. When we engage not only the naked eye but the growing eye as well, we begin to see the extraordinary within the ordinary. Our eye begins to grow. If this discussion of the growing eye sounds a bit suspect, like a UFO sighting by some New Ager who's been grazing too long on tofu, let's consider how the growing eye affects a writer's descriptions. Here's Annie Dillard describing the first moments of waking in a house on Puget Sound:

> I wake in a god. I wake in arms holding my quilt, holding me as best they can inside my quilt . . . .
> I open my eyes. The god lifts from the water. His head fills the bay. He is Puget Sound, the Pacific; his breast rises from pastures; his fingers are firs; islands slide wet down his shoulders. Islands slip blue from his shoulders and glide over the water, the empty, lighted water like a stage.
>
> —from *Holy the Firm*

Dillard's is a rapturous description, infused with spiritual awe. When she looks at the Pacific, she sees the Pacific, yes. But she sees more than the Pacific. Because she is looking with wonder, expectantly, the view expands to fill her growing eye. Puget Sound moves out of the realm of common sense and into the realm of the imagination. It's as if the writer is shining a flashlight from the inside of her subject, illuminating its inner workings.

In ancient myth, soothsayers, prophets and other clairvoyants were called *seers*, though many of them, like Tiresias of Greek legend, were blind. Because their eyes were not cluttered with external reality, so the theory goes, their inner eye could see more clearly into the heart and mind of the universe. The quest for internal vision continued with mystics, saints and monks, who practiced—and still practice—mortification of the senses. Through disciplines such as surrender, silence, darkness, fasting and meditation, they seek to "empty" their senses. The poet and priest Gerard Manley Hopkins emptied his vision regularly so that it could be "refilled." Once, for a period of six months, he refused to use his eyes. External reality, it seemed, only clouded the inner eye, his *insight.*

Few of us would go so far as Hopkins did, but there are less radical ways to shut out the world of appearances. Practicing fifteen minutes of meditation a day, directly before you write, can do wonders for your inner eye. Try it and see. Find a quiet place, close your eyes (or focus on a still object) and breathe slowly and deeply, from your diaphragm rather than your chest. Pay attention to your breathing, to its regular and sustained rhythm. Clear your mind of distractions, focusing only on the experience of the moment—your breathing, the silence.

If you find that your mind is wandering, take note of the distraction but do not dwell on it. Focus on what is taking place within yourself as you sit in the silence. You might want to try a technique used by hypnotists and Lamaze instructors: stare at a focal point until the distraction is removed. Or repeat a mantra or chant to bring yourself back to the present moment. Books such as Ira Progoff's *The White-Robed Monk* contain entrance meditations you can speak aloud, or listen to on tape, as a way of focusing attention on what you are about to write.

Another focusing activity is the "third eye" exercise I learned from Kenneth Koch's *Wishes, Lies, and Dreams.* At first I used the exercise only in my poetry-in-the-schools work, but I discovered that the third eye concept works equally well for adults. Imagine you have a third eye in the middle of your head, an eye that sees only what your other two eyes cannot see. Your third eye can see into any dimension of time and space, penetrating unseen mysteries. It possesses unlimited power. Well, almost unlimited. Remember, it can't see what the naked eye sees. The only way to engage your third eye is to refuse to use images perceived through the naked eye.

Sometimes the best way to describe our world is with our eyes closed. Daily life clouds our sight and our insight, especially when we spend time before televisions and movie screens where the visual world is even more frantic and fragmented than the world of nature, breaking into images lasting only seconds. Overwhelmed by visual stimuli, we can take in no more. The world has become a blur, each color and shape vying for our attention. Our naked eye becomes so filled that our inner eye refuses to see.

Fortunately, eyes come equipped with lids. We can lower them like shades when we've seen enough.

THE ALL-ACCEPTING EYE

There are other reasons for pulling the shades over our eyes. Anyone who looks long, hard and honestly at the world will see things he'd rather not see: children bald from chemotherapy, mothers stuffing fetuses down laundry chutes, refugees drinking raw sewage in order to be admitted into the camp's infirmary. What we do with these images will define, in part, our creative vision. Some writers seem incapable of ignoring the world's horrors; to deny them would be tantamount to artistic death.

For other writers, the unspeakable remains unspoken. Rather than confront the horror, they push it out of their mind's eye, training their attention only on what appears, on the surface, to be beautiful. Although this may seem to be the path of least artistic resistance, it probably isn't. Objects and scenes of unquestioned beauty are difficult to take in. Like the effect of a ravishing woman on a shy man, an overly beautiful sight might render a writer literally speechless. Vincent Van Gogh, in a letter to his brother, wrote that one particular olive grove was "too beautiful for us to dare to paint it or to be able to imagine it." Of course, being Van Gogh, he did dare, at least fifteen times, though none of the olive tree paintings ever satisfied him.

Another problem with unquestioned beauty is that it can quickly become' boring. Though a flawless, seemingly perfect subject might catch our eye momentarily (a *Playgirl* centerfold, this week's *Baywatch* chick), it is the flawed subject we are most likely to remember (Lauren Hutton's gap-toothed smile, Barbra Streisand's nose, the scar above Stacy Keach's lip). Flaws reveal the human, the vulnerable, in each of us. It's what my grandmother used to call "character," something she promised I would get someday, a quality more important and lasting than beauty. I inherited little of my grandmother's beauty, and, thus far, even less of her inimitable character. But I'm still hopeful.

In the meantime, I enjoy a well-placed crack in a piece of pottery, an ink-smudged letter, the errant cowlick in my nephew's hair. "What is always provocative in a work of art," wrote E.M. Forster, is "roughness of texture." As readers, he says, we long for descriptions "full of dents and grooves and lumps and spikes which draw from us little cries of approval and disapproval. When they have passed, the roughness is forgotten, they become as smooth as the moon."

How can we write descriptions that are "rough in texture" yet "smooth as the moon"? The first step, as I've said before, is to really *look* at your subject. Look with your naked eye and your inner eye. Most of all, look with an all-accepting eye. Accept every part of the subject, removing those conventional labels—*lovely, gross, sweet, inspiring, depressing*—that you normally associate with the image. Don't jump to conclusions. Try not to view the subject as you've been taught to view it. Look long enough and hard enough, and you're bound to find the "dents and grooves and lumps and spikes."

One of the biggest challenges we face as writers is describing something that almost everyone considers beautiful—a sunset, a rose, a new baby, the ocean. Although we want to write descriptions that are evocative and memorable, we end up filling our stories with phrases like "velvety petals" or "sparkling waves." When this happens to me, it's usually because I've proceeded, as my uncle used to say, "bass-ackwards." Rather than beginning with the image itself, I've begun with a label, judgment or conclusion about my subject, then merely provided details that back up my label. Let's say I want to describe a vase of tulips. My first thought is *beautiful, springlike, fresh.*

Already I've jumped to conclusions, providing labels before I've taken the time to consider my subject, the tulips themselves. My description is bound to fail. It will be no more than a series of clichéd, forgettable details concocted to support my judgment about the tulips.

But if I look before I leap, bringing forth the qualities of the tulips rather than merely labeling or explaining them, I might come up with a more memorable description, like Richard

Selzer's description of a vase of tulips delivered to a seriously ill man:

> ... They are the largest tulips of his life. A closer examination would have revealed that the long stems had been impaled on a bed of spikes and wired such that the distant hydrocephalic blossoms would respond to the least current of air. Placed on the window ledge, the evil heads are in a constant state of motion, nodding or shaking as if to vote yea or nay in the matter of his fate. At night the shadows of these flowers are magnified and thrown upon the wall—seven bald witches lunging for his thoughts. . . .
>
> There they are! On the wall! Sheeted by the moon, those caricatures of tulips, hunchbacked, swollen.
>
> —from *Raising the Dead: A Doctor's Encounter With His Own Mortality*

Another challenge we face is describing something commonly thought of as ugly, imperfect or disgusting. Again, we're likely to jump to conclusions. Rather than considering our subject firsthand and describing what we observe, we label it. Because we've already established, for instance, that slugs are disgusting, we go on to describe them as "slimy" creatures that leave "gooey trails." Cliché upon cliché.

But when we engage our all-accepting eye, when we look beyond surface prejudices and preconceptions into the actual nature of our subject, clichés disappear. In her poem "The Connoisseuse of Slugs," Sharon Olds transforms her subject with descriptive phrases like "naked jelly of those gold bodies,/ translucent strangers glistening among the/stones" and "glimmering umber horns/rising like telescopes." Her description forces us to see an old subject in a new way. We no longer have to choose between ugliness and beauty; they have realigned themselves, each side illuminating the other. When we engage our all-accepting eye, we discover the flaw that makes surface beauty interesting as well as the arresting detail that redeems a seemingly ugly image.

THE GLIDING EYE

It's 1873, and we're standing on the banks of the Seine. A small flat-bottomed boat cruises past. On its deck is a three-legged easel. The bearded man holding the paint brush is Claude Monet, who will soon come to be known as the father of impressionism. He works each day in this studio boat, floating down the river while the scenery passes by him, through him. Unfortunately, we can't see the scene through Monet's eyes. For one thing, we're standing on the bank, while he is moving. For another, we don't spend each day of our lives concentrating on the scene before us. And finally, we are not Monet, the "Raphael of Water" whom Cézanne once described as "only an eye. But my God, what an eye."

Monet's artistic vision, coupled with high emotional energy and a seemingly unquenchable passion for light, led him to create works that seemed to describe the most fleeting and fluid moments in nature. Realistic description was not Monet's goal. He was not struggling to reproduce reality but to coax a new reality out of the world his eyes saw. As one critic put it, Monet was "gliding with the light" rather than trying to conquer it. Monet not only chose to paint the most unstable of subjects— it is impossible to "capture" moving water—but he chose, at least part of the time, to paint it while he was in motion.

When we think of paying attention, we usually think of sitting still, of clearing our eyes and ears of distractions and concentrating on the object or scene before us. But sometimes the best way to be still—to still your mind and focus on your subject— is to get moving. Concentrating on your body may free your mind to discover its own path. Before you write, take a long walk, swim, lift weights, jog, dance or take a spin on your bike. You may find that the physical rhythms of the activity suggest the rhythms of sentences or poetry lines. This happened to me on the rowing machine; the even, repetitious strokes coupled with the whooshing sound of the machine led me to write a meditation on the heart, its iambic lub and dub.

If you hate exercise, take a tip from Monet and float down a river. Or take a long train ride, or set off on a motorcycle. As a child, I watched the world rush past the back window of our family's station wagon. When we slowed for intersections or stalled in heavy traffic, the pictures lingered; I studied them carefully, noting each detail. Then as we picked up speed, the scenes flickered by. Long car trips still turn my mind to reverie. If I'm a passenger, I record my images on paper; if I'm driving, I record them on cassette. The car is my floating studio, though the view passes more quickly than Monet's view and is more tightly framed. If you want to engage your gliding eye, set up a floating studio or set yourself in motion while the world rushes by.

THE CHILD'S EYE

For almost fifteen years as poet-in-residence for a large metropolitan school district, I worked side by side with children, encouraging them to read and write poems. I never ceased to be surprised by what they wrote:

> I have fierce, perfect muscles that you can see far away. I used to have a perfect mouth, till I lied.

> My parents got divorced and my dad got me.

> What's quieter than the rain Wednesday morning? Silence is the quietest thing that people break.

> Sometimes I feel kinda only.

Lines like these appeared every day, written by children of all ages, races, economic and achievement levels. Later, when they read the children's poems, adults shook their heads. "What happens to us along the way?" they lamented. "I used to be creative, too. Where did it go? Why can't I write lines like that? Kids!" they said, lifting their palms as if in surrender.

Although I, too, was impressed with the children's creativity, I had trouble believing that imagination is a gift bestowed freely in childhood only to be snatched away at adulthood. What about all those artists who continue their creative work well into old age? "Man's maturity," wrote Nietzsche, is "to regain the seriousness that he had as a child at play." This suggests a different

29

spin on creativity, an artistic seriousness at once playful yet highly concentrated, quite different from the buttoned-down serious-ness we often associate with adulthood. Like a child who manipu-lates a doll or a piece of string for the pure sensory pleasure of it, the imaginative writer takes pleasure in the purely descriptive moment, without hurrying the task.

Watching the children's faces as they wrote, I tried to guess what was happening within their minds. Some children smiled to themselves, smiles ranging from devilish to thoughtful to serene. Some laughed aloud, as if enjoying a private joke. Many scowled in concentration. A few cried unabashedly, tears drip-ping down onto the page. Yet no matter how different the ex-pressions on their faces, the quality of intense encounter was the same; each child was fully engaged in the task at hand.

Another thing I noticed as the children wrote was how often they changed their viewing perspectives. A child rarely looks at his world straight on. He lies flat on his back in the middle of a field, or peeks out from a hiding place, or climbs a tree and watches the scene from above. I used to spy from a crack in the hay mow floor as my grandfather milked the cows. From my vantage point, I could see only their smooth brown backs, the square white-speckled heads, and the swishing ropes of their tails. They had no feet, or so my eyes told me. These cows were dream creatures, and I imagined them floating in midair, list-lessly presenting their full udders to my grandfather's hands.

Suppertime brought no end to dreaming. Like most chil-dren, I was fond of partially obstructed views, and while the grown-ups weren't looking—which seemed to be most of the time—I crawled under the oak table to witness the drama of legs and feet. My grandfather often wore galoshes over his shoes; my aunt, in open-toed red pumps, crossed one stockinged leg over the other and swung it in my direction; my grandmother, who wore her stockings rolled below her knees, used her right foot as punctuation, stomping it adamantly to make a point.

Later in the evening, as my mother ironed a tablecloth for Sunday's upcoming dinner, I'd sit beneath the ironing board and let the white damask cover me like a cloud. Children love small spaces—tents, closets and department store clothing racks. These spaces provide a crowded security while also encouraging subterfuge. While hidden, a child can spy on the outside world without giving himself away, thus gaining an advantage over those whose secrets are now open to his view. He squeezes down into the smallest space possible, lies as still as he can, and holds his breath.

The moment does not last, of course, for a child at play is a child in motion. Soon he's spinning in dizzy circles, then stopping on a dime, gravity tipping him drunkenly towards earth as heaven swirls over him. Or he's on a swing, pumping his legs toward the highest branch. He throws back his head and the green world, broken by shards of sky, shatters into a thousand pieces. Who knows? Once grown, this same child might buy a studio boat, set up an easel and begin to describe the floating world.

Regaining the seriousness of play. Changing our viewing perspective. Hiding in small spaces and looking out. Setting ourselves in motion in order to watch the world swirl by. These are but a few of the ways we can regain the child's eye we thought was surely lost.

THE DREAM EYE

Every night as you sleep, the dream eye sets about to destroy your world—the world of logic, literal meaning, lock-step order and cause and effect. It dismantles daylight visions, razes buildings, ravishes the landscape in preparation for paving what Freud called "the royal road to the unconscious." *You're at the altar, dressed in a white bridal gown and rubber hip boots, blowing "I Do's" through a snorkel. Your father floats by, blinking his eyes, but they're not eyes. They're clear blue bowls where tiny minnows dart.*

In bed, you toss, flail, cry out in fear or exaltation. The bug of REM crawls beneath your eyelids. Then slowly, quietly, the dream eye begins its repair work, paving the road, raising the scaffolding, pouring the foundation. By the time you wake, dry-mouthed and woozy, the house is built, your old furniture rearranged, a few symbolic pictures framed. In some strange, inexplicable way, the pictures make sense. Not the kind of sense a news report makes, or an algebraic equation. The pictures make *dream* sense. Like art, they do not necessarily *mean* anything— that is, their significance cannot be separated out. The pictures are not asking to be understood and explained; they want only to be looked at with care and attention.

Our culture doesn't put much store in dreams, at least not the kind we have while we're asleep. Usually when we talk about dreams, it's in terms of daylight wishes, goals to attain, jobs to secure, hopes for our children's futures—things we assume are within our control. Nighttime dreams, on the other hand, are beyond our control. Perhaps that's why we discount their power to shape and reshape our lives. Many of us claim not to dream at all; others claim not to remember dreams.

And even those of us who say we value dreams often try to tame them, to analyze them, to make them *mean* something that our conscious, logical brains can use. We buy dream dictionaries that reduce our nighttime paintings to the sum of their parts: white, altar, blue, fishes, snorkel. We labor to find a lesson or moral: "The dream must be telling me not to marry Josh" or "Gee, maybe we shouldn't have an outdoor wedding, since it's obviously going to rain." Rather than give our attention to the dream itself, its shapes and textures and colors and emotions, we bypass its art, looking for logical answers. It's the equivalent of glancing at the Mona Lisa, then turning to our companion and saying, "Leonardo's saying that we should keep our secrets, it makes us more mysterious." Yes, dreams mean something, just as paintings do. But their meaning cannot be extracted like a motto for a bumper sticker.

When we stop trying to figure out our dreams, to apply our conscious minds to the pictures the unconscious is painting, we may begin to feel the power of their images. And we may find that those images emerge in our writing. The process can be as simple as keeping paper and pen on your bedside table, then, when you wake from a dream, recording everything you remember—the feelings, shapes, physical details, dialogue—without trying to decipher meaning.

When recording dreams, I use the present tense; it makes the scenes more immediate, bringing them more vividly to my mind's eye. The present tense verbs act as guides, leading me by the hand through the dream. The present tense is also helpful because it suggests *presenting* rather than explaining. It's as if I'm back in the dream and the scenes are emerging before my eyes as I watch. To use the past tense would suggest that the images had already been distilled, that they had acquired the weight of meaning and logic. I don't need dreams weighted with meaning and logic any more than I need didactic art. I need dreams that penetrate beneath my consciousness, that reveal the world of the imagination in all its strange and beautiful guises.

Once you get into the habit of recording your dreams, of replaying them directly onto a pad of paper or in a dream journal, you'll probably find you remember more of your dreams, and remember them in more vivid detail. After several months you'll have quite a collection of surreal images. If you reread them, you may see certain images repeating themselves. You may even see a pattern emerging. Beyond giving you information about your obsessions, fears and desires, these images can also provide entries into new poems or stories. (The underwater dream, by the way, was *my* dream, and the image of my father's eyes was the triggering image for what became an essay focusing on my father's uneasy relationship with water.)

Dream images can also help solve writing problems. They can provide insight into your characters or suggest a different plot direction for the story you've been working on. This does not mean you can simply retell a dream, detail by detail, and call it a story. Blow-by-blow descriptions of dreams are interesting only to the teller. If you don't believe this, try recounting last night's dream to your co-worker while you wait in line at the copy machine, and watch his eyes glaze over. Suddenly he glances at his watch, remembers a meeting he just has to attend, and is out of there—and just when you were getting to the good part, too. Though dreams can pave the way to a story, they are not the story itself. Images seen through the dream eye must be tested the way any image is tested by a prudent writer: by how it serves the story.

EXERCISES

1. Follow the example of poets A.R. Ammons and Jorie Graham: take up painting or sketching as a way of keeping your vision new. Or follow the example of writer Frye Gaillard, who claims to have a bad "visual memory." When he visits a place or interviews a subject, he takes detailed notes on what he sees, later expanding the notes into sensory descriptions.

2. Change your visual point of view. Stare at the same scene from several different focal points—lying flat on your back and looking up, peering through a peephole, looking down from a mountain, airplane or diving board. Or frame an ordinary scene in new ways. Look through a window. Roll a sheet of paper into a tube and study the scene through a new lens. Distort a realistic view by looking through prisms, kaleidoscopes or 3-D glasses. Then describe the scene through the lens of each eyepiece. For literary examples, read Theodore Roethke's "Child on Top of a Greenhouse," William Carlos Williams's "Nantucket," or James Wright's "Lying in a Hammock at William Duffy's Farm in Pine Island, Minnesota."

3. Listen to Paul Simon's "Fifty Ways to Leave Your Lover." Substitute "donnée" for "lover" and see how many ways there are to leave your story, to get beyond fact-for-fact's sake. ("Just drop off the key, Lee, and get yourself free.")

4. Make a list of images you find ugly, perhaps even disgusting, in objects, nature, people and yourself. Your list might include an amputee's stump, a crooked yellow tooth, wrinkles, a smoggy sky, cockroaches, stretch marks, a charred corpse, varicose veins, maggots, obscene graffiti, rubble from a bombed building. Then choose one image from the list and write a description that redeems that image, removing it from the world of ugliness and disgust.

5. Study a "beautiful" object until you discover an interesting flaw. Record the details you see, allowing the ugly and the beautiful equal weight.

6. Keep a dream journal in which you record not only night-time dreams but twilight imagery, daybreak reverie and simple

old-fashioned daydreams. Once a month, look through your entries, circling arresting images. Use one of these images in an opening line to a story, poem or essay. Or loan the dream to one of the characters in your story.

7. Change the way you record your images. Try writing on adding machine tape, restaurant napkins, or 3″×5″ cards. Or use unlined paper that encourages you to mix drawing with writing, to sketch characters or maps, and to write without the boundaries of margins or lines. Get out of your writing rut any way you can. Write in the dark with a lighted pen, or on a chalkboard, or with colored pencils. If the thought of filling a blank sheet of paper with description terrifies you, reduce the terror. Fold the paper in half, then in half again, and again. Your terror has now been reduced eightfold. Write one sensory detail on the folded section, then begin unfolding the paper, adding a detail to each section until the empty page is filled.

8. To engage your imaginative eye, change an ordinary or habitual act by adding a new dimension to it. For instance, eat the same flavor of ice cream in three different ways in three different places: straight from the carton while sitting in a bubble bath; out of a crystal goblet while sitting in a tree or under one; with your bare hands while shut up in a dark closet. Then, write a description of each experience.

9. If the previous experience is too kinky or messy for your style, try wearing headphones while you walk the same six blocks three times, varying the style of music each time. For one trip, a Strauss waltz; for another, heavy metal; for another, blues guitar. Notice how the same scene changes depending on the music you're listening to. Recently, while walking past the retirement home in my neighborhood, I was listening to Grieg's "Wand of Youth." Suddenly, the women in the window of the exercise room weren't old women in leotards and sweat pants, straining to lift their arms above their heads. They were pastel petals, ballerinas-of-the-folding-chair, their sinuous tendrils reaching. (I went straight back to my desk and recorded what I had seen.)

10. Reread one of your old descriptions. Circle adjectives that merely label or explain, replacing them with descriptive adjectives that evoke concrete, sensory qualities.

FROM EYE TO WORD: THE DESCRIPTION

Marvelous Truth, confront us
at every turn,
in every guise, iron ball,
egg, dark horse, shadow,
cloud
of breath on the air . . .

—from "Matins" by Denise Levertov

You've opened your eyes and stayed at the eyepiece, giving your attention to the world around you. You've engaged the eye of your imagination. And you've spent time reading the best literature you can find, poems and stories and essays rich in detail. You're eager to write a stunning description. Where do you begin?

Start with what's in front of your eyes. Description is word painting, and most painters begin with the subject before their eyes, whether it be a person, place, event or object. Georgia O'Keeffe collected objects—bleached bones, skulls, feathers, shells and stones. She called them her "treasures," and they filled her studio and her canvases. When she left New Mexico to return East, she crated a barrel of bones to accompany her. Later, the contents of the barrel provided the raw material for the first of her famous cow skull paintings; the background was provided by the blue pajamas of a friend's young son.

As you describe your subject, think of yourself as a painter of still life. You are painting a stationary subject, revealing its qualities as it remains in a fixed state. (Later we'll move on to action-based description.) Chapter two included Audre Lorde's description of a mortar and pestle, followed by an exercise in observation and description. If you haven't yet written a description of a common object, write one now, following the suggestions in chapter two. As suggested earlier, be sure to use specific nouns and only those adjectives that describe; avoid modifiers that label or explain.

When we write a description of a static subject—a pine tree, a deserted house, a rusted plow—we are in effect freezing the scene for ourselves and the reader. A frozen scene allows us to focus on our subject's permanent, fixed qualities. When an object or scene holds still, it gives us time to observe every detail. One way to focus on details is to describe the various parts that make up the whole. A tangerine, for instance, consists of rind, juice, seeds, fruit, pulp, grainy membranes, stem, blossoms and leaves. Describing each of these parts will force you to notice details you might otherwise overlook, what Chekhov called the "little particulars." Later you may decide you've included too many particulars. If so, you can always remove some of them or group them in a different way.

In description, the organization of details is as important as the details themselves. If you toss all the details at the reader without providing a pattern, he'll have trouble visualizing your word painting. So once you've described the details of your subject, you must order them. There are many ways to organize a description of a static subject—spatially, temporally or in terms of certain innate qualities.

In describing the tangerine, for instance, you might group the details by their common attributes—say, smooth, rough, edible or inedible. You could also organize the details in relation to a process that occurs over time—as the tangerine is peeled and eaten, for example, or as it evolves from seed to fully mature fruit. You might organize your description spatially, beginning at the inside of the tangerine and proceeding out, or from the outside in, ordering each detail to fit a visual schematic. (When you're describing a larger static subject such as a room or a forest, the same principles apply; the only difference is the size of your canvas. In chapter eight we'll discuss specific methods for organizing descriptions of place.)

Jim Crace uses spatial ordering in the opening to his novel *The Gift of Stones*. Notice how our mind's eye travels the landscape of the description, beginning with the top part of the father's arm and ending in the scar at the center of the stump:

> My father's right arm ended not in a hand but, at the elbow, in a bony swelling. Think of a pollard tree in silhouette. That was my father's stump. Its skin was drawn tight across the bone and tucked frowning into the hole left by the missing lower joint. The indented scar was like those made in the ice by boys with stones— a small uneven puncture, wet with brackish puss.

Regardless of how distasteful his subject might be, it's hard to discount the power of Crace's description. He manages not only to include specific, concrete details and order those details effectively; he also brings the description to life, proving that the description of a fixed, static subject needn't *feel* static. Good descriptions, you'll recall, follow Aristotle's dictum of revealing things "in a state of activity," and the best writers know how to make even stationary objects pulse with life. Later in this chapter we'll discuss how active, vivid prose can animate even the most static scene. For now, simply note Crace's strong verbs (drawn, tucked) and his use of figurative language (pollard tree, ice scars) which, taken together, lend "metaphorical life to lifeless objects."

Once you've painted a still life—that is, written a description of your subject in a fixed, permanent state—action-based description should be easy. Since your subject is in motion, you don't have to infuse it with life; you need only follow its movement with your mind's eye and describe what you see. The same principles that apply to describing a static object apply to action-based description. Begin by looking closely with your naked eye or the eye of your imagination. Visualize the scene. Break the subject or scene into its various parts, then order the parts for a smoothly flowing description.

A good place to start is to describe someone at work or play, performing a task involving several discrete steps. The details order themselves, since they occur chronologically. The following description from Jane Brox's essay "Bread" details the actions of a baker preparing loaves of Syrian bread:

> Flour swirled in a slant of light and lined the creases of the baker's neck, salting his hair. He doused the work table with flour and kneaded the dough until it felt soft as an ear lobe, then cut pieces off the mass and balanced them on the enamel scale. He flattened the pieces with the palm of his hand to make thin disks, which he slipped into the oven. In the intense heat of the fires the loaves puffed up, hollow in the center. Once out of the ovens they collapsed as they cooled, and he wrapped the bread in towels or muslin to keep it soft enough to fold around an olive or fresh cheese or a slice of cooked lamb.

If you were to underline each action the baker performs, you'd see that each phrase centers on an active verb. The baker douses, kneads, cuts, balances, flattens, slips, wraps and folds—eight strong verbs, eight steps in the process. Reading the description, we can visualize each movement, yet Brox's description is more than a series of chronological steps. The whole scene is alive with movement. Flour swirls around the baker's head, landing in the creases of his neck. Hollow-centered loaves puff up, then collapse. And through sensory details—in this case, details centered on the sense of touch—Brox takes us into the center of the baker's experience. We feel the dough in our hands, "soft as an ear lobe," and the heat emanating from the oven.

More basic even than Brox's strong verbs and sensory detail is her use of concrete, specific nouns. By naming the items of the baker's world accurately and precisely, providing what Aristotle called "the proper and special name of a thing," she invites us into the fictional dream: flour, dough, enamel scale, disk, oven towels, muslin, olive, fresh cheese, slice of lamb. Each noun anchors us, keeping us firmly planted in the world being described.

THE PROPER AND SPECIAL NAME OF A THING

It makes sense that Aristotle begins his discussion of description with the importance of the individual word, "the proper and special name of a thing." Naming is universally regarded as one of the first acts, if not *the* first act, of creation. In the Genesis account, God *said* let there be, and there was. The world sprang to life through the power of the word. Until *light* was spoken, the earth was formless, a void. But once light was named, and its fraternal twin, darkness, the world of possibility opened up. And the evening and the morning were the first poem.

Naming is so basic to the writing process, so intricately woven into every effective description, that we often overlook its importance. Yet without this first act, without a precise, significant and musical naming, no description can be attempted, no work of literature born.

But creating a literary work is not the same as creating the world, and we must forgive ourselves in advance for not being God. No matter how long we study a lake or our grandfather's handsaw or our husband's mustache, and no matter how hard we labor to bring forth a precise, significant and musical description of what we see, we will not be able to recreate reality. Nor to capture it. "I know I cannot paint a flower," wrote Georgia O'Keeffe, "but maybe in terms of paint color I can convey to you my experience of the flower or the experience that makes the flower of significance to me at that particular time."

Unlike visual artists, we have no brushes, no clay, no glazes, no many-colored palette to aid us in describing our world. And unlike performing artists, we have no keyboard, no trombone, no toe shoes, no tutu, no midair leap with which to stun our audience and ourselves. What we have is the alphabet, that small but loyal band of vowels and consonants.

Since the word is our only tool, we cannot afford to be imprecise, to say *knife* when we mean *scalpel*; fictional blood might be shed. Nor can we afford to squander five letters on saying it was a *green* tablecloth when green has nothing to do with the scene we are trying to portray. *Green*, although it is an accurate naming, will not serve in this case. And what is *ripple* doing in the middle of a poem about the weight of loneliness? *Ripple* weighs close to nothing. It tiptoes across the ear. It is a bad choice.

An Accurate Naming

The first test of naming is accuracy. Part of a writer's job is to learn the exact names of things and to have more than a passing acquaintance with them. When we read an essay by Richard Selzer, we trust he is naming the surgical instruments correctly. In the same way, we trust Annie Dillard to know the difference between a beetle and a scorpion, and to describe their exoskeletons precisely. And when poet Mary Oliver writes "long-billed curlew," we must be assured she does not mean "great horned owl." Though the reader may not know the exact name for everything in a piece of writing, he nevertheless expects the writer to know.

Every world has its own vocabulary, even those worlds that might seem simple or mundane, and precise naming takes us deeper into the world being described. You probably cannot write a convincing story about a beauty salon, for instance, without knowing the difference between a tint and a dye, or between a set-and-style and a permanent wave. It might also help to know how long each procedure takes, and how much it costs. If you're writing a story from the point of view of a high school biology teacher, you may need to know not only what your students are wearing but also how to properly prepare a slide and dissect a fetal pig, and how to fill out a midterm grade report.

Finding out the names of things, their histories and how they work often requires outside research. This applies to the writing of fiction and poetry as well as to nonfiction writing. In the midst of revising a short story about a girl who helps deliver a calf, I realized I knew almost nothing about the subject. I spent the next two days in the library, and the following day at a local farm interviewing a farmer. The best way to learn would have been to deliver a calf with my own hands, but it was winter and I had a deadline.

Before I sent the final version to my editor, I asked the farmer to read the description of the delivery. Other than an error in my use of the term *freemartin*, which I set about to correct, my description met the farmer's standards. "Yes ma'am," he said, "that's just how it is, you got it right. That's exactly how a calf is born, cord and all." (A freemartin, for those of you who are wondering, is the female twin of a bull calf. I've been waiting three sentences to tell you. Aristotle was right. What a joy to find "the proper and special name of a thing.")

A Significant Naming

Precision extends beyond mere accuracy. Although there might be several correct names for something, according to Aristotle "one word may come closer than another to the thing described . . . set it more distinctly before our eyes." For example, if you were describing a girl's white face, *milky, bloodless* and *alabaster* would all pass the correctness test; all refer to whiteness. Yet each word brings forth a different visual image. While milky skin calls out to be touched, *bloodless* connotes a sickly, perhaps deathly countenance. And *alabaster,* though it might look good on a statue, suggests an unearthly quality. Although all three girls have white skin—you named the color accurately—they are definitely three different girls. The one with alabaster skin belongs on a pedestal; the one with bloodless skin, in an ambulance. And the girl with skin of milky white? Well yes, go ahead. Reach out and touch her.

Word choice, then, refers not only to correctness but to precision of image. We must go beyond selecting the correct name for something. We must also select the word that will call forth the significant image, attitude and emotion our story requires.

A Musical Naming

Finally, our naming must be musically precise. That is, the sounds of our words must reinforce their imagistic and emotional content. To return to an earlier example, *ripple* is probably not the best word to use in a poem describing the weight of loneliness. Not only does the word *mean* something slight, almost insignificant; it *sounds* slight. The short *i* is a bantamweight vowel, the lightest, most childlike sound in our language. Furthermore, the word's consonants slide easily into one another like liquid evaporating into mist. As softly as it began, the word ends. Not with a bang, but a whimper.

A more weighty choice would have been a word like *stone* or *root* or *nobody*. Is there a vowel more heavy or sad than the long *o?* It hollows out the mouth, intones the deepest sorrow. In "The Philosophy of Composition," Poe discusses his choice of *nevermore* as the refrain in "The Raven." He wanted a word that was "sonorous and susceptible of protected emphasis," which led him inevitably to the long *o*, "the most sonorous vowel."

It isn't merely the long vowel that makes *stone* and *root* weigh more than *ripple*. Because they are one-syllable words, their individual heft is felt as we place them on the page or as we read them. And their ending sounds make a strong final impression. The *t* of *root* supplies an abrupt ending, closing down completely, while the *n* of *stone* remains before our eyes and deep in our throats, providing weight and texture to reinforce the word's heaviness. Later we'll discuss in more detail how the sounds and rhythms of individual words, phrases and sentences affect our descriptions. For now, it's enough to remember that effective description requires not only an accurate and appropriate naming, but a musical naming as well.

The Back-Door Technique

Sometimes the best way to name an object, person or scene is by way of what it is *not*. After reading "Sonnet 130," we don't know what the eyes of Shakespeare's mistress look like, only that they "are nothing like the sun." Likewise, in her cheeks, no roses; and in her voice, no music. From a list of what she is not, the reader fashions his own mental picture.

This sonnet has been categorized by some scholars as anti-Petrarchan, meaning that it purposely eschews the attributes an Elizabethan sonneteer might commonly assign to his beloved. But Shakespeare's poem goes beyond rebellion against established literary conventions. His technique of negation, describing his mistress in terms of what she is not, also allows him to avoid clichés (rosy cheeks, a musical voice) while leaving room for the reader to supply his own image of the beloved.

The technique of description-by-negation works well when the object being described is viewed as ideal—a mistress, a beautiful scene, a lofty idea. For these subjects, a direct approach would likely yield sentimentality or cliché. Arguably the most famous piece of writing employing the "back-door" technique is found in the New Testament, in the thirteenth chapter of the first letter to the Corinthians, often referred to as "the love chapter." Is there any subject that invites more sentimentality or cliché? Yet in his description of love (or "charity") the author is able to avoid these traps, in part by listing the qualities love does *not* contain:

> . . . charity envieth not; charity vaunteth not itself, is not puffed up . . .

> Doth not behave itself unseemly, seeketh not her own, is not easily provoked, thinketh no evil. Rejoiceth not in iniquity . . .

Describing by negation also opens up physical spaces otherwise closed to characters, narrators and readers. In Norman MacLean's *Young Men and Fire*, he details a scene that would be impossible for someone to witness and still live to tell about. In the following passage, he describes the last few minutes of several firefighters' lives:

> It is really not possible to see the center of a blowup because the smoke only occasionally lifts, and when it does all that can be seen are pieces, pieces of death flying around looking for you—burning cones, branches circling on wings, a log in flight without a propeller . . .

The back-door technique provides entry not only into physical landscapes but psychic landscapes as well. Describing something in terms of what you don't see, hear or know reinforces a feeling of emotional distance. In "The Secret Sharer," Joseph Conrad reveals, by way of negation, the aloneness the young captain experiences before the ship embarks:

> At that moment I was alone on her decks. There was not a sound in her—and around us nothing moved, nothing lived, not a canoe on the water, not a bird in the air, not a cloud in the sky.

You can also employ the back-door technique to create ironic or comic touches:

> The new secretary squeaked by his desk in crepe-soled oxfords. Marilyn Monroe, she wasn't.

Or to introduce a fantastic or surreal setting:

> What she saw in her dream bore no resemblance to her earthly, daylit home. Gone was the sturdy pin oak, the brick columns, the white fence stretching to the end of the driveway . . .

The back-door technique can also build suspense, demonstrating the confusion or disorientation of the viewer:

> Up in the sky, it's a bird, it's a plane, it's . . .

When the back-door technique is sustained, as in Ivan Turgenev's "The Tryst," it also builds rhetorical suspense. Here's Turgenev's description-by-negation of a birch grove in early autumn when the leaves first begin to fall:

> It was not the cheerful, laughing rustle of springtime, not the soft whispering, not the long conversation of summer, not the cold and timid stammering of late autumn, but a barely audible, dreamy chatter.

The repetition of "it was not" slows down the revelation—a kind of verbal teasing—and the reader rushes forward, eager to reach the descriptive climax. Okay, we gasp. If it's not this, and it's not this, and it's not this, then what is it? When we finally reach the phrase that actually describes the early autumn sounds, we're not disappointed, although the description consists of only five words: "a barely audible, dreamy chatter." By saving the actual description until the end of the passage, Turgenev holds our suspense.

THE POWER OF ACTIVE, VIVID PROSE

The most basic technique for making descriptions come alive is the use of active, vivid prose. Long before a character begins to move, before any "action" has begun, descriptive language quivers with life. Its nouns are specific and concrete, its verbs pulsing with movement, its syntax active rather than passive.

In active voice, the subject of the sentence is the doer of the action: *A freckled boy flung the newspaper onto the porch.* In passive voice, the object of the action (in this case, the newspaper) becomes the subject of the verb, although the object doesn't actively do anything: *The newspaper was flung by a freckled boy.* On rare occasions, the passive voice might be suitable—for instance, when you wish to emphasize a subject's passivity or victimization: *Walter Milquetoast was buffeted by the slightest breeze of chance.* In most cases, however, the active voice is the better choice.

If your descriptions lack vitality, examine your sentences. Are the subjects of your sentences the active doers of action? Or have you twisted your syntax so that a potentially vital act has become passive? Sometimes all you need to do to make a passive sentence active is to move the subject to the front of the sentence.

(passive)	The ship was rocked by rough sea winds.
(active)	Rough winds rocked the ship.
(passive)	The vote was passed by the neighborhood board of directors.

(active) The neighborhood board of directors passed the vote.

Moving the subject to the front of the sentence adds another benefit: unnecessary words disappear. Often the first to fall are filler phrases that begin with *there* and *it*. Starting your sentence with the most logical and active subject will sweep your sentences clear of unnecessary debris:

(cluttered) It is probable that summer will arrive later this year.

(direct) Summer will probably arrive later this year.

(cluttered) There were four beautiful models waiting outside Tim's office.

(direct) Four beautiful models waited outside Tim's office.

A note of caution: While you're sweeping, be sure you don't sweep away a phrase that might lend drama or rhythm to your description.

REMOVING FILTERING DEVICES

In *The Art of Fiction*, John Gardner mentions another stylistic tic that depletes the energy of a writer's language—the use of "needless filtering of the image through some observing consciousness." Phrases such as "he noticed" and "she felt" may not only clutter our sentences unnecessarily but also distance the reader from the sensory image we're trying to convey. In most cases, stating the image directly is more effective than filtering it through the narrator's, or a character's, consciousness, as in this example:

> The boy eyed the contents of his grandmother's room, noticing the tiny figurines arranged in tiers on the mahogany shelf. He saw the bouquet of miniature irises, the ceramic Cinderella slipper, the glass horse with the painted blue eyes. He felt a sadness sweep through him like an autumn breeze.

47

Once we've established the scene and clarified the point of view, we don't need to constantly supply filtering devices. In the preceding example, the reader knows, after the first few words, who is watching the scene. Unless there's a reason to focus on the boy's consciousness—that is, unless the point of the description is to demonstrate how intensely the boy is watching—the writing loses nothing, and gains much, by removing the filtering mechanisms "noticing," "he saw" and "he felt."

> The boy eyed the contents of his grandmother's room, the tiny figurines arranged in tiers on the mahogany shelf—the bouquet of miniature irises, the ceramic Cinderella slipper, the glass horse with the painted blue eyes. Sadness swept through him like an autumn breeze.

THE IMPORTANCE OF ACTIVE VERBS

Using the active voice and removing filtering devices are important steps toward fresher prose, but they won't guarantee sentences that call forth images. Once you've checked to be sure your sentences are active and direct, examine your verbs. Verbs are the foot soldiers of action-based description. They march in the front lines, toting the heavy artillery. It's hard to imagine a description involving movement that is not supported, in some way, by evocative verbs. Sometimes strong verbs are all it takes to paint a moving picture, as in this short poem by one of my former students, a fifth grader who used an apt pseudonym for his school principal:

> Mr. Grunch storms down the hall,
> Slings open the green door,
> Stomps to the front of the room,
> Spits out sparks.

An older and more experienced writer, like the novelist Joan Chase in *During the Reign of the Queen of Persia*, embeds verbs more subtly into her prose, but the effect is similar. Both writers succeed in setting their characters in motion, thus allowing the reader to "see" the scene unfolding. In this scene, Chase's narrator describes the actions of a group of boys who have gathered to wait for their beautiful neighbor, Celia, to arrive on the scene:

> One early spring evening when Celia was fourteen and the rest of us girls thirteen or nearly so, Uncle Dan came home, carrying the sack of groceries Aunt Libby had ordered over the phone, and saw a troop of boys sprawled around on the porch or hanging from the railings and balustrades. He stopped and asked them if there was some problem, had their mothers forgotten something at the market. They slunk off sideways and kicked the porch steps. But when Celia walked through the front door they came alive and in a fevered sprint backed away, running and hollering, to the far road, their speeding eyes in retreat still fastened on Celia, who smiled vaguely with a certain regal privilege.

Although setting a character in motion is the most direct way of showing action, a character doesn't have to move for verbs to perform their descriptive work. In "For a Godmother," poet Allison Joseph describes the godmother's face, "its bones pushing up under pale skin/like something unrelieved." Here, the bones take on a life of their own through the movement implied by *pushing*. In the same way, Pam Durban's opening description in her story "This Heat" comes alive through the use of strong verbs. Even after the character has died, the action continues:

> . . . his heart finally set him free, and he staggered and fell and blew one bloody bubble that lingered, rising and shimmering, then burst, leaving a shower of blood like rust spots on his pale skin.

Rising. Shimmering. Burst. Verbs set this picture in motion. Durban not only tells us that Beau Clinton died; she shows it happening. A writer need not be bound by flat statements like "It was a rough sea," when verbs like *tumble* and *roil* and *seethe* wait to spill from her pen. Look what two seventh-graders did, through the use of active and specific verbs, to freshen the time-worn images of sun and autumn:

Leaping down the old
brown twigs,
sun beam scampers through
an early morning ballet.

October is a beggar,
snatching golden leaves,
knocking on doors.

CAUTIOUS USE OF LINKING AND HELPING VERBS

Although most verbs convey action, not all verbs are created equal. Linking verbs (*appear, seem, was, were* and other forms of *being*) and even some verbs associated with the five senses (*look, taste, smell, hear* and *feel*) serve mainly as grammatical constructs and should not be confused with descriptive verbs that call forth pictures in the reader's mind. For instance, in the sentence "The woman looked strange and distracted to everyone else," *looked* is not an active verb; it merely links the subject (the woman) to labeling adjectives.

It's easy to determine if a particular verb is serving only as a link. A linking verb, one that expresses a state of being, always requires an adjective to complete its meaning, while an active verb does not.

(linking)	The soup, though creamy and mild, *tasted* funny.
(active)	Bart *tasted* the soup, curled his lip and spat.
(linking)	Beatrice *appeared* sweet-tempered and mild to her co-workers.
(active)	Beatrice *appeared* in the doorway wielding a potato peeler.

Although it's often necessary to use them, linking verbs or verbs that refer to states of being cannot take the place of active verbs when it comes to effective description. The same can be said for helping verbs. Helping verbs like *would, can, might, must, should* and *may* serve mainly to indicate tense; they express no action. In addition, helping verbs can clutter your sentences unnecessarily. When they are not necessary for meaning, try removing them and watch the energy flow into your sentences.

(cluttered)   Every Sunday morning Eliza would stand in front of the mirror and sob.

(revised)   Every Sunday morning Eliza stood in front of the mirror and sobbed.

EXAMINE YOUR ADVERBS AND SUFFIXES

At the beginning of the chapter I warned against using adjectives that merely label or explain. Another kind of modifier to avoid in descriptive writing is the adverb that merely modifies or amplifies. Words like *very, extremely* and *quite* serve only to show the extent to which a quality is present; they contribute little, if nothing, to the word painting. All adverbs should be examined. (I started to write "examined closely," but what other way can one examine?) Adverbs like *closely* sneak up on us, and before we know it, we're writing phrases like "ravishingly stunning" or "hurrying quickly."

Sometimes we insert an adverb because our verb is too weak to stand alone. Trying to conjure up a word picture, we write "walked seductively" or "talked softly." We can avoid using empty adverbs by using stronger verbs to begin with. Rather than "walked seductively," we could write "slinked," perhaps, or "vamped." "Talked softly" could become "whispered" or "murmured."

Sometimes we destroy a perfectly good word by adding a suffix like *-ful, -ment* or *-tion* or *-ance*. In the process, verbs become adjectives, adjectives become nouns. Suffix by suffix, our writing expires. Bureaucrats, politicians, educational administrators and newscasters are famous for their ability to turn a concise, direct statement into pure gobbledygook by adding unnecessary suffixes, as are some student writers hoping to impress a teacher:

(cluttered)   Being *fearful* of every new situation was an *indication* of the *sordidness* of Billy's past.

(revised)   Billy's fear of every new situation indicated his sordid past.
(or, more directly:)
Because of his sordid past, Billy feared every new situation.

(cluttered)   The *experience* of meeting Babs had brought about a *transformation* in the *reality* of Caleb's life.

(revised)   Meeting Babs had transformed Caleb's life, making it seem more real.

Removing cumbersome suffixes can restore words to their original vigor and force unwieldy sentences into order. Your writing will thank you, as will your readers.

LENDING METAPHORICAL LIFE TO EMOTIONS AND IDEAS

Through action-based description, almost anything can come alive—human characters, of course, and animals, but also inanimate objects, forces of nature, emotions and ideas. In the following example, a seventh-grader describes the experience of playing a trumpet, his choice of verbs setting in motion every element in the scene—the trumpet, the conductor's baton, the musical notes, even the emotion that has been waiting to erupt:

> The golden brass bending and sliding,
> The notes trickling like a mountain stream,
> As the conductor's baton waves my way,
> The notes come flowing like a caged bird let free.

It's difficult to describe an abstract idea or emotion without first embodying it through sensory and concrete images. One way to lend metaphorical life to an abstraction is to use vivid verbs, as in the earlier example, "Sadness *swept* through him . . . " In *Soul on Ice,* Eldridge Cleaver transforms an abstract idea (the 1960s social and political revolt that began with Rosa Parks's refusal to give up her seat on a segregated bus) into a concrete, pulsing entity:

> And as the spirit of revolt crept across the continent from that wayward bus in Montgomery, Alabama, seeping like new life into the cracks and nooks of the northern ghettos and sweeping in furious gales across the campuses of southern Negro colleges, erupting, finally, in the sit-ins and freedom rides—as this swirling maelstrom of social change convulsed the nation, shocking an unsuspecting American public, folk music, speaking of fundamental verities, climbed slowly out of the grave; and the hip lobe of the national ear, twitching involuntarily at first, began to listen.

As important as it is in forming memorable description, action becomes meaningless when it is not tempered by its opposite, stillness. Action that continues nonstop, without pause or variation, ceases to hold our attention; it is the *change* in the picture that captures our eye. In puppetry, for instance, the use of stillness can be a more dramatic gesture than a forceful or repetitive action. Let's say that a witch puppet is dancing around a cauldron, her pointed hat darting up and down, her shrewish cackle screeching in time to the music. The audience is clapping, bobbing their heads in rhythm, enthralled by the motion onstage—for the moment, at least.

But this moment will not hold.

An amateur puppeteer, believing it will, continues shaking his puppets in frenetic, often senseless movement. Soon the audience loses interest. Their hands drop, lifeless, into their laps; their eyes dart sideways. Enough already, the audience is thinking. Let's get back to the story. We want to see what happens next.

Ironically, what happens next is often *nothing*—at least, when a skilled professional is manipulating the scene. The nothing that happens is that the witch stops dancing, the hat stops bob-bing, the cauldron stops bubbling, the music stops thumping. The witch freezes, her broom lifted in midair. She holds her pose. One second, two. The eyes of the audience refocus on the stage: silence, suspense. Something is about to happen, they can feel it.

Even the most energetic, vigorous, quick-on-the-trigger prose cannot sustain itself indefinitely. In Cleaver's description, the steady thump of strong verbs and the rollicking rolling syntax catches our attention and we grab on, riding its power and rhythm. We're heading somewhere, we're not sure where, but we feel the power snowballing, gathering weight as it tumbles headlong toward the end of the paragraph, where "folk music, speaking of fundamental verities, climbed slowly out of the grave; and the hip lobe of the national ear, twitching involun-tarily at first, began to listen."

By the time this phrase appears, we've already downshifted, felt the variation in rhythm, the slowing syntax. The verbs re-cede and soften: "climbed slowly," "began to listen." At the semicolon, we take a breath. The wind changes direction; the action slows, stops. The storm is over for the moment, calming the stage in preparation for the next storm, the next turn in the story.

When Aristotle wrote that description lends "metaphorical life to lifeless objects," he was demonstrating the close, often inseparable, connection between action-based description and figurative language. One often leads to the other. In the stu-dents' poems, the sunbeam's *scampering* leads to a ballet meta-phor; the notes' *trickling*, to the simile of a mountain stream. Cleaver's choice of active, often violent diction—"seeping," "sweeping," "swirling," "convulsed"—leads inexorably to the image of a whirlpool, signifying the dangerous, churning nature of the sixties. And his description ends with another brilliant metaphor, "the hip lobe of the national ear." Yet even then, he does not let up on the verbs. The ear of the nation *twitches*— what a perfect choice for the sudden, spasmodic motion of a nation caught in the turbulence of a decade.

THE IMPORTANCE OF CONCRETE DETAIL

A friend who is fond of slogans, self-help tapes and refrigerator magnets once gave me a bumper sticker that reads, "Don't sweat the small stuff." I thanked her politely, took the bumper sticker home, excised the "Don't" with a felt-tipped marker, and placed the sticker over my writing desk. A writer's job, after all, is to sweat the small stuff. Without the small stuff, no large stuff can follow. "No ideas but in things," wrote William Carlos Williams, the father of imagist poets.

Ideas exist, of course, floating noiselessly above our heads, infused with ether. But how does one paint an idea? Or one's idea of an idea? It *is* possible, however, to paint a cow's skull or a white flower—that is, a representation of a cow's skull or a white flower—and allow the idea to rise from the embodied object. When she was asked about how she came to paint the famous *Cow Skull: Red, White and Blue,* O'Keeffe responded that she painted "my cow's head because I liked it."

I love the way O'Keeffe calls her painting "my cow's head," taking personal possession of the thing itself and revealing her attachment to it. Why is it that so often in our writing, we fail to describe the *things* of the story, the poem, the essay? Maybe we don't believe anyone would be interested in the ordinary objects of our world. Or perhaps we feel the task is simply beneath us. After all, we're trying to make Art, right? We're trying to move the reader to a new place, reveal Truth with a capital "T." Once, in a college writing class, I questioned a student about why he had typed his poem in all caps. I was stalling for time, trying to find something positive to say about the poem, which was filled with phrases like "the anxiety of my being" and "the chaos of undefined modernity." He looked up, his mouth spreading into a smug smile: "I didn't want anyone to miss the obscurity."

I swear, that's what he said. And I had to hand it to him; he'd certainly accomplished his purpose. No reader could possibly miss the obscurity.

I nodded mutely and moved on to the next writer. Eight of the twelve lines of her poem were devoted to describing a button.

It was a small black plastic button, smooth as a wet stone, slippery to the touch, nothing special, the kind of button you can buy in any fabric store (four buttons to a card, two dollars and forty-nine cents). Painstakingly, the writer had described its shine, its four tiny holes, the way the needle made a "scritching" sound as she tried to stitch the button onto a blue seersucker jacket. The man wearing the jacket was the narrator's dead father, propped up in a casket a few hours before the viewing. The daughter, who had noticed that a button was missing, had hurried to the store for a replacement.

That's all she wrote; those were the twelve lines. But beneath the workmanlike description of a button, the poem was living and breathing on its own. The button was a button, yes. But it was also the embodiment of a daughter's grief, her attempt to fill the missing space. Sewing on the button was the last chore she would ever perform for her father.

I've mentioned that the poet had taken pains to describe the button. The work of accurate description can be painstaking and difficult, and it often goes unpraised, like most menial labor. In some ways, a writer *is* a menial laborer, laying stone by stone what John Gardner calls the "proofs" of the story, those closely observed details that convince the reader the events really happened or might have happened. Much of our writing energy is expended not in illuminating the deep mysteries of theme and symbol but in simply performing the physical tasks of the story, such as moving a character from the bed to the refrigerator. Or describing a small black button.

Why spend eight lines of a twelve-line poem to describe a button? After all, such description requires valuable time and energy, not only for the writer but for the reader as well. Why not just mention the button, then move on to a memory of the narrator and her father, or to a lyrical riff on the joys of the father-daughter bond? Why is it so important to sweat the small stuff?

Keeping alive the fictional dream is the most obvious reason to sweat the small stuff. But it is not the only one. Equally important is the power of concrete detail to engage not only the mind of a reader but his emotions as well. A poet can drone on and on about how her father's death has affected her. She can use abstractions like *grief* and *pain* and *emptiness* until the proverbial cows come home, without moving the reader.

If it is difficult to write about grief or pain or emptiness without first embodying these concepts, it is equally difficult to write abstractly about a father's death. The subject is too large; the writer cannot compete with it. But let that same poet thread a needle, take a small black button in her hand, stitch it to a dead man's jacket, and the reader enters the poem with her. Word by carefully crafted word, the world of grief shrinks until it can fit through the eye of a needle. Finally, it is the small things that break our hearts.

The necessity of concrete imagery applies to prose as well as to poetry. "The fiction writer," said Flannery O'Connor, "has to realize that he can't create compassion with compassion, or emotion with emotion, or thought with thought. He has to provide all these things with a body; he has to create a world with weight and extension." Before an idea, emotion or abstraction can take on imaginative weight and substance, it must be embodied in sensory, concrete detail.

THE WAY TO A READER'S HEART

When a reader fully believes our story, both intellectually and emotionally, he moves in and unpacks his bags. No longer a tourist living out of a suitcase, ordering room service and watching suspiciously from his hotel window as the natives bustle on the street below, he has become, for the moment at least, a native himself. He changes into comfortable clothes, strolls the avenues, eats in open-air cafes, even tries the local catch-of-the-day. He turns another page in the book. Anything is possible. Who knows? He might even fall in love.

When we give careful attention to the things of the story, what Gardner calls "moment by moment authenticity" of detail, our reader is fully engaged. He is not only taking in information, he is responding emotionally to that information. Like our narrator, the reader, too, wants to kiss the girl with the coral lipstick. He, too, wants to brush the strands of hair from her eyes. Could it be he's falling in love?

If our reader continues turning pages, his blood pressure may rise, his hands tighten into fists. She's been cheating on him all along—he should have known. If he could just get his hands on the guy, he'd . . .

What has happened is that we have done our job well. Through the use of concrete and sensory detail, through page by page rendering of the story's world, we have penetrated layers of the reader's consciousness, blasting right through his neocortex and into the mammalian and reptilian brain.

Human beings have a three-layered brain. The top layer is the most recent layer in evolutionary terms. Without it, we would not be fully human. The neocortex takes in information and categorizes it. It enables us to reason, to contemplate, to reach intellectual insights and process abstractions; words like *grief* and *fear* actually mean something to the neocortex. However, although the neocortex can understand the concept of grief or pain, it cannot *feel* it. I think of the neocortex as a gentleman in formal attire, sitting upright in a wingback chair, puffing leisurely on a pipe (he is, of course, not inhaling). His head may nod slightly, in agreement or detached interest, but be assured he is not keeping time with the music. He is no head-banger; he presents no danger on the dance floor. The neocortex is not capable of producing a physical response, a gut reaction.

That ability is housed deeper, in the mesocortex, the early mammalian brain, which is capable of feeling anger, passion, sexual love and other emotions. When a reader feels desire for a character in your story—say, the girl with the coral lipstick—his mammalian brain is engaged.

And when the reader feels threatened, when his very survival as a fictional lover is called into question, his reptilian brain is activated. He wants to punch the other guy. Though we might like to imagine we're above such brutality, the truth is that no matter how civilized we become, we all possess a reptilian brain capable of almost anything when our survival is threatened. You need look no further than front page headlines to be reminded of this fact. "I just snapped," said Mike Tyson when he was questioned about biting his opponent's ear during a match. "I cannot tell you why I acted like I did—I can only say I thought I might lose."

Few of us wish to produce such primitive emotions in our readers. However, we *do* want our readers to respond not only intellectually but emotionally to the words we write, the scenes we set, the characters we create. Without an emotional response, the reader will not sympathize with the plight of our characters or care about what happens to them. And if a reader doesn't care what happens to the character, why turn the next page? If a reader isn't invited into the room of our poem or story by means of sensory detail, why would he wish to remain? Why spend time in a place you not only can't imagine, but feel nothing for? And *feeling*, remember, resides below the neocortex. It lives beneath abstraction and explanation and analysis, in the living breathing world of the real, a world created by the writer who patiently and carefully handles, again and again, the objects of her story.

EXERCISES

1. Make a list of terms associated with your vocation or avocation, or with a line of work you're interested in, perhaps a job your main character holds. In *On Fire*, Larry Brown lists some of the equipment of his fireman's world:

> . . . ladders, axes, forcible entry tools, rappelling gear, ropes, safety belts, breathing apparatus, nozzles, generators, a Hurst Tool (Jaws of Life), flashlights, pike poles, entry saws, boltcutters, fire extinguishers . . .

After you've made your list, choose several terms from the list and expand them into descriptive phrases. Combine these phrases to make a complete, sensory description. You might try the "I love" technique that Brown employs:

I love my old torn-up boots, the toes skinned and
burned, my wrinkled gloves, sootstreaked and charred,
my dirty coat and frayed turnout pants.
    I love to go down on the floor and see the smoke over
me, worm my way forward to the fire, the hose hard as
a brick, the scuffed rubber on the end of the fog nozzle.
I love the two-and-a-half-inch hoses and the big chrome
nozzles that no man can hold, the red axes and the
pry bars and the pike poles that we tear down ceilings
with . . .

2. Write a description for an article of clothing that will appear in a catalog unaccompanied by an illustration. Your job is
not only to describe the item accurately but also to entice a
customer to buy it. Begin with the basics: name the article precisely and list available colors (be inventive!) and fabrics. Then
describe, in detail, each distinguishing feature. Finally, set the
fantasy scene for the customer. Where might he wear the item?
How will this article of clothing change his image, his life?

3. Starting with the same article of clothing (see exercise
two), write another description. This time, imagine you own
the item. It is, in fact, your favorite piece of clothing. Your sister
(or brother or best friend) has written to you, asking to borrow
the item to wear for an upcoming event. She's never seen the
item, but she's heard through the grapevine it's quite a find.
You don't want to loan it to her, but you don't want to tell
her that. Write the description you'd include in your response.
Remember, you're trying to convince her it's *not* such a find
after all.

4. Write descriptions for five different entrees to be served
at an upscale restaurant. These are descriptions the waiters will
recite, word for word, to diners. Be sure to include not only the
name of the dish and its ingredients but also details about how
it will be prepared and served.

5. Choose a piece of furniture in your home that holds at
least four objects. I'd probably choose my writing desk, which
is crowded with coffee cups, pens, books, rubber bands, a sleeping cat, unsent letters, photographs and mementos. You might

choose your dresser or the dining room table. Before you begin to describe the objects, select a method for ordering your description. You might decide, for instance, on spatial ordering, working from right to left or from front to back. You could order the objects in terms of size, shape, texture or any other sensory quality. Or you might describe the objects in order of their significance—emotionally, practically, or aesthetically.

6. Describe a person in action, preferably at a task with clearly delineated steps. Watch your daughter wash the car, or take notes (mental or actual) as your husband plants a tree. You might also write a description directly from memory. Maybe it's been forty years since you've seen your uncle milk a cow, but the moment remains in your mind as clearly as if it happened yesterday. As you write the description, think of breaking the larger action into small, detailed movements. Let the verbs lead the way.

7. Using this chapter's suggestions for using the "back-door technique," describe an object or place in terms of what it is *not*.

8. Following Flannery O'Connor's advice about writers providing a concrete body for emotions, scan your writing for any abstract term for an emotion (words like *love, grief, anxiety* and *guilt*). Rewrite a section that contains an abstraction, substituting concrete images that suggest the feeling. If you find it hard to remove the abstraction completely, try anchoring it with a concrete detail. For instance, instead of writing, "I feel a heavy guilt every time I go home," you could write, "Guilt comes in the door with me, dragging its heavy suitcase."

9. Choose an inanimate subject—an object, place, idea or emotion—and describe it using active verbs. Refer to the selections from *Soul on Ice* and *The Gift of Stones* as examples.

THE NOSE AND MOUTH AND HAND AND EAR OF THE BEHOLDER

So far we've been talking mainly about eyes, but eyes are only one-fifth of the sensory plot. Consider how the world first makes itself known to an infant. Long before the eyes focus—on light, the mother's face, the yellow rattle being shaken—the nose and mouth and hands and ears have already begun their work. The taste of first colostrum on the tongue. The milk-scent of mother, the lilt and pitch of her voice, the braille of her soft veined breast.

Since ours is a visually oriented culture, it's easy to think of description solely in terms of seeing. "Paint pictures with your words," we tell our students. "Describe that character so I can really see him." Rarely do we ask to *hear* the character, the rhythms of his dialogue or the squeak of his boots on the linoleum. And we almost never request information about how characters (or places or objects) *feel* to the touch, or how they *smell.* And *taste?* It's barely mentioned in polite company.

Yet ignoring the other senses in your writing is like sitting in a gourmet restaurant wearing ear plugs, work gloves, and a surgical mask over your nose and mouth. Sure, you can still read the menu. You can even enjoy the artist's palette, the purple radicchio curled on top of the mixed greens. You can hold your wine glass to the light and admire its fluted stem. But you can't hear the clink when you raise the glass for a toast. Or the sibilant intimacies from the couple in the next booth. And what about the hot crusty roll the waiter just placed with a tong on your bread plate? It looks hot, it looks crusty, but how will you know unless you pick it up with your bare hands, feel its weight and shellacked surface, break it open and feel the steam escaping from the soft center? You swirl the butter knife in the small white crock, spread a smear of herb-speckled butter on the bread, lift it to your mouth. Were you not wearing a mask, you might detect the scent of rosemary even before the bread touches your lips.

SMELL

A picture may be worth a thousand words, but a scent is worth a million. If this were one of those scratch-and-sniff books, you could slide a fingernail across the page and smell the restaurant bread I've just slathered with rosemary butter. Perhaps if we thought of description in terms of a child's scratch-and-sniff book, our writing would be more inviting to the reader, and more emotionally evocative.

Of the five senses, smell is the one with the best memory. It's been thirty years since my high school prom, and I've long forgotten whether my date had blue or brown eyes. I've forgotten the timbre of his voice, too, and the endearments he insinuated into my ear as we were dancing. But each time I catch a whiff of English Leather shaving lotion, he returns to me. It happened just last week. A middle-aged man walked past me on his way to the dairy section, and I had to physically restrain myself from ditching my grocery cart and following him. In that instant, I was transported to the balloon-strewn gymnasium of a Southern California high school. Such is the power of smell, our most primitive sense, the one most directly linked to memory and emotion.

One of my friends is afflicted with a rare disorder known as anosmia; his sense of smell is absent. When he first told me this, I was so astounded I said something like, "Oh my God, I'd rather be blind!" He was hurt by the remark, for which I immediately asked forgiveness, casually brushing off the seriousness of his disorder. But if truth be told, it's hard to imagine living without the sense of smell. Where would we store our memories? And how could we enjoy the present pleasures of the bed, the table, the scented bath?

Smell is why cartoon dogs rise toward the ceiling and float, on visible scent waves, toward their meals.

Smell is why real estate agents advise sellers to bake something—preferably bread or chocolate chip cookies—before a prospective buyer comes to call.

Smell is why some of us marry certain men, and why, after twenty years, we still want to be near them.

Smell is why cyber-sex will never wholly catch on.

For even in this scrubbed, disinfected, sanitized, deodorized society, our noses still work fairly well. Some work better than others; these belong to perfumers and wine tasters and chefs and firemen, and to forensic pathologists who conduct autopsies (only a small percent of the population can detect the odor of arsenic.)

Although the rest of us may not use our noses so directly in our work, the sense of smell is nevertheless an important, if subliminal, part of our lives. Many writers rely heavily on this sense during the writing process. "You can smell the poem before you can see it," says Denise Levertov, suggesting that smell not only evokes strong memories but also triggers imagery. Maybe that's why the German poet Schiller kept rotting apples in his writing desk. Their odor, he said, helped him to write.

Whenever I want to write about adolescence, I need only catch a whiff of vinyl, and I'm back in 1962. Vinyl is the smell of September, of fresh beginnings. It's three-ring binders and zippered pouches and collapsible rain bonnets. It's the first day of school. I'm sitting in the front row, sharpened pencil poised. Miss Suchek opens a new box of chalk and takes out a piece, long and white and as yet unbroken. She writes the year's first equation on the board. Anything is possible.

Another writing day I'm working on the same story, set in a seventh-grade algebra class. My cat comes in from the rain and leaps onto my lap. Wet fur. Wet wool. It's still 1962, but now it's November. Things have begun to sour. The smell of wet wool brings back cloakrooms, winter coats, cold rain, radiators hissing in the classroom. Already today Miss Suchek has broken two pieces of chalk on the same equation. I'm clammy from the radiator steam seeping into my sweater. Will seventh grade ever be over?

Since smell is the most direct of our senses, you'd think it would be easy to describe a particular scent. On the contrary. In *A Natural History of the Senses,* Diane Ackerman calls smell "the mute sense, the one without words," then goes on to explain the weak connections between the smell center and the language center of our brains: "We can describe a sight using visual adjectives—but when we try to describe smell, it's usually in terms of other things . . . usually we resort to describing how they make us feel."

She's right. If you were to look back at descriptions you've written that employ the use of smell, you'd probably find lots of adjectives suggesting an odor's effect on you, or on one of your characters. For example, you might have written that the smell of rotten eggs was nauseating or repulsive, or that the scent of a woman's perfume was intoxicating. You might also have shown a character's physical reaction to a particular smell, saying "he recoiled from the stench" or "he inhaled deeply the woman's scent." In *As I Lay Dying,* Faulkner uses this method to suggest the stench of Addie's body days after her death. He never directly describes the odor; instead, he mentions such details as the changing direction of the wind and the townspeople covering their noses and mouths as the death wagon passes.

Although these methods—using an adjective to describe a character's feeling toward a particular smell, or showing his physical reaction to that smell—can be effective, they are indirect methods of description. They do not call forth directly the quality of the subject. *Nauseating* is not the odor that eggs give off. And although *intoxication* might describe your reaction to smelling a woman's perfume, *intoxication* is not the scent itself (despite the fact that a perfumer named it so).

If this perfumer were asked to describe the qualities of his new scent, "Intoxication", he might press his nose to the test tube. *Musky,* he'd say. Or *minty,* or *floral,* or *acrid,* in the same way a wine taster might describe a particular wine's bouquet as *nutlike* or *fruity* or *oaky*. Yet despite the range of descriptive adjectives at his disposal, the perfumer would still be naming the aroma in terms of something else. *Floral* suggests that the perfume smells like a flower; *musky,* that it resembles the odor of a musk deer or perhaps a ripe muskmelon.

Writers, also, often evoke smells by describing them in terms of other smells. This works especially well on a reader who has no firsthand experience with a particular scent. For instance, a New Yorker who's never known a summer in the deep South may not even know what kudzu *is*, let alone how it smells. But after reading Mary Hood's story, "How Far She Went," the reader will be able to imagine it:

> The heat of the day had broken, but the air was thick, sultry, weighted with honeysuckle in second blood and the Nu-Grape scent of kudzu.

By describing the kudzu vine in terms of a grape soda, which most people have smelled, Hood provides the reader with an entry into the sensory territory of the book.

Another descriptive technique for evoking a smell is to confine it to a particular place, especially a place weighted with history. In the following description from Joan Chase's *During the Reign of the Queen of Persia*, the smells of the kitchen are intensified by the accumulation of years:

> Both men were smoking; the air held it low because the kitchen was steamy from cooking and the storm windows sealed us in, the smoke blending with the milk smell of the room, that room soured every inch by milk slopped and strained, churned and set by, year after year, maybe seventy of them passed altogether.

Like most readers, you might never have brought pails of milk in from the barn, waited for the cream to rise, or churned butter. But you've known the stale smell of closed-up rooms and the odor of milk left in the carton beyond its expiration date. Because you've witnessed how time has its way with things, you're able to enter the kitchen of Chase's novel.

To evoke the atmosphere of this particular kitchen, Chase also mixes the smell of milk with the smell of cigarettes and the steam of cooking food, thus creating a collage of smells, a layering of senses that takes us deeper into the world of her novel. Mixing two or more smells is another technique for bringing forth the qualities of a place, an object or a person. One of my college boyfriends smelled like motor oil, cigarettes and Dial soap. A strange and complicated combination, perhaps, but then, most memorable things *are* complicated. How would you describe a high school gymnasium during a basketball game? Can you bring forth at least two distinct, even contradictory, smells? How about an August afternoon on the beach? Try to get beyond the salt smell of the shallows. Perhaps a scent of coconuts floats by—the girl in the yellow bikini, her body oiled with tanning lotion. Beside you, an open can of beer warms in the sun. Mix the three smells together and see what you have, then invite the reader in.

Another way to intensify a description using smell (or any other sense) is to temporarily mute the other senses. I'm not referring to actual mortification of the senses, like poet Gerard Manley Hopkins's refusal to use his eyes. However, the concept of stripping away the senses is one that writers can apply to descriptive passages. When we refuse to rely solely on one sense—most writers favor the visual—the other senses will naturally come to the foreground. Remember Blind Man's Bluff, the party game of childhood? Suddenly the blindfolded child seemed to grow longer arms, more sensitive fingers. He had to—or risk bumping into a tree.

Though we certainly don't want to blind our characters in order to call forth sensory description, we can metaphorically darken their worlds. In this excerpt from Naomi Shihab Nye's story "The Cookies," the narrator recalls going door to door with her grandmother to sell Girl Scout cookies to elderly neighbors in an old apartment building:

> Hand-in-hand we climbed the dark stairs, knocked on
> the doors. I shivered, held Grandma tighter, remember

still the smell which was curiously fragrant, a sweet soup
of talcum powder, folded curtains, roses pressed in a
book. Was that what years smelled like?

Because the stairways were dark, the girl could not rely on
her eyes for sensory information. What other circumstances
might put a character, literally, in the dark?

Maybe he's in bed trying to sleep. Suddenly, smells are more
distinct. What *is* that odor? Is something burning?

Or he's bound and blindfolded by kidnappers. For days he
tries to identify his surroundings and attackers solely through
smell and hearing.

Or maybe he's just blind with love. (Does closing our eyes
when we kiss intensify the aroma of our lover, the flavor of the
kiss? Perhaps. At any rate, it cuts down on distractions.)

By refusing to base our descriptions merely on visual imagery
and by placing our characters in situations where vision alone
will not serve them, we force other sensory possibilities to the
surface. A blind man probably isn't born with stronger powers
of hearing, smell, taste or touch than the rest of us. He's just
forced to use them more. And without the distraction of visual
imagery, he's able to focus more purely on other means of
perception.

When discussing techniques for descriptive writing, it's easy
to get carried away, to forget the most basic of Aristotle's max-
ims: "the proper and special name of a thing." Sometimes the
best route to a reader's nose is a straightforward naming of the
thing itself. Something as simple as "The room filled with the
smell of ripe peaches" may be enough to coax a reader into
your fictional dream.

TASTE

Dwelling in close proximity to smell is taste. So close, in fact,
that it is difficult to separate the two. As Diane Ackerman writes
in *A Natural History of the Senses*, "Smell and taste share a common airshaft, like residents in a high rise who know which is
curry, lasagna, or Cajun night for their neighbors." Everything

that has been said about describing smells applies to describing tastes. Like smell, taste elicits strong physical and emotional responses. It's not the sight of blood, but its scent and taste that draws the shark to its victim. In the same way, the reader can be pulled viscerally into a description that employs smell and taste as well as sight. And, like smell, taste conjures up memory. Marcel Proust, a genius of sensory description, wrote that "when from a long-distant past nothing subsists, after the people are dead, after the things are broken and scattered, taste and smell alone . . . remain poised a long time . . ."

Though both senses present rich opportunities for evoking emotion and memory, both present challenges to us when we employ them in descriptive passages. Smell isn't the only "mute" sense; for some writers, the vocabulary of taste extends no further than a mention of the food's name. Sometimes it's enough, as Aristotle suggested, merely to name the object precisely. Fried chicken. Buttermilk biscuits. Merlot. But the effectiveness of that technique depends a great deal upon a reader's associations with the food being named. To launch me directly into bliss, a waiter need only mention Häagen Dazs Chocolate Chocolate Chip; but another diner, say, someone allergic to chocolate or someone who's nursing a toothache, may react quite differently.

Moving beyond a straightforward naming, a writer can describe a taste in terms of the tongue's gustatory map: sweet, salty, sour and bitter. But tongue-bound adjectives carry us only so far. *Sour*, for instance, can describe not only a lemon drop, but buttermilk that's gone bad. The sour of sour cream presents yet another variation, as does a whiskey sour.

These limitations of taste description don't seem to affect the writings of Marcel Proust. His descriptions are so evocative that they elevate tastes and smells almost to the status of characters. For the narrator of *Remembrance of Things Past*, these twin senses were the gateways to the past; in particular, the taste of a madeleine tea cake was the key to memories of his childhood in the village of Combray. With the first taste, the village "rose up like a stage set" in his mind; visual images followed the gustatory.

Years ago my neighbor, a novelist, was so taken with Proust's description of madeleines that he decided he must learn to bake them. As a result, every few months a package of these delicacies arrives at my doorstep, usually accompanied by a descriptive passage that my neighbor just couldn't resist sharing with a fellow writer. Later, sitting together and sipping citrus-scented tea, we *ooh* and *ahh* over Proust's words. Perhaps no writer is more effective in bringing forth the flavors of the world.

Let's return to Proust's treatment of the madeleines, those little cakes soaked in tea. One descriptive technique he uses is to borrow qualities from the other senses. From the sense of sight, he borrows color and shape: the cakes are described as "squat" and "plump," shaped like "the fluted valve of a scallop shell" which is "richly sensual under its severe, religious folds."

From the sense of smell, he borrows "a decoction of lime-blossom."

And borrowing from the sense of touch to describe the madeleines soaked in tea, he writes that when "the warm liquid mixed with the crumbs touched my palate . . . a shudder ran through me." Here, Proust suggests not only the physical properties of the tea—in this case, warmth—but also his bodily reaction to that warmth. If the madeleines had been crunchy, Proust might have included their crispy snap; had they been spicy, he might have described the degree of heat or discomfort the spiciness induced, perhaps a tingling sting at the edges of his lips.

Another of Proust's techniques is to set the scene in which the cakes were consumed, a childhood scene the adult narrator is recounting. The madeleines were served to him on Sunday mornings at Combray, when he went into his aunt's bedroom to wish her good morning. The aunt, after dipping a piece of cake in her tea, would hand it to him. Over time, the taste of the madeleine became inextricably mixed with the memory of those Sunday mornings, the shared intimacy between an aunt and nephew.

Atmosphere—including time, place, mood and surrounding details—is an important element in the enjoyment of any food. A chicken salad sandwich, for instance, might be a forgettable lunch when eaten on a paper plate while you're alone on a Saturday afternoon staring at a television screen. Take that same sandwich, put it on a white china plate on a glass-topped table overlooking the Pacific ocean at dusk while you sit beside your newest lover, elbows touching, and it becomes a gourmet feast you'll remember for years.

After a while, the Pacific breeze begins to disturb the latent flavors in the air, so that it isn't just chicken salad you're tasting, or the slice of Bermuda onion, or even the seeded wheat bread on which the mixture is spread. Is it possible to taste the ocean? My five-year-old nephew can, or so he tells me, his head leaning out the car window—and we're still five miles from the beach. He slurps up a summer evening, too, pronouncing it delicious. He knows the taste of Play-Doh, the dog's fur he presses close, the plastic ball that smacks him in the face. Blood, too, from a cut on his lip. I remember that taste. Once, during a junior high softball game, I tripped over third base and landed face-first: blood rust, mixed with the scent of wild onion and the briny sting of tears.

Our tongues know more flavors than merely those of food and drink. We chew on a blade of grass, bite the end of a cigar, suck on a cinnamon-flavored toothpick. We fluoride our teeth, swish mouthwash, down vitamins that taste of iron, swallow cherry cough syrup. Our mouths know the taste of a dental hygienist's rubber gloves, the cardboard X-ray slide we bite down on, the flat dry taste of a tongue depressor. Late evening, after giving our baby a bath, we press our mouth affectionately to his stomach, tasting the sweet mixture of talcum and Johnson's Baby Oil and innocence.

Innocence? Well, what else to call the sweetness that rises from the baby's skin? Sometimes, as in the advertisement for Mounds bars, a taste seems "indescribably delicious." Or merely indescribable. That's when abstractions can help fill in the blanks. Athletes tell of tasting defeat or victory; a vocalist sings "Love Is in the Air." And a writer, struggling to convey the bittersweet taste of a doomed lover's kiss, writes "Her mouth tasted like roses and sorrow."

TOUCH

Touch, by definition, is an intimate sense. It requires a body's immediate presence. The eye can see across long distances, the ear hear faraway noises, the nose detect aromas far removed from it. But in order to feel something or someone, we must be close. A well-written description that employs the sense of touch bridges physical and emotional distances. It can wrap a soft quilt around the reader, deliver a bracing slap across the face, or render him helpless in sensory bliss. That's what happened to me as I listened to Gail Galloway Adams read from her novel, *The Eye of Madame X*:

> Next day Madame brushed my hair like Momma does at home. There is real surrender in letting my head be tugged by a rattail comb in someone else's hands. First she parts, scoring my skull like a map, separating strands into smooth threads. Little teeth nip hair by hair out of tangles and the preliminary comb is ritual before the hair brush. That begins with bristles skimming like sea urchins down the contours of my head. Madame lifts the brush quickly off my neck to make the hair fly, like a held music phrase; each strand slips back like a whispered note. With my eyes closed, I pretend I'm underwater, head bumping, and sand scratches my scalp, currents tug me like seaweed ropes; I shiver. Bristles quiver near my ear, tiny nylon nails.
> "You cold?"
> "No, I'm fine. Makes me shiver."

The scene Adams sets is charged with physical intimacy, due in part to the private nature of the act she describes. Unless you're a cosmetologist, you probably don't brush the hair of a stranger, nor do you allow a stranger to brush yours. Not all touching is created equal. We often shake strangers' hands, share crowded subway seats where physical contact is unavoidable, squeeze past fellow airplane passengers on our way to a window seat.

But to allow someone access to your head, your scalp? This requires trust and surrender. At the salon, the stylist greets you, ties a cape around your neck. You glance in the mirror: a bibbed child. Your feet dangle high off the ground. Gently she lowers your head into the sink, turns on the water, tests it with her hand—a maternal gesture. You close your eyes, you can't help it. If she's a good stylist, she encourages you to let go, don't worry, she'll support your head. Then her hands are working, her fingers scratching, massaging, loosening the scalp. "Marry me," you whisper, and she laughs, wrapping your head in a warm white towel.

It's clear what Adams's description did to me. The writer so strongly evoked the feeling of being taken care of, of giving oneself over, literally, to another's hands, that I did what any willing reader does. I took it personally, extending her scene to include a reverie of my own. I recall that when I first heard Adams's description, and later, when I read her words, I reacted viscerally. Like the narrator, I too shivered; I even closed my eyes. Many writers could describe a hair-brushing scene, but how many could cause physical symptoms in their readers? And how does Adams accomplish this task, beyond merely choosing a scene of physical intimacy?

First, following Aristotle's suggestion, she accurately names the objects of the story's world: rattail comb, little teeth, bristles, strand, tiny nylon nails. Then she describes, patiently and precisely, the act itself. The hair isn't merely brushed and combed; it is tugged, parted, scored, separated, nipped, untangled, lifted. The writer breaks one broad generic act into its specific and significant steps, taking time with each one because, in this case, each step matters. Every part of the process is necessary to call forth the emotional quality of this particular scene, in which the narrator first begins to trust Madame, to take her into her confidence.

We know that the narrator is physically affected by Madame's brushing: "I shiver." Madame notices this: "You cold?" Thus, the reader is given two proofs of what the narrator is feeling. Since touch is a passive as well as an active sense, a speaker's or character's physical reaction is an effective technique for evoking the sense of touch.

When physical terms no longer suffice to describe her sensations, the narrator breaks into metaphor and simile. Madame's brushing has taken her beneath her physical self, into an underwater world where bristles are like sea urchins and "currents tug me like seaweed ropes." The brushed hair, alive with static, holds in air "like a held music phrase; each strand slips back like a whispered note."

It's fitting that Adams describes the scene in terms of music, for much of her description's effectiveness is due to its attention to language, to carefully selected diction and musical phrasings. The tingling effect is suggested by the repetition of the short *i*. Lightly and quickly, the words tickle our ears the way a comb tickles our scalp: *nip, bristles, skimming, lifts, slips, whispered, quiver.* Adams's phrasing reinforces this effect. During the preliminary parting and scoring, the sentences are broken into short segments. Then, as the brushing continues and the narrator gives in to the sensual experience, the sentences grow longer, more leisurely, suggesting the rhythms of sex—which happens to be the subject of a subsequent section of Adams's novel.

SOUND

"The ear writes my poems, not the mind," said Stanley Kunitz in a PBS interview. "The ear is the infallible test." Prose writers, too, often speak of the important role sound imagery plays in the writing and revision process. Some claim to hear an inner voice—the narrator's or a particular character's—that dictates the rhythms, diction and tone of their language. Others focus on the musical interplay among words, on lyrical cadences, a kind of sound-for-sound's-sake that results in stories resembling tone poems.

Still others focus on the sounds of the physical world as a way of pulling the reader into their fictional dream. Early on in Mary Hood's "How Far She Went," the grandmother hears at a distance "the pulpwood cutters sawing through another acre across the lake. Nearer, there was the racket of motorcycles laboring cross-country, insect-like, distracting." Later in the story, after discovering that their lives are threatened by the men on these motorcycles, the woman and her granddaughter hide from the men, crouching in the silence and hearing "the glissando of locusts, the dry crunch of boots on the flinty beach, their low man-talk drifting . . ." After several terrifying moments, one bike started up. "The other ratcheted, ratcheted, then coughed, caught, roared." Finally, when the motorcyclists were gone, "crickets resumed and a near frog bic-bic-bicked."

Within these brief passages, Hood demonstrates several methods for evoking the sounds of a fictional world. First, she names specifically the sound the character hears: "the pulpwood cutters sawing." Sometimes it's enough to merely state directly what a character or narrator hears—"the screen door slamming" or "a bluebird calling high and sweet"—without attempting to reproduce the particular sound through audio likenesses.

Another common way to suggest a sound is to modify it through the use of adjectives. Rather than "the sound of slippers," for instance, you could write "the soft sound of bedroom slippers." Hood uses this technique with "the dry crunch of boots." Often, however, adjectives merely label the quality rather than bring it alive for the reader. Hood's descriptive phrase escapes cliché partly because she employs an adjective not usually associated with the sense of sound. We expect to see adjectives like *loud, harsh, high-pitched* or *deep* in sound descriptions. But *dry*? Hood's choice is surprising and new.

Hood completes the image by giving further descriptive information, thus providing a setting or context for the sound: "the dry crunch of boots *on the flinty beach* . . ." By the time this image appears in the story, the reader is ready to receive it, to add it to the other sensory proofs that have been offered. The dryness of the air has long been established. The reader has learned, by an accumulation of details, that it's August, there has been no rain in some time, and there will be none on this day. Even the leaves know it; they have turned over, "quaking, silver."

When Hood names the motorcycles' sound a "racket," she is moving a step closer to imitative sound imagery. Though "racket" does not suggest the exact sound a motorcycle makes, it is nevertheless a more evocative auditory choice than "loud sound" would have been; its harsh consonants grate more irritatingly on the ear. In the same way, "crunch," though not strictly onomatopoeic, comes closer to evoking the sound of boots than "noise" would.

Onomatopoeia is one of the most effective ways to help a reader imagine a particular sound. Words like *boink, sizzle, slosh* and *yakety-yak* attempt to represent things by the sounds they make. Though no word can reproduce an actual sound, you can sometimes imitate a sound by substituting an onomatopoeic word for a more general word. For example, "the sound of bedroom slippers" could become "the hush of slippers," or "the whisper of slippers," if softness is the quality you wish to evoke.

I encourage my students to keep lists of favorite sound words, those that employ onomatopoeia as well as those that merely suggest a sound's quality. Although adult students occasionally come up with interesting lists, the children's lists never fail to startle. After listening to Carl Sandburg's "Jazz Fantasia," one fourth grader, who titled his list "Words With Personality," came up with seventy or eighty words during one class period. The list included not only the standard *whiz* and *pop* and other single-syllable explosions fourth grade boys are so fond of (*burp, belch, fart,* etc.) but also words like *rustle* and *shuffle,* and an occasional invented word: *wind-swish* for a weeping willow during a breezy rain, *honk-shoe* for his father's snoring. My favorite was *plinkle,* which the boy invented for a story about his sister plucking violin strings. When I questioned him about why he didn't use *pluck,* he shook his head adamantly. "Pluck is too deep," he said. "Hers is more like the way an angel would do it. You know, plinkle."

Although isolated sound words provide an entry into description, they take a writer only so far. After all, how often does a word appear in isolation? Furthermore, a sound word that is overly boisterous may call attention to itself, robbing a phrase or sentence of its overall effectiveness, thus distracting the reader from the fictional dream. Any word that becomes too big for its own britches should be questioned at length before you let it loose on your story or poem.

That goes double for any word whose sound, however musically intriguing, is not reinforced by its sense. It may be true, as one witty personage noted, that *syphilis* is the most beautiful word in the English language; however, try using it in a story, and see how far its musical beauty gets you. The opposite theory also holds true. Some words that purport to suggest beauty simply can't musically carry the message. Take *bucolic*, for instance. Does an uglier word exist? Not for me. It sounds like something a baby would do to a burp rag, or worse. In the case of *bucolic*, for my money at least, sound and sense simply do not make a happy marriage.

On the other hand, some sounds and meanings were meant for one another; Henry James suggested "summer afternoon" as the most beautiful phrase in our language. The words' meanings not only call forth warmth and leisure and, for some reason I don't quite understand, youth; they also *sound* lazy and languid. *Summer afternoon* takes its time; it's not going anywhere soon. And the living is easy, phonetically speaking—the open vowels, the liquid roll of the repeated *r*'s.

Although selecting an evocative sound word is important, more important is how the word operates within a given phrase, sentence, or paragraph. In Mary Hood's story, *ratcheted* helps us hear the motorcycle starting up, but it's the combination of the sputtering phonemes and syntax of "ratcheted, ratcheted, then coughed, caught, roared" that sends the motorcycle, finally, on its way. *Glissando* is a beautiful word in isolation, but Hood's phrase "the glissando of locusts" is even better, not only for the cumulative effect of its sound but for the surprise of its metaphor.

Just as metaphor can connect a reader to the smells, sights, tastes and textures in a story, it can also call forth the *sounds* of a fictional world. The motorcycles, the reader learns, were "laboring" through the countryside. They were "insect-like," a description that calls up not only their movement but also their monotonous drone. In contrast, the "glissando of locusts" suggests the graceful slide of music.

Having been presented again and again with the auditory proofs of Hood's story, the reader comes to equate the motorcycles' racket with irritation, cacophony, mechanical intrusion, and finally, terror. When the terror subsides, what remains are the sounds of nature, providing euphony, peace and release: "Their roaring died away. Crickets resumed . . ." and, as the grandmother and her granddaughter made their way toward home and safety, insects "sang in the thickets, silencing at their oncoming."

SYNESTHESIA

"It smells like sparkling gases" and "tastes like a mouthful of bees," wrote the little girl. Tammy was a fourth grader in a poetry class I was teaching, and we'd spent the hour writing color poems. She'd chosen silver, which she said was her favorite color. Most of the other children had chosen the expected blue or green or red, and many of their descriptions were good, some even astonishing—"Red is a mad crayon/foaming at the color" and "Green is fresh/like a new pair of lungs." But only Tammy's poem employed synesthesia, the phenomenon in which one stimulation evokes sensation in another.

I was not in her class long enough to find out more about Tammy, to see if this example was typical of the way she perceived the world. Quite possibly it was. She may be one of those rare persons—1 out of 500,000—in whom sensory perceptions are mixed. Though some synesthetes claim to "smell" certain colors or musical notes, the auditory-visual mix is the most common. Many famous artists and composers have this ability, as do some writers, Baudelaire and Samuel Johnson among them. Nabokov, a famous synesthete, called his ability "colored hearing."

I've never read anything to suggest that Georgia O'Keeffe experienced synesthesia. Why, then, can I almost hear the tones and rhythms pulsing from her painting *Music, Pink and Blue I*? Perhaps O'Keeffe, although she was not physiologically wired for synesthesia, was *emotionally* wired to receive multisensory messages. Or maybe, in the process of working long and hard in her medium, she discovered connections she had not known were present. After Tammy handed in her poem about silver, I began to devise assignments that I hoped would jump-start my students into writing more unusual sensory descriptions. "What does your name taste like?" I asked. "Can you smell red, or yellow, or green? How would you describe yourself—or a sunset, or an object—to a blind person? What colors and shapes are your dreams and emotions? How do they move?" Here are some of the children's responses.

I Answer the Blind Man

What does a sun look like
going down over the ocean?

It's like touching a rose
after it has rained.
It's like hearing a river
flow downstream.
I like picturing in your mind
the sun halfway in the water
and the golden rays on the ocean.

    Maria, 5th grade

My Cat Dreams

My cat dreams.
His dreams are like an ocean.
Waves of different dreams roll onto shore.

    Mary, 4th grade

Freedom

Freedom is like putting three strawberries
in your mouth at a time,
touching the wet coldness of it,

> looking at the redness,
> hearing the crisp wonder in the air.
>> Tiffany, 3rd grade

We've already noted the strong connections between smell and taste; it's difficult to write a description evoking one without suggesting the other. However, other sensory connections—for instance, the relationship between hearing and sight, or between taste and touch—may not come so easily. We may have to trick ourselves into surprise by giving ourselves assignments that require mixing the senses, or by seeking out literary examples of synesthesia to use as models.

In her novel *Stones for Ibarra*, Harriet Doerr mixes the visual and tactile with the auditory. Sara and her husband have just arrived in Ibarra. It's dark, too dark for them to see the interior of the house where they will sleep. Although the night is alive with leaves rustling, a coyote crying, the "quick, light feet of possums and raccoons," Sara, having fallen asleep quickly, hears none of these noises. It's only when the physical noises cease that she stirs from sleep:

> Sara sits up in her cot. "I think I hear frost," she says to her sleeping husband.
> Four hours later they awake shivering to a sudden dawn that floods up behind the eastern mesa and stains half the sky coral.
> Now the house is revealed, and the garden.

It's possible to see frost, touch frost, perhaps even taste frost. But Doerr's character also hears it. Within her highly charged emotional space, her sensory perceptions stir, wake and leap boundaries, until she is able to hear the unhearable. In the same way, the adolescent narrator Darl, in Faulkner's *As I Lay Dying*, was able to actually *feel* silence:

> Then I would wait until they all went to sleep so I could lie with my shirt-tail up, hearing them asleep, feeling

> myself without touching myself, feeling the cool silence
> blowing upon my parts . . .

In describing the way silence felt, Faulkner moves a step beyond Doerr, into the realm of abstraction. Frost, although it makes no audible sound, is still a sensory and concrete object. Silence, on the other hand, has no weight or texture; it is a condition, a quality, an *abstraction* that nevertheless manages to evoke a sensory response.

A NOTE ABOUT ABSTRACT DESCRIPTIONS

> . . . I love abstractions, I love
> to give them a nouny place to live,
> a firm seat in the balcony
> of ideas, while music plays . . .
>   —Stephen Dunn, from "Loves"

Literary rules, although not *made* to be broken, often are, even the most basic and sacrosanct dictum (I tremble as I write this!) of employing sensory, concrete details. There may be instances where *abstract* description better serves the story, poem or essay.

"Wait a minute," you say. "An abstract description? I thought you said . . ." You're right, I *did* say that description is a body composed of three parts: word, story and *image*. And I'll stick by that assertion. I'll even go so far as to say that the chief quality of description is its imagistic power, its ability to make us, as Aristotle put it, "see things." Most of the time—perhaps as much as ninety percent of the time—a concrete sensory description is the best way to accomplish that task.

But then again, there is that other ten percent. Consider Chekhov's "The Lady With the Pet Dog," a story filled with passages such as:

> . . . in his character there was something attractive and elusive that disposed women in his favor and allured them. . . .

Chekhov's description of Gurov meets few of Aristotle's criteria. It fails in "making people see things," it does not show Gurov in a state of activity, and it employs no metaphor. Yet, in its abstract and static way, the description is effective in supporting the story of a man who experiences love through intellect rather than emotion. As readers, we sidetrack Gurov's body and the physical, concrete world his body inhabits, entering the fictional dream through the door of abstract description. We dwell beside Gurov, in the room of his intellect, the place where Gurov is most comfortable.

More commonly, a writer will mix concrete and abstract descriptions within the same passage. Tim O'Brien uses this technique throughout his Vietnam story, "The Things They Carried," in his catalog of items the American soldiers carried.

> They carried Sterno, safety pins, trip flares, signal flares, spools of wire, razor blades . . . . Taking turns, they carried the big PRC-77 scrambler radio, which weighed 30 pounds with its battery. They shared the weight of memory. They took up what others could no longer bear. Often, they carried each other. . . . They carried infections. . . . They carried the sky.

Luke Whisnant, in his novel *Watching TV With the Red Chinese*, employs a similar technique in the narrator's description of his new neighbors, three Chinese men who've recently moved to the States. In the following example, Whisnant not only mixes the concrete and abstract within the same passage but also within the same sentence, so that idea words like *existence* and *approach* share space with *boxer shorts* and *soap scum*:

> They wing it, they wing everything: their poverty-line existence, their faded Mao jackets and crisp new white boxer shorts dripping dry on the bathroom radiator, their wobble-legged card-table desk and concrete-block bookcase approach to the Land of Plenty, their soap-scum sinked, bare-lightbulbed, no-Cuisinart kitchen,

bottom-line basics—everything rigged, secondhand, cast off, and recycled.

We've already dealt at length with techniques for describing concretely and specifically, and you've been cautioned against making sweeping abstractions, of "telling" the reader instead of "showing." (Remember the student who typed his poem in all caps so the reader wouldn't "miss the obscurity"?) But, in truth, good writing is a dance between showing and telling, between scene and summary, between the concrete and the abstract. John Gardner calls these two ways of describing "discursive" and "poetic." The discursive mode, he says, is most often used by essayists and "is by nature slow-moving and laborious, more wide than deep." In contrast, the poetic mode is dependent on concrete images, using little or no explanation.

Later on, in the chapter on plot, we'll discuss the dance between showing and telling in more detail, suggesting ways that description can orchestrate the movement between them. By suggesting the possibility of abstract description, I am not trying to confuse you. I am trying instead to confuse the issue—or at least, to open it up for discussion. Only confusing issues are interesting, just as only that which entangles us in a maze can qualify as a*maz*ing.

EXERCISES

1. Keep a sensory journal for a month, devoting each weekday to one of the five senses. For example, if you choose Monday as "scent day," then every Monday during the month you'll describe in detail three things you smelled that day. If Tuesday is "sound day," describe in detail three sounds you heard that day. On Saturdays and Sundays, either take a break from writing or look back over your week's descriptions and combine some of them into longer descriptions. On the second Monday, begin the process again. After a month you'll have at least twelve descriptions for each of the senses. Read over your descriptions,

pulling out memorable sections that might work into a new poem, story or essay.

2. Make a list of all the items you associate with a particular sensory quality. For instance, if you choose "white" your list might include linens, bridal veil, snowy field, vanilla ice cream, bandages, eggs and powdered sugar. Choose four or five of the items, expand each into a descriptive phrase, and shape your descriptions into list form. Or choose one of your items to expand into a fully rendered description that can stand alone.

If you have trouble expanding your description, try using question triggers—who, how, where, when, what kind, in what way—to elicit details. Let's say the first item on your list is an egg. Visualize the egg. Then ask yourself questions about it.

Where is it? In a straw basket lined with dish towels? Beneath a broody hen? On the top branch of a tree? On the embroidered panel of a child's Easter dress?

What kind of egg is it? A duck egg, dinosaur egg, a boiled egg? Is it round, oval, misshapen, tiny?

Continue asking questions until a complete image begins to form. In this line from his list poem "Varieties of Quiet," John Witte answers the questions *what, what kind, who* and *where* to form an evocative description:

> There is a quiet on the almost invisible eggs the killdeer
> lay in the dead grass behind our house.

Other sensory categories might include sweet, sour, bumpy, smooth, curly, slick, silent, scratchy, swirly, crunchy, black, swift, slow, bitter or noisy.

3. Describe a place (a forest, swimming pool, library, etc.) solely in terms of one sense. Mute the other senses while you explore just the smells, for instance, or the textures of the place.

4. Describe a place or a person by mixing two or more smells—like my description of my college boyfriend, who smelled of motor oil, cigarettes and Dial soap. Or focus on a sense other than smell, using the same technique of mixing two or more sounds, tastes, textures or sights to form a complex, perhaps even contradictory, sense impression.

5. Write a short description of a place or person that combines a concrete detail with an abstraction. Here's a sentence from Amy Tan's *The Joy Luck Club* that does exactly that:

> . . . And she had a daughter who grew up speaking only
> English and swallowing more Coca-Cola than sorrow.

After you've written a sentence or two, write a whole paragraph of description that freely mixes the concrete and the abstract. Refer to the passages by Whisnant and O'Brien.

6. Employ synesthesia. Describe an object, place, person or idea by using one sense to suggest another. What color is the silence in your bedroom? What is the shape of your grandmother's laughter? What smell emanates from fear?

7. Using Proust's description of madeleines as a model, describe a food you particularly enjoy. Borrow from the other senses to expand your details. You might even include the setting in which the food is consumed and all the environmental factors that contribute to your enjoyment.

8. Make a list of words that, as one of my young students put it, "feel good when they land on your ear." They might be onomatopoeic (buzz, sizzle) or simply words whose sounds suggest particular qualities or emotions. Here's a list of some of my favorites: whisper, rumble, slosh, shuffle, hollow, plush, slap, rustle, hiss, snap, squeak, crack, glop, tweak, whing, splat, slosh, chuckle, whoosh, willow, hush. After you've listed thirty or more, create sound clusters by combining several words with similar qualities into one descriptive phrase. Using my list, for example, you might write "the plush whisper of her slippers in the hall." Although you can't completely ignore the *sense* (meaning) of the words, for this activity pay more attention to their *sounds*. Allow your ear to guide you. (This exercise is a variation on the word basket exercise detailed in the next chapter. With the word basket technique, you use index cards rather than lists. I prefer index cards because I can physically move the words around to form different combinations.)

FIGURATIVELY SPEAKING: A "PERCEPTION OF RESEMBLANCES"

Reality is a cliché
from which we escape by metaphor

—Wallace Stevens, from *Opus Posthumous*

In my large extended family, we have a term for any strange, aberrant or overly imaginative ability. We call it the NQR factor ("Not Quite Right") and we assign a quotient to all family members based on symptoms they display, beginning at birth. One nephew, whose favorite zoo animal is the "gazebo" and who likes to sleep on my convertible "crouton" rather than alone in the guest room where he is assailed by "all kinds of mares, night- and day-," tests high on the scale. A toddler niece who enjoys wearing underwear on her head is a potential candidate for a seismic rating. And being a professional puppeteer puts my husband at the top of the list.

I follow at a respectful distance. Poets are, by definition, borderline NQR. Sometimes we even get paid for it. On a rainy Wednesday morning, my phone rings. The man at the other end of the line identifies himself as a business writer; a mutual acquaintance has given him my name. "He says you can help me with my writing. It's too cut and dried. It needs something. I'm not too keen on that fancy stuff, but . . ."

"Fancy stuff?" I say.

"Similes and symbols and all that. I'm just trying to get across information. With me, what you see is what you get."

"How can I help you?"

"I thought you could help make my writing more poetic. You know, more descriptive. I've got all the important stuff down. I just need to stick in some metaphors and similes."

Tempted though I am to schedule a consulting appointment with the caller (it's been a slow month, and I could use the money), I find myself, of all things, being honest. I tell the man that yes, I'd be happy to look at his writing, but no, I won't help him "stick in" metaphors and similes. That's not the way it works, I say. Metaphor isn't something you insert after the fact. It's not just something you say, a mere figure of speech; it's a way of perceiving the world.

He thanks me politely and hangs up. I hadn't meant to be discouraging, but talking about metaphor always has this effect on me. Is any literary term more misunderstood? How many times have I seen students "stick in" a simile or metaphor right before they hand in a first draft? For that matter, how many times have I stared at one of my own dying sentences, laboring to conjure a figure of speech that might save it, only to have the manuscript returned by my editor with the sentence marked "Seems contrived"?

Of course it seemed contrived. It *was* contrived. In my desperation for the telling phrase, the perfect image, I forgot my own advice: Metaphor, like all components of successful description, begins in the eye and ear of the beholder. It isn't a fancy embroidery stitch, something with which to embellish the surface of a written piece. It's the whole cloth out of which the writing is formed. Even Aristotle, who tended to view metaphor as separable from language, something which could be grafted onto a piece of writing to achieve a specific effect, nevertheless conceded that the source of metaphor could not be willed. "It is the mark of great natural ability," he wrote, "for the ability to use metaphor well implies a perception of resemblances."

Does this mean that as far as metaphor is concerned, a writer either has it or he doesn't? Is the ability to experience the world metaphorically an inborn trait, like my family's NQR factor? Some writers seem to have been born wrapped in a caul of figurative language. Similes seep through their pores; they breathe in metaphor. Although many of these writers are poets, being a poet does not guarantee a metaphoric bent. Conversely, being a prose writer does not preclude viewing the world through the lens of metaphor. The use of figurative language seems more closely related to a writer's natural temperament than to the form or content of the writing. Some gifted poets use little or no metaphor, while prose writers like Zora Neale Hurston take long luxurious swims in its waters:

> Janie stood where he left her for unmeasured time and thought. She stood there until something fell off the shelf inside her. Then she went inside there to see what it was. It was her image of Jody tumbled down and shattered. But looking at it she saw that it never was the flesh and blood figure of her dreams. Just something she had grabbed up to drape her dreams over . . . She had no more blossomy openings dusting pollen over her man, neither any glistening young fruit where the petals used to be. She found that she had a host of thoughts she had never expressed to him, and numerous emotions she had never let Jody know about. Things packed up and put away in parts of her heart where he could never find them.
>
> —from *Their Eyes Were Watching God*

Like the ongoing debate of nature vs. nurture, the debate of whether metaphor can be learned could go on indefinitely. For our purposes, let's consider that both sides, nature and nurture, play a role in a writer's use of figurative language. Yes, it appears that some people are more naturally tuned to receive messages from the metaphoric universe. But we can all increase our ability to recognize resemblances in the world around us. And once we recognize these resemblances, we can learn to shape and reshape the expression of the resemblances, the metaphors we have been given.

WHAT IS METAPHOR?

Thus far, I've been using *metaphor* and *figurative language* synonymously. Because metaphor is the mother of universal connections, I view all forms of figurative language—in fact, all original turns of phrases—as metaphor's offspring. *Figurative language* is too cold and confining to describe the "perception of resemblances" that radiates from the natural world and the world of the imagination; the phrase places too much emphasis on the words being used rather than on the perception beneath the words. However, for purposes of clarity I'll defer to centuries of literary criticism and define my terms in more traditional ways.

Literal language means, literally, what it says. It follows the denotation of a word, its meaning as defined by the dictionary. *Figurative language*, on the other hand, doesn't mean exactly what it says. It strays from denotation and moves toward connotation, those overtones a word acquires over time. Figurative language usually implies (or overtly states) a comparison between two things. These comparisons are called *figures of speech.*

Metaphor has traditionally been considered the most prominent figure of speech. It derives from the Greek *metaphora*, which breaks into two parts: *meta* ("over") and *pherein* ("to carry"). Moving vans in Greece are often marked with the word *Metaphora* to suggest the transfer of items from one place to another. Metaphor occurs when one thing, or part of one thing, is carried over into another. An imaginative transfer takes place.

Usually, this carrying over is accomplished through images. These need not be visual images, although figures of speech usually form sense impressions; abstractions almost never act as transfers. The earliest uses of *metaphor* stretch to include any transfer of a word from its ordinary application to another application, whether it involves a comparison or not. In contemporary usage, however, metaphor suggests a comparison between two seemingly unlike things.

A metaphor always requires two parts, two sides, to complete its equation. The critic I.A. Richards calls these two sides the "tenor" and the "vehicle." The tenor, the main subject or the "general drift," is usually a thing but can also be an idea, an emotion or some other abstraction. The vehicle is the concrete image that embodies the main subject, supplying it with weight, shape and substance. For instance, in "He carried his guilt like a heavy suitcase," *guilt* is the tenor and *suitcase* is the vehicle.

In the passage from *Their Eyes Were Watching God,* Hurston's tenors (main ideas) include time, thought, emotions and dreams. Her vehicles (concrete objects and images that carry the main ideas) include a shelf, a drape or blanket, pollen, fruit, petals and "things packed away." But Hurston does more than simply show relationships between tenors and vehicles. Reading the passage, I didn't think, "Oh yes, Janie's heart is like a closet lined with shelves of memories." I didn't visualize a blanket draped over a dream, or imagine pollen floating down on a man. Instead, I was taken into a world I'd never entered before, Janie's inner world of disillusionment and lost dreams.

Effective metaphor does more than shed light on the two things being compared. It actually brings to the mind's eye something that has never before been seen. It's not just the marriage ceremony linking two things; it's the child born from the union. An original and imaginative metaphor brings something fresh into the world. In the interaction between two things being compared, a new image or idea is formed.

METAPHOR AND SIMILE: FRATERNAL TWINS

Some scholars don't distinguish between simile and metaphor, or between metaphor and other figures of speech, considering the differences among figures of speech to be mostly surface differences. But even surface differences are worth examining. Digging beneath the surface, we might discover variations that, however slight, affect our writing in important ways. Take simile and metaphor. At first glance, they seem to differ little from one another. Both are comparisons between two things.

> Simile: Your hair is like a dark river.
> Metaphor: Your hair is a dark river.

In this example, the surface difference between the two statements is the appearance of "like," which calls to mind the definition I memorized in sixth grade: *A simile is a comparison using "like" or "as."* Actually, this is an inadequate definition. *Like* and *as* aren't the only connectives that appear in similes. *Than* is another; so are verbs like *resembles*. The sixth-grade definition is inadequate also because it suggests that any phrase comparing two things using *like* or *as* is a simile. Not true. "Your hair is like your sister's hair" is not a simile. Both simile and metaphor require comparisons between things that are unlike in kind.

The use of connectives isn't the only quality that distinguishes metaphor from simile. They differ also in the degree of likeness they suggest. Simile is usually limited to one likeness, whereas metaphor often implies a whole range of like qualities. In metaphor, because the comparison between the two things is implied rather than stated, the reader is free to imagine additional qualities the things might share.

Another form of metaphor, implied metaphor, carries free association a step further. In traditional simile and metaphor, both parts of the comparison are stated.

Simile: "Your *hair* is like a dark *river*."
Metaphor: "Your *hair* is a dark *river*."

Both statements contain "hair" and "river," the two sides of the metaphorical equation.

In implied metaphor, however, only one side of the equation is stated:

Implied   "Your hair twists and meanders across the land-
metaphor: scape of your shoulders."

Here, the tenor of the metaphor ("hair") is present, but the vehicle ("river") is merely implied through the use of "twists," "meanders" and "landscape." An implied metaphor uses neither a connective (such as "like" or "as") nor any form of the verb "to be."

Metaphor is implied comparison. Simile is comparison made explicit. By its very construction, a simile calls attention to itself as a figure of speech. It not only shows the relation between the two things being compared, it *explains* the relationship through *like* or *as* or some other connective. Metaphor, on the other hand, suggests that the imaginative transfer (from one thing to another) has already occurred. In metaphor, one thing is not only being compared to another; it *is* the other. For this reason, metaphor often carries more emotional intensity than simile. Not always. In some cases, a deeply felt, resonant simile can carry as much weight as a metaphor. I'll never forget the opening simile to a poem written by one of my second-grade students:

> When my mama sit down, it's like the whole world be resting.

Despite the student's grammatical shakiness (or perhaps because of it—who can fathom the mysteries of literary wonder?) this remains one of the most effective similes I've ever encountered. The inclusion of *like* does not detract from the apt comparison, the simple yet effective visual image, or the complexity of the sentiment. I can almost feel the weight of the mother as she sinks, exhausted, into the chair. More than that, I sink with her. The whole world sinks. Yes, mama, it's been a long day. Kick off your shoes, put your feet up. Rest awhile.

THE EXTENDED FAMILY: OTHER FIGURES OF SPEECH

Metaphor and simile, though the most fundamental figures of speech, aren't the only possibilities open to us. Choices abound.

Hyperbole is an exaggerated metaphor or simile. In hyperbole, you overstate the comparison. Your boss is a weasel or a rat or pond scum. Your lover is more stunning than heaven's brightest star. James Lewis MacLeod's story "The Jesus Flag" opens with hyperbolic brilliance:

> If God, in cursing Lot's wife, had turned her into a pillar of sugar, instead of salt, Mrs. Wilhelper would have fit the bill. With her tight bun hairdo and her squat body resembling a bush, she was five feet three inches of sweetness as determined as a dump truck. She had two sayings—"Too Sweet for Words" and "Perfectly Marvelous"—which she unloaded on every aspect of the uni-

verse as relentlessly as a manure spreader covering a green field.

Though hyperbole is used primarily for comic touches, it can also be employed for serious, even tragic effects, as in these lines describing a gifted child pianist:

> He was born with the ears of a dog.
> He could hear his mother's skin decay,
> the soft give
> as her cheeks sagged just barely more.
>
> —from the poem "The Prodigy" by Lola Haskins

In **personification**, an inanimate object, a force of nature or an abstract term is spoken of as if it were a person. Although the distinguished critic John Ruskin disapproved of phrases that ascribe emotion to nonhuman phenomena (he called this figure of speech "pathetic fallacy"), modern writers often employ personification with stunning results:

> When laborers imported from Haiti came to clear the land, clouds and fish were convinced that the world was over . . . Only the daisy trees were serene . . . . It took the river to persuade them that indeed the world was altered. That never again would the rain be equal, and by the time they realized it and had run their roots deeper, clutching the earth like lost boys found, it was too late. The men had already folded the earth where there had been no fold and hollowed her where there had been no hollow, which explains what happened to the river. It crested, then lost its course, and finally its head. Evicted from the place where it lived, and forced into unknown turf, it could not form its pools or waterfalls, and ran every which way.
>
> —from *Tar Baby* by Toni Morrison

Since most writers are persons (chimps write, too, and some baboons), personification comes naturally to us. We know how people feel and act, so we can easily extend those feelings and actions to the world of vegetables and minerals. Personification also works in the opposite way. By describing the emotional worlds of inanimate objects or aspects of nature, you can suggest the emotional worlds of your human characters.

Animism, closely related to personification, also attributes life to an inanimate thing, an idea or a natural object; the difference is that animism does not imply *human* life. Cathy Smith Bowers uses this technique skillfully in her poem "The Love." In Bowers's first line, which alludes to a Thomas Wolfe quote, she begins with an abstraction, but the abstraction soon grows a body. Though not a human body, it is nevertheless a living entity capable of emotion:

> The love that ended yesterday in Texas
> crawled out of the sea
> fresh-eared and barnacled,
> his lashed eyes astonished
> at the shook-out world . . .

Animism avoids the "pathetic fallacy" inherent in most uses of personification, while still infusing descriptions with energy. In both personification and animism, this energizing is accomplished predominantly through the use of strong verbs.

Paradox creates a relationship that seems, at first glance, to be contradictory, but upon reflection, makes sense. Since the most intriguing characters, emotions and ideas contain at least two sides—and sometimes more—paradox can suggest emotional complexities and provide the mystery all good writing requires. "She loved John too much to stay with him" gets our attention; it makes us want to know more, and we continue reading in part to unravel the paradox. Paradox can also suggest conflicts that will emerge later in the story. If you're having trouble finding the center of conflict within your plot or character, try writing an opening sentence that contains a paradox.

In **metonymy**, we refer to something not by its own name but by something closely related to it. The President is "the White House." "From birth to death" becomes "from cradle to grave." And who's watching the baby? Not a mother, but "the hand that rocks the cradle." In **synecdoche**, a subset of metonymy, we use part of something to stand for the whole of it, or vice versa. "Lend a hand," we cry, although we require more help than a single hand could provide. As you can see from these examples, it's difficult to find a fresh example of metonymy, and nearly impossible to come up with one of your own. But that doesn't mean you can't try.

An **analogy** is a comparison between two relationships, and it contains four parts: A is to B as C is to D. Although many writers are fond of analogy, for my money, analogic constructions are overly clever and complicated, too reminiscent of standardized tests and no. 2 pencils and empty bubbles waiting to be filled. When it comes to proportional metaphor, I'll step aside and let better minds than mine have their say. My favorite analogy is from Franz Kafka: "A book is an axe for the frozen sea within."

Allegory is a story or description where each element—each person, place, thing and idea—is metaphorical. In addition to providing one-on-one correspondences, the elements "add up" to something greater than the sum of their parts, some overriding idea or message. Bunyan's *Pilgrim's Progress* and Kafka's "In the Penal Colony" are classic examples of allegorical narratives. The problem with allegory is that its literal elements aren't important in their own right. The objects, characters and places in an allegory stand more for abstract ideas than they do for themselves. Whereas a story using symbols has two independent lives, the literal and the symbolic, an allegory often can't stand alone as a literal story.

A **conceit** is a long, complex comparison between two things that are extremely unlike. Like allegory and analogy, conceit requires a great deal of ingenuity and logical plotting on the part of the writer. When conceit isn't skillfully accomplished, it calls attention to itself, thus distracting the reader from the fictional dream. However, in the hands of a master such as the metaphysical poet John Donne, this technique can yield metaphorical surprises, as in "A Valediction: Forbidding

Mourning,'' in which separated lovers are compared to the legs of a compass.

Symbols are such important and complex figures in poetry, fiction and nonfiction that they warrant more than a brief explanation. Remember our discussion of tenor and vehicle, the two sides of a metaphor? The tenor is the general idea that requires concreteness before it can be fully understood; the vehicle is the embodiment of the tenor. In both metaphor and simile, the tenor is stated. In symbolism, it is not. In symbolism, only the *vehicle* shows itself. A symbol is a visible sign—an object or action—that points to a world of meaning beyond itself.

Although symbolism works by the power of suggestion, a symbol is not the same as a meaning or a moral. A symbol cannot be an abstraction. Rather, a symbol is the thing that points to the abstraction. In Poe's ''The Raven,'' death isn't the symbol; the bird is. In Crane's *The Red Badge of Courage*, courage isn't the symbol; blood is. Symbols are usually objects, but actions can also work as symbols—thus the term ''symbolic gesture.'' Since actions speak louder than words, a single symbolic gesture can reveal more about a character than pages of dialogue. Anna Karenina throws herself under the wheels of a train, Cinderella's stepsister slices off her toes so her foot can fit into the slipper, and Hemingway's Kino finds the pearl of great price.

An object or action may come to symbolize a world greater than itself, but first it must justify its existence—as an object or an action—in the world of the story, the poem or the essay. For a symbol to work effectively, the real world must precede the symbolic. The necklace in Guy de Maupassant's story may come to symbolize surface appearances and human vanity, but first it must be a necklace. The laundry in Richard Wilbur's ''Love Calls Us to the Things of This World'' may come to represent angels or souls ''bodiless and simple/As false dawn,'' but first it must be washed, rinsed and hung out to dry.

A symbol means *more* than itself, but first it means *itself*. Like a developing image in a photographer's tray, a symbol reveals itself slowly. It's been there all along, waiting to emerge from the story, the poem, the essay—and from the writer herself. Symbols are powerful figures, capable of bearing the weight of a hundred lesser metaphors. When a symbol grows organically from its source—character, setting, conflict, plot, language and from our own passions—it can enrich our writing. But when it feels forced, self-conscious or merely *placed* over a piece of writing, it brings the whole house down with it.

DISCOVERING ORIGINAL METAPHORS

The description from Zora Neale Hurston's novel, quoted earlier in this chapter, succeeds not only because of its striking and sustained metaphors but also because those metaphors appear to be deeply felt, springing organically from an authentic source. The writer has not "stuck in" metaphors after the fact; rather, they appear as natural outgrowths of the way the narrator sees, and feels, her way through the world. Hurston's metaphors reflect a perception of resemblances richer and deeper than any mere figure of speech.

When images emerge naturally, when the perception of resemblances makes itself known, it's not *fancy* at work, but imagination. (The distinction between fancy and imagination was first made by Samuel Taylor Coleridge in *Biographia Literaria*.) In fancy, the writer is concerned with making or assembling images; fancy is a mechanical facility that calls attention to its own construction. When my editor wrote "Seems contrived" in the margin of my manuscript beside the drummed-up metaphor, she was distinguishing between imagination and fancy. Fancy relies solely upon labor. When we're employing fancy, we feel ourselves reaching out, fetching. That's why our results often seem farfetched; we've fetched them from afar.

Imagination, on the other hand, isn't a mere assembling of likenesses but an almost effortless blending of images into a unified whole. But how does this blending occur? How can we encourage metaphors to emerge organically in our writing? Coleridge offers a hint: the difference between fancy and imagination depends, in great degree, upon the emotional involvement of the writer. Images, he says, "become proofs of original genius only as far as they are modified by a predominant passion."

"Original genius." Hmm. Originality is a subject that comes up often in literary discussions. My students, especially those of college-age and beyond, talk a lot about originality, by which they seem to mean something weird or odd or completely, dazzlingly incoherent. Some expend enormous amounts of effort trying to look and act the part of the "original" artist, searching out the funkiest clothes and the latest night spots, leaving little energy for their writing. Some complain that their metaphors are hopeless, that they just can't think of anything that's new enough, strange enough.

"Everything's already been said," one student moans. "And by better minds than mine."

"I don't have an original bone in my body," says another.

"Did you hear what you just said?" I say. "That's exactly where your originality lies. In each bone of your body." I go on to explain the root of *originality*: *origin*. Origin, as in source, spring, primary being. We are most original when we are most ourselves. Only then are we close to our first source, our fueling passions.

Discovering the source of original passion should be the most natural thing in the world, right? "It's as clear as the nose on your face," my grandmother used to say. In fact, the nose on our face isn't clear to us at all. It's clear only to others, or to ourselves when we're looking in a mirror. Sometimes we are simply too close to our origins to recognize them. When our writing is going well, it's often because it's springing naturally from an original source. We are writing from our passions. This doesn't mean we are necessarily writing *about* our passions, or even about *ourselves*. But our passions, the sources of our originality, are fueling the writing. When we are writing from the center of ourselves, our metaphors are organic, unforced, springing from imagination rather than fancy.

Beginning writers, especially children, usually draw naturally on original sources. They don't know any better, and ignorance serves them well. They write only, as Samuel Butler once advised, "what refuses to go away," what matters most to them. Those of us who have been writing for a while sometimes lose our way. The act of writing—that solitary, sometimes joyous and sometimes agonizing but always passionate act—gets mixed up with publishing and competition and success and failure and reviews and deadlines. We forget why we began writing in the first place. Like the nouveau millionaire who leaves the little town that formed him, we forget where we came from. We lose our origins—and with it, our originality.

FINDING YOUR PERSONAL CONSTELLATION OF IMAGES

The poet Stanley Kunitz, who has written and published for over seventy years, once called the sources of a writer's originality her "constellation of images." If a writer never discovers her constellation, Kunitz said, she may produce adequate, even good, work; but the work will never rise above superficiality. In Kunitz's poems, his constellation of images revolves around the central star, his father. The loss surrounding his father's death (his father committed suicide six weeks before Kunitz was born) supplies the metaphor that informs everything he writes. Kunitz calls his father's suicide the "nexus" linking every image, every metaphor, of his work.

An early event in your life can shape your metaphorical constellation. For me, it was the death of an infant sister the year I was born, an event that shaped not only my role in the family drama but also the images of death and survivorship that would eventually emerge in my poetry, fiction and nonfiction. For many years after I began writing and publishing, I was not conscious of my personal metaphor, my "one small grief" as I would later call it. I discovered my constellation of images partly through the writing process itself and partly through the comments of editors and readers; it was as plain as the nose on my face, at least to them.

Little by little, as I studied the metaphors running through my work, the clues came together: sidekicks, sisters, decoys, hand-me-downs, skin grafts, rubber dolls, twins, doubles, even my penchant for compound words. Dead and lost children haunted my fiction, as did childless women and men. Even my comic stories contained images of the double—remember my reference, in an earlier chapter, to the freemartin, the female calf of a twin bull? To this day, I continue to work and rework the central myth of the double. If my metaphors are original, it's simply because they arise organically from my origin, my life source.

Childhood events aren't the only forces that shape a writer's vision. Your present-day preoccupations, interests and obsessions provide you with original metaphors, as do the subjects you discover through research or accident. Look back over your writing. Reread your stories, poems and essays, noting successful images or metaphors, those passages that seem to have sprung from imagination, not fancy. Notice what you've taken time and care to describe—description is one of the entries into metaphor. If you keep a journal or a writer's notebook, reread old entries. Circle recurring images, descriptions, or isolated words; if the entries are stored in a computer, you can even do a search to see how often a particular word or phrase occurs. This process can help you discover your inner "constellation of images," the ruling passions that fuel your most original work.

Too coldhearted or objective an assessment won't help at this delicate stage. Like the centipede who was proceeding quite nicely, thank you, until he stopped to consider which leg went after which, we don't want to become too preoccupied with the how and when of each step of the writing process. But a calm, inquisitive approach to our own processes can be instructive. Paying attention to recurring motifs in our work can help us discover the sources of our originality. It can also increase our ability to extend isolated metaphors, resulting in richer, fuller descriptions.

EXTENDING METAPHORS

Once you've discovered your original images, you can use and reuse those images in new ways. Monet's overwhelming passion for water served him well throughout his career. Even when he wasn't painting water he was painting water. His smokestacks and meadows seem liquid, his trees mast-like, his trunks and branches like rivers. In the self-portrait of 1917, his cheekbones seem to be made of wave-like particles. Even his brushstrokes are watery. Monet extended his ruling metaphor to include not only ordinary water, but mist, fog and ice—even steam from passing locomotives.

One way to write richer descriptions is to extend one of your original metaphors. Let's say you've discovered images of plants recurring in your work. But they're merely mentioned, then abandoned; they aren't leading to full-fledged descriptions. Try writing down all the words or images you associate with plants—you might use a thesaurus to get started. Free associate, listing everything that comes to mind. Your list might include leaf, bud, stem, seed, water, roots, compost, moss, darkness, green, swamp, trowel, greenhouse, oxygen, rubber boots, roses, thorns. As you continue, one image will lead to another; *thorns* might lead you to write *blood*, for instance, which might lead to *circulation*.

If the words in your list begin to diverge from your original idea, don't worry. You can always return to your root word—or you might find that the free association journey leads to more interesting connections than you'd planned. If you're especially tuned to the sounds of words, their musical qualities might lead you further into the metaphorical world. This happens to me often, and it always surprises me. When I began "Sidekick," which later evolved into a long catalog poem, I thought it would be a short lyric. After all, I had only two images—the image of a comic's straight man, and Michelangelo's image of the martyred St. Bartholomew being reunited with his flayed skin. But as I began to write, one word called up another. "Straight man" led to "ploy," which led to the rhymed "decoy." The image of "decoy" demanded "bobbing," which called, musically and visually, for "back up singers with their benign doo-wops." The metaphor kept growing in this way, propelled not by an overall idea or motif, but by the actual process of placing one word after the other.

The shapes, rhythms and sounds of words suggest other shapes, rhythms and sounds, which can extend a single metaphor, forming a universe of connections. We can also extend a metaphor by studying the technical world from which the metaphor emerged. Your isolated and spotty plant images, for instance, might expand into full descriptions if you consult a gardening book, a botany text or schematic drawings that depict a plant's inner workings. In his novel *Ingenious Pain,* Andrew Miller describes a boy's fascination with William Harvey's sketches of the human body:

> But it is the pictures which snare him: the world beneath the skin; the skein of guts, the globes and bulbs of the great organs; the sheets of muscle strapped around the trellis of the bones; the intricate house of the heart, veins and arteries radiating, curling, branching into tiny tributaries.

Although the boy is presented as a character, not the author himself, the description has the feel of firsthand observation. Perhaps, like the curious boy, Miller stared at Harvey's sketches until he began to see the other worlds contained within the world of the body—the skeins and globes and trellises and houses. Our metaphors can grow out of research, eye-search, and even I-search, that ransacking of memory that so often yields surprise treasures. In the case of your plant images, for instance, can you recall an early experience that shaped the obsession? The memory may contain within it details you'd temporarily forgotten.

An isolated metaphor, when given attention, can yield a whole family of metaphors, resulting in rich and sensual descriptions. Sometimes we're not sure where an image is leading, but we feel instinctively that it is important. At this point, we may feel the way Ingmar Bergman says he feels when he's first conceiving a film:

> It is a mental state . . . abounding in fertile associations and images. Most of all, it is a brightly colored thread sticking out of the dark sack of the unconscious. If I begin to wind up this thread, and do it carefully, a complete film will emerge.

Winding up the thread of a metaphor requires patience and trust. We must believe that connections will be made along the way. Provided that our metaphor has emerged from imagination rather than fancy, these connections will probably grow naturally as the writing proceeds. But what about those times when our metaphors do not grow naturally, when an isolated image remains a single thread we're unable to wind into a fully developed description?

Sometimes the best thing to do is to stop worrying about it. Metaphor is only one of many methods for achieving effective description. In fact, too much metaphor can harm our writing, calling attention to itself, or to *ourselves*, at the expense of the fictional dream. In *Writing Fiction*, Janet Burroway suggests that "metaphor is to some degree always self-conscious" and that a bad metaphor "produces a sort of hiccup in the reader's involvement." Prose writers, especially, might wish to heed Aristotle's advice: Overuse of metaphor can make prose too much like poetry. Even if your aim is more poetic prose, metaphor may not be the best way to achieve the goal. Your reader may suffer for your overindulgence.

However, if you feel that your work lacks imagination and you wish to increase your power to perceive metaphoric resemblances, you can take some practical steps. Two have already been suggested—that you write directly from your passions, those things that "refuse to go away," and that you begin to trace the "constellation of images" that emerges in your life and work.

Another step is to respect your natural writing style and stay true to it, trusting that metaphors will emerge in their own good time. My friend, the writer Frye Gaillard, confesses that metaphor does not come easily to him. Instead, he focuses on word choice and on the cadences of his sentences, two of his natural writerly gifts. By focusing on what he does well and avoiding any self-conscious "sticking in" of metaphor simply for the sake of metaphor, his writing proceeds smoothly. Occasionally he's even rewarded by the appearance of an apt, original figure of speech that grows organically from his attention to the diction and rhythms of his language.

As in John Lennon's adage about life, metaphor sometimes happens while you're busy doing something else. You can exercise the muscles of metaphor even when you're not writing, through any activity that tricks your mind into making connections between seemingly unlike things.

- Play games that require divergent thinking. My favorite is "Object," where participants sit in a circle and pass around common household utensils like colanders, eggbeaters and chopsticks, miming imaginative uses for each object. Chopsticks, for instance, can become antennae or drumsticks or tiny oars.
- Spend time with children. Build forts from popsicle sticks, whittle swords from broomsticks, or create self-portrait collages out of vegetables, fruits, seeds and pods.
- Each day, move something in your house to a different spot. Turn it upside down or inside out, or use it for a new purpose. A quilt can become a tablecloth; an ashtray, a soap dish.
- Visit an art gallery or a craft fair and enjoy the creations of artists who see the surreal, whimsical and extraordinary worlds hidden within the ordinary.
- Every morning, instead of reading the newspaper, read a poem, especially one rich in metaphor. When author Gina Berriault was interviewed after winning the Book Critics Circle Award for *Women in Their Beds: New and Selected Stories,* she said she often reads poetry as a way of preparing herself to write. She even cited a line from the Chilean poet Pablo Neruda—"There is no space wider than that of grief"—as inspiration for one of the stories in the collection. Poetry reminds us of the metaphorical connections in our world.

The characters in our stories can also inspire metaphor, opening up possibilities our "author selves" have forgotten to see. By imagining ourselves inside the skin of someone else— which is what fiction writers do all the time—we free ourselves to see things in a new way. Viewing the world through the lens of our characters allows dormant parts of our personalities to emerge. For example, in my daily public life, my speech is, for the most part, carefully considered; I don't trust myself with spontaneous outbursts, one-liners and colorful epithets.

My writing self is another story. It creates characters like Regina Ratcher, a feisty fourteen-year-old from a poverty-pocked town in North Carolina. Regina capitalizes on her love of hyperbole, puns, clichés, and all lowly forms of figurative language by writing advertising copy for local businesses. What a delight to speak through her mouth. All the silly phrases I deny myself are freed from bondage, like Regina's motto for Gotch's Taxidermy (*Forever Yours: The Look of Life Without the Trouble*) or her newspaper ad for Lloyd Batson's Full Service Exxon (*Jesus is Lord. We pump, you relax.*)

Perhaps one of your characters is fond of simile or paradox, or his speech is more colorful than yours. Let him have his say. He may surprise you with a striking metaphor that your author self would never allow. Looking through his eyes, you may begin to see the ordinary world anew, noticing connections you have never seen before. They're there, just waiting to be discovered. "Life," as Regina is fond of saying, "is just one big extension cord."

AVOIDING THE PITFALLS OF METAPHOR

Let's say you've begun to explore your personal constellation of images, that "perception of resemblances" that lies beneath any successful use of figurative language. Your metaphorical well is filling from within, spilling over into the outside world, where you've begun to notice connections you've never seen before. These connections are emerging in your writing, taking the form of simile, paradox, personification, even symbol. Since you're writing from your passions and origins, your metaphors are original. But are they fresh? Beyond that, are they effective? Do they sustain the fictional dream of your story, poem or essay?

The most obvious test of an effective metaphor is its freshness—not only of vision, but of expression. Clichés are dead metaphor. When they were first born, they were lively, original figures of speech. The first time someone wrote "proud as a peacock," it was fresh; the second time, it was imitative. Now it's a cliché. It's hard to escape cliché—it's as comfortable as an old shoe. (The old-shoe cliché just sneaked up on me. That's the way clichés are. If you aren't vigilant, they'll slide right into your writing.) Unless you're using a cliché intentionally—for purposes of humor, irony or as an integral part of character development—it doesn't belong in your work.

Sometimes we don't realize we're using a cliché. Maybe it hasn't been around long enough to acquire full-cliché status like "white as snow" or "silver-tongued devil." It might be an expression borrowed from politicians, pop culture or the media, like "my plate is full," "getting in touch with your inner child," "couch potato" or "surfing the Internet." A metaphor doesn't have to be decades old to be stale; any overused expression qualifies, however recently it might have been coined. There I go again with another cliché: "to coin a phrase." Actually, coining a phrase might not be such a bad idea. If we had to pay every time we used a stale expression—a kind of syntax sin tax—we might be more careful about allowing clichés into our descriptions.

In our attempt to use fresh expressions and to avoid clichés, we may go too far in the opposite direction. *Far* is the operative word here. You've already been warned against fetching metaphors from afar—that is, straying too far from your origins and passions. Farfetched also refers to anything that seems strained, improbable or unnatural. A farfetched metaphor not only calls attention to itself; it calls attention to the differences between the two things being compared rather than to their likenesses. Although a metaphor, by definition, compares two unlike things, if they are *too* unlike, the reader will focus on the strangeness of the metaphor rather than on the images being created. Yes, perhaps a character's teeth *could* be compared to stalactites or stalagmites. But do you really want your reader to fixate on subterranean images, when all you were trying to show was that the teeth were sharp?

The main goal of metaphor is not merely to point out resemblances but to create, through these resemblances, a fresh and vivid image. Like other descriptive techniques, metaphor usually accomplishes this task through concrete, sensory details.

Although I've never actually seen an eagle diving off a cliff into the ocean, when I read the second stanza of Tennyson's "The Eagle," I feel as though I have:

> The wrinkled sea beneath him crawls;
> He watches from his mountain walls,
> And like a thunderbolt he falls.

Tennyson's figures of speech—the wrinkled sea crawling and the falling thunderbolt—appeal to my senses, bringing the imagined picture into sharp focus. They clarify, rather than blur, the picture. His metaphors and simile, rather than calling attention to themselves as figures of speech, illuminate the scene, bringing it vividly to the eye of my imagination.

Tennyson's metaphors and similes are not only concrete and sensory; they are also precise. Not literally precise, of course. Figurative language, by definition, deviates from the literal. Literally speaking, waves are not wrinkles, and the sea has no knees on which to crawl. But within the world Tennyson creates, the figures of speech are accurate; they follow natural laws. In contrast, a phrase like "her tears gushed like a geyser" is inaccurate. Tears might trickle, drip, even flow, but they cannot gush like a geyser, and saying that they do distracts the reader from the sense impression you're trying to create—unless you're intentionally employing hyperbole to accomplish some literary purpose.

Figurative language, like surrealism or fantasy, is not a screen to hide behind. Using metaphor does not absolve us from writing clearly and accurately. Unfortunately, government officials, businessmen, academics and advertisers so often use figures of speech as substitutes for clear communication—or worse, to deceive, evade or manipulate—that it's tempting to think of metaphor as an easy out. Clear, direct thinking is hard; communicating those thoughts precisely is even harder. Easier to run for cover, hiding behind clichés, vague or mixed metaphor, or overworked figures of speech.

"Dazzle me with clarity," the poet Cathy Smith Bowers tells her students. She's asking for a lot. It's easy to merely dazzle, to fill our poems and stories with figures of speech that leave the reader stunned, yet confused:

> A vacuum waits to be filled, if not with precious stones, with scarabs, fat and scarred. Birds of crimson plume, sky blue, or white fluff with rufous trim, compete for precious gems beneath a sunflower moon. The stylish meet at first light for revels. Yard birds rush in to fill a void like circus clowns.

This description may dazzle, but it doesn't dazzle with clarity. It took three readings for me to figure out what is happening: birds are gathering at an almost-empty bird feeder. The writer, carried away by metaphor, does not anchor his metaphors with clear, direct language. Nor does he consider how the metaphors are interacting with one another. Not only is the description crowded with images—vacuums, scarabs, sunflowers, moons, gems and clowns—but the images don't work together for an overall effect. The writer has scattered his forces.

We scatter our forces when we use too many metaphors, or when our metaphors cancel each other out. This happens in succinct passages as well as in long descriptions:

> The neighborhood bullies hover like vultures, plunging
> in names like daggers and carting away the bones.

In this example, "vultures" and "bones" work well together, but "daggers" cancels out a potentially effective image. The reader is left not knowing where to put his attention. Just when he's conjured up a mob of vultures, he's asked to provide them with knives. It just doesn't work.

Figures of speech require space and time in which to accumulate meaning, and the reader needs room to imagine the connections. If you write "The woman brandished a hairbrush, skipping toward him like a schoolgirl on holiday," you'll derail the reader. Which meaning is intended? Is the woman warlike or girlish? Is her gesture a physical threat or a playful tease? *Warlike?* you say. *Oh, no, I didn't mean warlike. I just meant that she's swinging the hairbrush as she moves toward him.*

The problem here is more fundamental than mixing metaphors; it's a problem with word choice. In an earlier chapter we discussed the importance of naming an object precisely and accurately. The same principle applies to effective figures of speech. Any word used in a metaphor or simile must pass the precision test; figurative language is no excuse for sloppy diction. "Brandish" suggests that a weapon is being used. If you're going to use "brandish," you need to know both its denotation and its connotation, to ensure that your diction is precise.

Knowing the precise meaning of words will help us avoid mixed metaphors like "He was steeped in the aurora of her hair." "Aurora" is not just a pretty word. If you look it up in the dictionary, you'll see that it means "a flashing luminosity visible in the night sky." And "steep" has nothing to do with the night sky—or any sky, for that matter. It means "to soak in liquid, to be immersed."

Writing a mixed metaphor isn't the worst sin a writer can commit. We're all allowed a few along the way. Even the most successful writers, whose editors are paid to catch such things, sometimes fail to be accurate. Here's Ian Fleming at his metaphorical worst: "Bond's knees, the Achilles' heel of all skiers, were beginning to ache." The problem with such writing isn't simply that the metaphors are mixed. The real problem is that *since* the metaphors are mixed, the reader is unable to conjure the image in his mind's eye. Should he visualize a knee or a heel? An imprecise metaphor, or one in which two or more vehicles fight for dominance, cannot create a unified impression in the reader's mind.

PRECISE, ORIGINAL *AND* EFFECTIVE METAPHOR

In the earlier discussion of "the proper and special name of a thing," we noted the importance not only of a precise naming but of a significant and musical naming as well. The same principles apply to figurative language. An effective metaphor or simile is *significant* when it calls forth an image that reinforces the overall description. When John Edgar Wideman, in his memoir *Brothers and Keepers,* describes the grass surrounding the penitentiary where his brother is incarcerated, his simile is not only precise but significant. It reinforces the regulated sameness of such institutions, a soulless uniformity evident in the prison's physical property as well as in its human property:

> Grass grows in the margin between the spiked fence paralleling the river and the asphalt lot. Grass clipped harshly, uniformly as the bristle heads of convicts in old movies about prison. Plots of manicured green define a path leading to steps we must climb to enter the visitors' building.

Because of Wideman's precise simile, we can visualize both the grass and the convicts' severe haircuts; each side of the simile supports the other. The significant details that surround the simile—"spiked," "clipped" and "manicured"—further support the simile rather than canceling it out. The larger constellation of words and images—"margin," "between," "define," "plot," even the seemingly innocuous "we"—is also significant, suggesting the boundaries not only between convict and visitor but between brother and brother.

Wideman's description also passes the third test of "the proper and special naming of a thing." It is musically appropriate. "Spiked," "bristle," and "clipped" appeal to our ear as well as to our eye. The repetition of "i" provides musical unity, while the harsh, brittle consonants reinforce the brusque treatment both the grass and the prisoners receive.

Wideman's use of figurative language succeeds on every level. His simile is *original* because it appears to spring naturally from his origins, the source of his passions. It is *effective* in its precision, in the suggestiveness of its sound, and in the significance of its details. Every element extends and deepens the simile, the larger descriptive passage, and finally, the entire memoir. We are left with a perception of resemblances, each one illuminating the other, and all of them illuminating the whole.

EXERCISES

1. Make a "word basket" for your writing desk. Fill it with words recorded individually on index cards or slips of paper, one word per card; the more cards, the more possibilities. (You can also purchase ready-made word kits; some are even magnetized so you can create poems and stories on your refrigerator. I prefer to create my own list of words from my personal "constellation of images.") Concrete nouns, strong verbs and sensory adjectives work best for me, but I also include some abstract words. Here's a partial list of the words in my basket: blossom, moon, plow, white, melt, deep, stream, edge, hollow, circle, wave, willow, root, parting, hand, crown, hayloft, kites, pianos, mirror, follow, gloss, nibble, home, song, sorrow, mercy, skin, window, wonder.

The object of the exercise is to trick your mind into making metaphorical leaps you might not otherwise make. Once you've filled your word basket, select at random four or five cards, spread them out on your desk, and combine two or more to form a simile, metaphor or other figure of speech. For instance, from the list above you might combine *nibble* and *kites* to form "kites nibble at the sky." *Blossom, sorrow* and *song* might form "Sorrow blossoms into song." Once the metaphorical connection is made, you can reword your metaphor: "Yellow kites take bites of the sky" or "Sorrow's song is a blossom."

You may find that this exercise produces farfetched metaphors, which you've been warned against using. The word basket is merely a technique for exercising your metaphor muscles; once you get used to freely associating disparate images, you may find that metaphors arise more naturally in the context of your stories or poems.

2. Locate a simile in one of your stories, poems or essays. Rewrite the simile first as a metaphor and then as an implied metaphor. You'll probably find that the conversion requires more than simply removing "like" or "as," particularly when you're writing an implied metaphor, which relies solely on supporting details. (Verbs may be your best route into implied metaphor.) After you've written all three versions, choose the one

that most effectively serves your literary purpose.

3. Select from one of your stories a character you'd like to develop more fully. Using hyperbole, describe her physical appearance, demeanor, personality or movement. Limit yourself to one main vehicle for your hyperbole; then expand it. For instance, rather than saying that Gloria is slim as a willow reed, pale as the far side of the moon, and aggressive as a pit bull in heat, choose one of the hyperboles and expand it into a full description.

4. Write a description of a natural object, idea or emotion using personification or animism. Again, verbs are natural entries into both figures of speech. If you're animating "greed," for instance, ask yourself how greed moves or acts. Does it grab, clutch, or seize? Does it devour? The verbs might be enough to suggest personification or animism, or you could allow the verbs to lead you further in the writing process. If greed grabs, perhaps it has tentacles. If it devours, it might have a mouth. What kind of mouth?

5. Using paradox, write a description of one of your characters. You can apply the paradox to a physical description of your character or to your character's motives or emotions. In either case, choose two qualities that seem to be contradictory; then place them side by side. For instance, you might write that Eloise's face was "scarred and beautiful" or "beautifully scarred." Thinking in paradox may require engaging the all-accepting eye we discussed in chapter two. When you use paradox, you're allowing both sides of the mystery equal weight. One way to do this is to join the two sides with "and" (which is a democratic, equal-opportunity conjunction) rather than with conjunctions like "but," "or" or "yet" (which emphasize the opposition between the two sides.) Another way is to use a modifier (an adjective or adverb) that seems opposed to the word it's modifying (like Eloise's "beautifully scarred" face).

The same principles hold if you're describing a paradox in your character's emotions or motives. What does your character want? Rather than state it as a single, unequivocal desire, break the desire into two opposing parts and give each of them equal weight.

6. If you haven't begun to identify your personal "constellation of images," search through your stories or poems for recurring images or motifs, or ask someone familiar with your work to point them out. If your word processor has a "find" feature and you suspect that a certain word or phrase is part of your constellation, you can search your writing for evidence of a pattern. Once you've identified recurring images, you can use this knowledge for "seeding" new stories or poems.

7. Search your work for any metaphor that seems clichéd, strained, farfetched or simply inaccurate. Either rewrite the metaphor in a fresh way or remove it altogether. If a passage contains several metaphors close together, none of which relates to the others, consider removing all except the most effective one. Or expand the passage so the metaphors are spread over more area, giving the reader time to let one metaphor fully settle before moving on to the next.

BRINGING CHARACTERS TO LIFE THROUGH DESCRIPTION

W hen Broadway composer Stephen Sondheim was asked about his creative process, he replied, "If you told me to write a love song tonight, I'd have a lot of trouble. But if you tell me to write a love song about a girl with a red dress who goes into a bar and is on her fifth martini and is falling off her chair, that's a lot easier, and it makes me free to say anything I want." As we've already noted, it's hard to write effectively about a large, abstract subject—grief or anger or love—without first "sweating the small stuff." Remember the student writer who demonstrated, through a description of a small black button, the grief over her father's death? In Sondheim's case, the concept of love is embodied in a girl, but not just any girl. This is a particular girl in a particular place wearing a particular dress and drinking a particular drink. By the time the song is over, the girl may come to signify love, but first she has to put on the dress, take her place on the bar stool, and order a drink.

The characters in our stories, songs, poems and essays *embody* our writing. They are our words made flesh. Sometimes they even speak for us, carrying much of the burden of plot, theme, mood, idea and emotion. But they do not exist until we describe them on the page. Until they are anchored by our words, they drift, bodiless and ethereal. They weigh nothing; they have no voice. Once we've written the first words—"Belinda Beatrice," perhaps, or "the dark-eyed salesman in the back of the room," or simply "the girl"—our characters begin to take form. Soon they'll be more than mere names. They'll put on jeans or rubber hip boots, light thin cigarettes or thick cigars; they'll stutter or shout, buy a townhouse on the Upper East Side or a studio in the Village; they'll marry for life or survive a series of happy affairs; they'll beat their children or embrace them. What they become is up to us.

The girl in Sondheim's scenario acquires weight and substance through the physical details Sondheim supplies. First he provides a setting. In our mind's eye we see her sitting at the bar, wearing a dress that Sondheim also provides. But it's not just any dress. This dress is *red*—a detail both sensory and significant, suggesting a certain kind of girl (passionate or showy perhaps) or suggesting, at the very least, the passionate and showy aspects of the girl's nature. The drink is another significant detail. Other girls might drink chardonnay or lite beer or frothy pink drinks with paper umbrellas on the side. The girl in the red dress drinks martinis. Note the plural. Not one martini, but five.

Sondheim doesn't stop with identifying the girl and providing her with weight and substance through significant details. He also sets her in motion, thus following another of Aristotle's dictums for vivid descriptions—that whenever possible, we show our subjects in a state of activity. As a result, the reader not only sees a picture in his mind's eye; he sees a *moving* picture. The girl in the red dress is falling off her chair.

If the description were to continue, we might hear the girl speak. Her choice of words, her syntax, the timbre of her voice and the rhythms of her speech would add other elements to her characterization. We might also overhear what others at the bar are whispering about her. We might even gain access to the girl's inner world—hearing her unspoken words, feeling her fears, dreaming her dreams. Once we're situated inside, we might look out through her eyes and describe the world as it appears to her (and now to us) from our unsteady perch on the bar stool.

Our characters come alive through all these descriptive methods, and more. We establish characters by direct physical description, by our choice of sensory and significant details about the character and his surroundings, and through description of a character's movements and speech. Less directly, we describe our character through the eyes of other characters, by evoking a character's private world of thoughts and feelings, and by describing what the character sees through his own eyes.

CHRISTENING YOUR CHARACTERS

We begin by naming our characters or by identifying them in some way—"the grocer," "my aunt," "the little girl in the front row"—the reader can keep track of them. If you're writing nonfiction, you have little choice as to what to name your characters. They already have names, which you may choose to use or not to use, depending on your purposes. If you're writing fiction, choices abound. Like a prospective parent, you have the power to name your child anything you want. Not that you would, of course. A loving parent doesn't slap just any old name on her child. She carefully considers her choice. How will it sound when coupled with the surname? Should she choose a name with an ethnic flavor, one that suggests the family heritage? Maybe she should name him after his father, or after a famous person—a heavyweight boxer, a saint, an actor. What impression will the name make later on—on teachers, peers, future employers?

When we name our characters, we should use the same care we'd use in naming our children. A name is often the reader's first introduction to a character, and first impressions are important. "Queen Esther Alexander Pratt" announces itself, while "Sybil Rumple" stands in the shadows. An Alfred J. Petticoat might take mincing steps toward us; a Sam Slade probably won't. (If he does, however, or if Alfred turns out to hold a black belt in karate, you may still be on firm fictional ground, particularly if your goal is to surprise the reader.)

Suzanne Newton's novels are filled with memorable names, which often show up in her titles—*M.V. Sexton Speaking*, *What Are You Up To, William Thomas?* and *I Will Call It Georgie's Blues*. "The names just come to me," she says. "Intuitively, I know they're right." Newton's creative energies aren't spent in coming up with the perfect name but rather in inventing the background details that support her choice to the reader, especially if the name is a particularly strange one. Here's the scene from *Reubella and the Old Focus Home* in which the main character introduces herself.

> "Well, do you wish to be called 'Miss Foster?' "
>
> I felt myself turning red. "No, ma'am. My name's Reubella. R-e-u-b-e-l-l-a. I was named for my grandparents, Reuben and Ella Foster. My mom and dad didn't know, when they named me, that there was a virus by a similar name."
>
> I expected them to burst out laughing again, but they didn't. Instead they murmured polite things like "What an interesting name!" "Unusual!" and so forth.
>
> "It isn't easy going through life with a name like a virus," I told them, "but I have tried not to let it be an obstacle between me and my goals. I don't answer to a nickname. If people are interested in communicating with me, they have to use my real name."

If, unlike Suzanne Newton, you have trouble thinking of appropriate names for your characters, you can start by scanning the phone book or the obituary pages. Baby books are helpful too; some even list derivations. I prefer the obituary pages because you can see the whole name, middle initial, nickname and all. Be careful, though. If you find a name you like in its entirety, change it a little for your own protection; writers have been sued for less. As you're browsing, you might run across names that, though inappropriate for your character, are just too good to pass up. File them away for future stories. Some writers keep address books filled with characters' names.

Once you've used one of the characters in a story, you can also include beside his name any important details you might be apt to forget. This technique comes in handy if you're writing a long novel, a group of interrelated stories, or a novel series in which the same characters reappear. Mystery writer Margaret

Maron records all important information about her characters—physical descriptions, biographical data and other details revealed through dialogue and summary—to ensure consistency from book to book. Recording names and other details will also keep you from using the same name, or names too close in sound or flavor, for various characters.

Occasionally, real-life encounters provide us with better names than we'd find in the phone book. Some seem too good to be true, which probably means we can't use them. I once taught a student named Tarantula, a small brown girl who liked to bite her classmates. There's no way I could use that name, coupled with those details, in a story. It would feel forced, as if I'd thought of The Big Idea first, then hunted around for a name to serve my idea. Certain names suggest larger ideas and themes, even symbols: Destiny, Beulah, Pandora, Jesus. But unless you're writing an allegory or a parable, you should be cautious about using a name with symbolic overtones. Eudora Welty often uses such names, but she's quick to defend her choices. When a critic asked if her choice of "Phoenix" for the character in "A Worn Path" was consciously chosen to work as a symbol, Welty responded, "It's boring to think that things would be offered for symbolic reasons only, and it would be ridiculous too." The name was chosen, she said, because it was "an appropriate Mississippi name," and because it fit not only the locale but the time period in which the story takes place.The names we give characters do more than merely suggest personality traits. They also establish characters in time and place, and suggest ethnic and religious backgrounds, social and financial status, even parental aspirations (much is expected of a Muhammed Ali Johnson, for instance).

A character's nickname also provides descriptive clues for our readers. "Stretch" and "Spider" bring forth visual images; "Butter Bean" and "Buffy" suggest geographical and social classes. Since a nickname is usually given by close friends or family, it also offers insight into a character's personal relationships as well as suggesting a character's history and the events that have shaped him. Relating how a character got his nickname can open up a straightforward narrative, providing background information that might otherwise be difficult to insert. In one of my stories, I wanted to show the close relationship between the orphaned teenaged narrator and her older brother, but I didn't want to use flashbacks. His nickname provided the narrative vehicle I needed:

> Brick's not his real name, but I've never called him anything else. His real name is Reginald Brewster . . . My father's name was Reginald, but I never knew him. Aunt Mag's shown me pictures, so I see where Brick got his skin and hair . . . The name fits perfect. I mean, there he is, with that reddish-orange hair, a color you can't put your finger on, and pale skin with sprinkles of freckles across his forehead and down the back of his neck, and light reddish hair all over his arms, and even on his legs when he wears shorts . . . Most people think he got his name in school after he started playing football and they found out how strong he was. He's a tackle. Guys who make the mistake of running into him never do it again . . .

When I completed the passage, I was surprised to see that the nickname had not only provided a way to insert background information; it had also focused the details of my physical description. Since physical description of a character is such an important element of most fiction, and since it's often difficult to select the telling detail from so many possibilities, I was happy when the name "Brick" came along to help.

PHYSICAL DESCRIPTION OF CHARACTERS

Once we've named a character, we provide him with a body— how else will he move through the world of the story? Unfortunately, description that relies solely on physical attributes too often turns into what Janet Burroway calls the "all-points bulletin," which reads something like this: *My father is a tall, middle-aged man of average build. He has green eyes and brown hair and usually wears khakis and oxford shirts.*

This description is so mundane, it barely qualifies as an all-points bulletin. Can you imagine the police searching for this suspect? No identifying marks, no scars or tattoos, nothing to distinguish him. He appears as a cardboard cutout rather than as a living, breathing character. Yes, the details are accurate. Some even border on sensory—green eyes, brown hair. But they don't call forth vivid images. We can barely make out this character's form; how can we be expected to remember him?

When we're describing a character, factual information is not sufficient, no matter how accurate it might be. The details must appeal to our senses. Phrases that merely label (like "tall," "middle-aged" and "average") bring no clear image to our minds. Since most people form their first impression of someone through visual clues, it makes sense to describe our characters using visual images. "Green eyes" is a beginning, but it doesn't go far enough. Are they pale green or dark green? Even a simple adjective can strengthen a detail. If the adjective also suggests a metaphor—"forest green," "pea green" or "emerald green"—the reader not only begins to make associations (positive or negative), but also visualizes in his mind's eye the vehicle of the metaphor—forest trees, peas or glittering gems.

The problem with intensifying an image only by adjectives, as you can see from these examples, is that adjectives encourage cliché. It's hard to think of adjective descriptors that haven't been overused: bulging or ropy muscles; clean-cut good looks; frizzy hair. If you use an adjective to describe a physical attribute, make sure the phrase is not only accurate and sensory but fresh. In "Flowering Judas," Katherine Anne Porter describes Braggioni's singing voice as a "furry, mournful voice" that takes the high notes "in a prolonged painful squeal." Often, the easiest way to avoid an adjective-based cliché is to free the phrase entirely from its adjective modifier. For example, rather than describing her eyes merely as "hazel," Emily Dickinson remarked that they were "the color of the sherry the guests leave in the glasses."

Making details more specific is another way to strengthen physical descriptions. In the earlier "all-points bulletin" example, the father's hair might be described as "a military buzz-cut, prickly to the touch" or "the aging hippie's last chance—a long ponytail striated with gray." Either of these descriptions would paint a stronger picture than the bland phrase "brown hair." In the same way, his oxford shirt could become "a white oxford button-down that he'd steam-pleated just minutes before" or "the same style of baby blue oxford he'd worn since prep school, rolled carelessly at the elbows." These descriptions would not only bring forth images; they would also suggest the background and personality of the father.

Although the techniques for describing a fictional character are similar to those for a nonfictional character, nonfiction creates additional challenges. Let's say you're writing an essay about your brother, whose most distinguishing characteristics are his bald spot, his paunch and his stutter, none of which he likes to be reminded of. You love your brother, and you don't want to hurt his feelings; however, you want to create an accurate portrait. If he were a fictional character, you'd have no problem. A fictional character won't show up at two o'clock in the morning, demanding to know what right you have to embarrass him this way. A fictional character won't weep, slam a door in your face or disown you. A brother might. At some point in the writing process you'll have to decide what's more important—accurate, sensory and significant description, or your brother's feelings.

Specific details can strengthen our descriptions, but if we include too many specific details, we defeat our purpose of providing a visual image of our character. Here's the kind of description I wrote after my first creative writing teacher advised me to make my details more specific:

> Rosa Guy stood in the doorway, dressed in a blue denim jumpsuit with silver braid. Her face was bright and shiny, as if she'd just scrubbed it with complexion cream or Dove soap. Yellow earrings, in the shape of sunflowers, dangled from her tiny pink ears. Her neck was thick and veiny. She was broad-chested, like a female wrestler from Channel Nine's Monday Night Wrestling. Her hips

were wide, but her feet were as long and narrow as the
oars my grandfather uses when he rows his canoe.

Yikes! Where is the reader supposed to focus attention? True,
the details are sensory and specific, but are they significant?
What overall impression was I trying to make? In the previous
chapter we discussed how a figure of speech fails when images
are too farfetched or mixed, or when one image cancels out
the other. The same principle applies to physical descriptions.
Too many details, however sensory and specific, overload the
reader. When my husband builds a puppet character, he
chooses one or two physical details to focus on. He says that
beginning builders provide too many features, resulting in what
he calls the "Salad Bar Puppet." There's no need to overload
your plate, he says. Select a few distinguishing features and ignore the others.

In describing characters, we need to select details carefully,
choosing only those that create the strongest, most revealing
impression. One well-chosen physical trait, item of clothing or
idiosyncratic mannerism can reveal character more effectively
than a dozen random images. This applies to characters in nonfiction as well as fiction. When I write about my grandmother,
I usually focus on her strong, jutting chin—not only because
it was her most dominant feature but because it suggests her
stubbornness and determination. When I write about Uncle
Leland, I describe the wandering eye that gave him a perpetually distracted look, as if only his body were present. His spirit,
it seemed, had already left on some journey he'd glimpsed
peripherally, a place the rest of us were unable to see.

Besides including too many details, beginning writers also
tend to clump details of physical description together, usually
at the beginning of the story or when the character is first mentioned. There's no need to frontload your story with physical
descriptions, or to reveal all your details at once. Details can
accumulate as the story progresses. This technique protects
your readers from overly long or static passages, while providing
the series of proofs that help sustain the fictional dream. According to Flaubert, an object in a story has to be mentioned

three times in order for the reader to be convinced of its existence. The same can be said for physical description. If you describe a character's freckled skin only once, the reader may not remember it. But if you mention it again, even briefly, you increase the chances that the detail will be not only remembered but believed. Look back at the passages of physical description in your stories or essays. Are all your descriptive details about a character lumped together at the beginning of the piece or when the character is first introduced? If so, you might try breaking up the passage into smaller sections, then scattering these sections throughout the work.

You don't have to confine your descriptive proofs to scenes in which the character appears. Photographs can provide a smooth entry into physical descriptions. In Tim O'Brien's story "The Things They Carried," he introduces Martha through one of the photographs Lieutenant Cross carries in his wallet:

> It was an action shot—women's volleyball—and Martha was bent horizontal to the floor, reaching, the palms of her hands in sharp focus, the tongue taut, the expression frank and competitive. There was no visible sweat. She wore white gym shorts. Her legs, he thought, were almost certainly the legs of a virgin, dry and without hair, the left knee cocked and carrying her entire weight, which was just over one hundred pounds.

Photographs supply visual clues to a character's *past*. We can also portray characters by imagining how they might look in the future, a kind of descriptive time travel. In Andrew Miller's novel *Ingenious Pain*, the narrator describes a young boy named Sam, "an agile, scrawny, wonderfully ugly boy of eleven years." The description continues:

> At fifteen he will be untellable from a red-faced son of the plough in spotted neckerchief and leather breeches, roaring in some market town. By thirty he will be one of these at the table; still lusty, but already half broken by work and worry, drinking to forget.

Although visual physical description is the most common way to introduce a character to a reader, it's not always the most effective way. As we discussed in an earlier chapter, description that involves smell, hearing, touch and taste often draws the reader in more quickly, and more emotionally, than description that relies only on sight. For memorable characters who come alive on the page we need to supply more than visual clues.

A character's scent, for instance, can reveal his age, background, lifestyle and environment. (Helen Keller claimed to be able to tell a person's occupation by the way he smelled.) When my nephew comes in from outside and climbs onto my lap, I can tell not only where he's been but what the weather is like. When he smells fresh, like pine or cedar, I know it's cool and windy, and he's been swinging on the tree swing out back; when he smells like a wet puppy, I know the afternoon's turned hot and steamy, and he's been running hard. Great Aunt Bessie, a recurring character in my essays and fiction, appears not through the world of smells, but through sounds I associate with her oldness—the swish of taffeta down the hall, the clonk of heavy heels and the mechanical clack of her loose dentures.

Study your descriptions. If you find you've included only visual description, try adding other sensory details. What smells might suggest your character's occupation or preoccupation? Formaldehyde, paint thinner, motor oil, furniture polish, Lava soap, bourbon, wintergreen breath mints, wood smoke? How does his wife's skin feel? Silky and smooth, or dry and scaly? When he holds her, does he sink into womanly flesh or impale himself on bone? Is her laugh shrill as a whistle or low and raspy, a lifetime smoker's laugh? Our characters are more than mere holograms or still photographs in an album. Their bodies are microcosms of texture and aroma and sound, reflecting the private and public worlds in which they move.

DESCRIBING CHARACTERS THROUGH THEIR ENVIRONMENTS

As the old saying goes, everybody has to be *somewhere*. Fictional characters are no exception. Once we give our character a name and body, we put a roof over his head or, at the very least, give him a place to roam. The world we create for the character includes not only physical spaces—a home, workplace, neighborhood—but historical settings as well. Since I'll be discussing setting in another chapter of the book, I'll confine my remarks at this point to those elements of setting that directly reveal a character's character—not only his occupational and personal environment, but also his belongings, the objects that fill his world.

Often when I have trouble developing three-dimensional characters, it's because I haven't provided them with a suitable background against which to shine. For a long time, one of my characters refused to show herself. Her name was fitting, her actions believable and her internal conflict absorbing. But I could not visualize her; she did not feel real. She lacked a world in which to move. Once I found the right workplace for her (a greenhouse) and the right digs (a basement apartment on the premises) she fleshed out nicely. I could imagine her "wearing a dark green smock, watering ferns or pinching back wild vines, her face white and vulnerable against the leafy background of scheffleras and palms." The greenhouse also provided a setting for her first meeting with the man who would become the father of her child. Since he happened to be a *married* man, the underground apartment mirrored their illicit relationship, deepening the internal conflict that drove the story to its conclusion.

A character's immediate surroundings can provide the backdrop for the sensory and significant details that shape the description of the character himself. Environment can also mirror a character's emotional state. If your character doesn't yet have a job, a hobby, a place to live or to wander, you might need to supply these things. Once your character is situated comfortably, he may relax enough to reveal his secrets. On the other hand, you might purposely make your character uncomfortable—that is, put him in an environment where he definitely doesn't fit, just to see how he'll respond. Let's say you've written several poems about your grandmother in the kitchen, yet she hasn't begun to ripen into the three-dimensional character you know she could become. Try putting her at a gay bar on a

Saturday night, or in a tattoo parlor—or at Appomattox, serving her famous buttermilk biscuits to Grant and Lee.

In describing a character's surroundings, you don't have to limit yourself to a character's present life. Describe the house where he grew up or the room he shared with his twin brother. Childhood environments shape fictional characters as well as flesh-and-blood people. In Flaubert's description of Emma Bovary's adolescent years in the convent, he foreshadows the woman she will become, a woman who moves through life in a romantic malaise, dreaming of faraway lands and loves. We learn about Madame Bovary through concrete, sensory description of the place that formed her. In addition, Flaubert describes the book that held her attention during mass, and the images she particularly loved—a sick lamb, a pierced heart.

> Living among those white-faced women with their rosaries and copper crosses, never getting away from the stuffy schoolroom atmosphere, she gradually succumbed to the mystic languor exhaled by the perfumes of the altar, the coolness of the holy-water fonts and the radiance of the tapers. Instead of following the Mass, she used to gaze at the azure-bordered religious drawings in her book. She loved the sick lamb, the Sacred Heart pierced with sharp arrows, and poor Jesus falling beneath His cross.

Characters reveal their inner lives—their preoccupations, values, lifestyles, likes and dislikes, fears and aspirations—by the objects that fill their hands, houses, offices, cars, suitcases, grocery carts and dreams. In early scenes of the film *The Big Chill*, we're introduced to the main characters by watching them unpack the bags they've brought for a weekend trip to a mutual friend's funeral. One character has packed enough pills to stock a drugstore; another has packed a calculator; still another, several packages of condoms. Before a word is spoken, even before we know anyone's name, we catch glimpses of the characters' lives through the objects that define them.

What items would your character pack for a weekend away? And what would she use for luggage? A leather valise with a gold monogram on the handle? An old accordion case with decals from every theme park she's visited? A duffel bag? Make a list of everything your character would take: a Save the Whales T-shirt; a white cotton nursing bra, size 36D; a breast pump; a Mickey Mouse alarm clock; a photograph of her husband rocking a child to sleep; a can of Mace; three Hershey bars.

We already know many things about your character, and you haven't even described her yet. Or have you? Description doesn't have to be direct to be effective. There are lots of techniques for describing a character indirectly, through the objects that fill his world. Write a grocery list for your character—or two or three, depending on who's coming for dinner. Show us the character's credit card bill, or the itemized deductions on his income tax forms. Have your character host a garage sale and watch him squirm while neighbors and strangers rifle through his stuff. Which items is he practically giving away? What has he overpriced, secretly hoping no one will buy it? Write your character's Last Will and Testament. Which niece gets the Steinway? Who gets the lake cottage—the stepson or the daughter? If your main characters are divorcing, how will they divide their assets? Which one will fight harder to keep the dog?

SETTING CHARACTERS INTO MOTION

I admit right off that this is a subject dear to my heart. Since my husband is a professional puppeteer, at least half our livelihood depends on his ability to make inanimate objects come alive. To aid a puppet's movement, he sometimes uses wires, rods, string, monofilament, cables, even motors, but his favorite puppets are the simplest ones, those that rely solely on the motions of his hands. He asserts that a puppet's appearance is not nearly as important as what it is able to do. "Puppets aren't dolls," he says. "The essence of puppetry is movement." Without movement, an intricately carved figure, beautifully painted and costumed, is only that—a figure, a pretty doll on a shelf. Conversely, the most humble object—a piece of fabric, two blocks of foam, a dust mop—comes alive through adroit movement. The dust mop becomes a mischievous puppy; the foam blocks, two local politicians belaboring a moot point; the sheet of blue fabric, undulating waves rocking a drowned Annabel Lee into eternal sleep.

Writers, like puppeteers, must breathe life into inanimate creatures. Our characters, mere black marks on white paper, cannot actually walk, talk, make love or war, scramble eggs or strum guitars. But they must *appear* to. So after we've given them substance—bodies, names, histories, occupations, preoccupations, houses and cars—we set them in motion. One character flicks cigarette ash onto the carpet, another character vacuums it up. In fiction, as in life, actions speak louder than words. We learn about characters by watching them move.

The earlier "all-points bulletin" description of the father failed not only because the details were mundane and the prose stilted. The description suffered also from lack of movement. When my students are writing portraits in poetry or prose, I encourage them to conjure a mental image of the person being described, complete with concrete, sensory physical details. Then I ask them to place the person in a particular setting and to be as specific as they can—the father is not just "in the house" but "in the brown recliner." I remind them that setting implies time as well as place. The time they select may be clock-bound (six o'clock, sunrise, early afternoon) or bound only by personal history (after the divorce, the day he lost his job, two weeks before his sixtieth birthday).

Then, following Aristotle's dictum of "using expressions that represent things as in a state of activity," I ask the students to set the person in motion. Again, it's important to be as specific as possible. "Reading the newspaper" is a start, but it does little more than label a generic activity. In order for readers to enter the fictional dream, the activity must be *shown*. Often this means breaking the large generic activity into smaller, more particular parts: "scowling at the Dow Jones averages," perhaps, or "skimming the used car ads" or "wiping his ink-stained fingers on the monogrammed handkerchief he always keeps in his shirt pocket.'' These three actions describe three very different fathers. Besides providing a visual image for the reader, specific and representative actions also suggest the personality of the character, the emotional life hidden beneath the physical details.

As we've said earlier, verbs are the foot soldiers of action-based description. However, we don't need to confine our use of verbs to the actions a character performs. Well-placed verbs can sharpen almost any physical description of a character. In the following passage from Marilynne Robinson's novel *Housekeeping*, verbs help bring the description alive even when the grandmother isn't in motion:

> . . . in the last years she continued to settle and began to shrink. Her mouth bowed forward and her brow sloped back, and her skull shone pink and speckled within a mere haze of hair, which hovered about her head like the remembered shape of an altered thing. She looked as if the nimbus of humanity were fading away and she were turning monkey. Tendrils grew from her eyebrows and coarse white hairs sprouted on her lip and chin. When she put on an old dress the bosom hung empty and the hem swept the floor. Old hats fell down over her eyes. Sometimes she put her hand over her mouth and laughed, her eyes closed and her shoulders shaking.

Notice the strong verbs Robinson uses throughout the description. The mouth *bowed* forward; the brow *sloped* back; the hair *hovered*, then *sprouted*; the hem *swept* the floor; hats *fell* down over her eyes. Even when the grandmother's body is at rest, the description pulses with activity. And when the grandmother finally does move—putting a hand over her mouth, closing her eyes, laughing until her shoulders shake—we can visualize her in our mind's eye because the actions are concrete and specific. They're what playwright David Mamet calls ''actable actions.'' Opening a window is an actable action, as is slamming a door. ''Coming to terms with himself'' or ''understanding that he's been wrong all along'' are not actable actions. This distinction between nonactable and actable actions echoes our earlier distinction between showing and telling. For the most part, a character's movements must be rendered concretely—that is, shown—before the reader can participate in the fictional dream.

Action-based description does more than bring a character to life by painting a vivid, moving picture. A character's actions also reflect how a character moves morally and psychologically through the world of the story. Mystery writer Margaret Maron says there are some things a character simply cannot do as part of his moral landscape. The writer, she says, cannot successfully force a character to perform an action that goes against his personal morality without first changing the character himself. We can't just wind up our characters as if they were spring-loaded toys. Action, in and of itself, is not sufficient. The actions we give our characters must be chosen carefully to represent not only the character's outer life but his inner life as well.

DESCRIBING A CHARACTER'S INNER LANDSCAPE

When Hollywood announces the opening of a movie made from one of my favorite novels, my first reaction is to climb into the pages of the book, pull the cover over my head, and fall back into the fictional dream. The last thing I want to do is see the movie. It's like that invitation to my thirty-year college reunion that arrived a few weeks ago. Do I really want to see what Mike McGraw looks like now? I mean, I have his senior picture, the wrist corsage pressed between two pages of my yearbook, and three decades of gauzy, airbrushed memories. Why fly all the way to California to dance with some impostor wearing Mike's name on his lapel?

That's the way I feel about an actor playing the part of my favorite fictional character. For months I've lived within the world of the story, wearing the character's skin and looking out through his green, penetrating eyes. Now, on the forty-foot screen, it's Harrison Ford or Liam Neeson or Tommy Lee Jones, and no matter how skilled his portrayal, he can never be more than an actor playing a role. He stomps or stumbles or rolls onto the scene, wearing a three-dimensional body that leaves nothing to my imagination. The character that breathed from the pages of the novel is gone, and nothing short of opening the book and climbing back into its pages will revive him.

Although the novelist described the character well, what was left unsaid was as important as what was said. My imagination created the rest. Like all absorbed readers, I created the character partly in my own image. Such is the power of literature. No other medium—not stage or screen or television—allows us to participate so fully in the writing, producing and directing of the fictional dream. That's why books will never become obsolete. Novels, short stories, essays and poems allow the reader to complete what the author began.

Those of us who write for the page can learn much from the fields of playwriting, cinematography, scripting, and oration— about showing instead of telling, setting the stage, and bringing a character to life through actions, dialogue and stage directions. But at a certain point, our writerly paths diverge. Although the road of the filmmaker or screenwriter may be broader, more public and populated, and more likely to be paved with coins, our road has more twists and turns, more hidden entries and exits, and more possibilities for revealing the mysteries of the human heart. Those of us who write for the page can travel to places a camera can never travel, the internal landscape and mindscape of our characters and ourselves.

Description is not strictly external. We don't always have to use concrete, visual details to describe our characters, and we aren't limited to describing "actable actions." We don't even have to follow Aristotle's dictums of making people "see things" or of "using expressions that represent things in a state of activity." Aristotle, after all, was schooled in drama and rhetoric, which are public, oral traditions that rely solely on outward signs to achieve their effects. Since he'd never read a novel— there were no novels to be read—Aristotle had no idea of how to portray the inner life of a character.

I wonder what Aristotle would have thought of the novels of Milan Kundera, who uses little outward description of characters or their actions. Kundera is more concerned with a character's interior landscape, with what he calls a character's "existential problem," than with sensory description of person or action. In *The Unbearable Lightness of Being*, Tomas's body is not described at all, since the idea of *body* does not constitute Tomas's internal dilemma. Teresa's body *is* described in physical, concrete terms (though not with the degree of detail most novelists would employ) only because her body represents one of her existential preoccupations. For Kundera, a novel is more a meditation on ideas and the private world of the mind than a realistic depiction of characters. Reading Kundera, I always feel I'm living inside the characters rather than watching them move, bodily, through the world.

With writers like Kundera, we learn about characters through the themes and obsessions of their inner lives, their "existential problems" as depicted primarily through dreams, visions, memories and thoughts. Other writers probe characters' inner lives through what characters see through their eyes. A writer who describes what a character sees also reveals, in part, a character's inner drama. In *The Madness of a Seduced Woman*, Susan Fromberg Schaeffer describes a farm through the eyes of the main character, Agnes, who has just fallen in love and is anticipating her first sexual encounter, which she simultaneously longs for and fears:

> . . . and I saw how the smooth, white curve of the snow
> as it lay on the ground was like the curve of a woman's
> body, and I saw how the farm was like the body of a
> woman which lay down under the sun and under the
> freezing snow and perpetually and relentlessly pro-
> duced uncountable swarms of living things, all born with
> mouths open and cries rising from them into the air,
> long-boned muzzles opening . . . as if they would swallow
> the world whole . . .

Later in the book, after Agnes's sexual relationship has led to pregnancy, then to a life-threatening abortion, she describes the farm in quite different terms:

It was August, high summer, but there was something definite and curiously insubstantial in the air . . . In the fields near me, the cattle were untroubled, their jaws grinding the last of the grass, their large, fat tongues drinking the clear brook water. But there was something in the air, a sad note the weather played upon the instrument of the bone-stretched skin . . . In October, the leaves would be off the trees; the fallen leaves would be beaten flat by heavy rains and the first fall of snow. The bony ledges of the earth would begin to show, the earth's skeleton shedding its unnecessary flesh.

By describing the farm through Agnes's eyes, Schaeffer not only shows us Agnes's inner landscape, her ongoing obsession with sex and pregnancy, but also demonstrates a turning point in Agnes's view of sexuality. In the first passage, which depicts a farm in winter, Agnes sees images of beginnings and births. The earth is curved and full like a woman's fleshy body. In the second scene, described as occurring in "high summer," images of death prevail. Agnes's mind jumps ahead to autumn, to dying leaves and heavy rains, a time when the earth, no longer curved and womanly, is little more than a skeleton, having shed the flesh it no longer needs.

When a character describes a place, in effect we get two descriptions for the price of one—a glimpse of the external place as well as insight into the describer's internal world. The same principle applies when one character describes another character. The reader not only glimpses the second character through the eyes of the first but gains insight into the inner life of the describer, as well as to the relationship between the two characters. In Tom Wolfe's *The Bonfire of the Vanities*, we are introduced to Lawrence Kramer's wife through the eyes of her husband, who has been fantasizing about having an affair with a young woman. The Kramers live in a small apartment, and their bed is almost as wide as the bedroom, which means they have to crawl to the edge of the bed in order to reach the floor. His wife is doing just that as Kramer awakes.

He woke up to the pitch and roll of his wife crawling down to the foot of the bed . . . Now she was standing on the floor and bending over a chair to pick up her bathrobe. The way her flannel nightgown came down over her hips, she looked a mile wide . . .

A third, more subtle method of indirect description involves rendering a character's inner landscape through cadence, syntax and diction. In this method, the writer imagines herself into a character's mind, then attempts to reproduce the internal rhythms of a character's thought patterns. In *Praying for Sheetrock: A Work of Nonfiction*, Melissa Fay Greene takes us inside Fanny's mind as she recalls a difficult childhood "in a world that consisted of her cot, the field, the kitchen and the church."

Night, dawn, noon, dusk, night. Bed, field, table, field, church. Sleep, pick, eat, pick, pray . . .
   Bed, field, table, field, church. Bed. Field. Table: a hollow gallop of wooden bowls on a wooden table. Field. Church: a chase through dark woods and clinging vines, barefoot behind her grandmother, who carried a pair of church shoes for the girl in one hand. Bed. Field. Table. Field. Church: dry, upright, mumbling heat. She slumped against her sisters and snored. Bed. Field: endless. Table. Field: dirt filled her fingernails, eyes, ears, nose, hair. Church. Bed. Field: she weeded, hoed, and picked until the sky and air whirled brown and thistly around her, and her small fingers moved, delicately plucking so as not to get pricked, even in her sleep. Bed.

Through the use of repetition, cycling and recycling the same words through recurring staccato rhythms, Greene describes Fanny's world from the inside out. Rather than being told what Fanny looks like from the outside, we feel the weight of Fanny's weariness and the monotony of her days.

All three of these techniques—showing a character's inner life through thoughts, dreams and fantasies, describing the world that passes before a character's eyes, and rendering a character's interior rhythms—are indirect methods of description. That is, the writer does not directly describe a person, scene or event, but rather processes the description through the character's consciousness. Once we depart from direct authorial methods (such as physical description of a character, his environment and his actions) and enter a character's internal world, we must consider how the character's consciousness filters the description and shapes the telling of the tale.

EXERCISES

1. If one of your characters doesn't yet have a full name, give him one, including a last name and a middle name or initial. Try out different names to see which one best fits his personality and actions, or give him a completely inappropriate name, one that goes against expectations. Then give him a nickname and invent the story behind it; describe him, physically or otherwise, in terms of his nickname. Finally, give the character the name he secretly wishes he has, the one he's always dreamed of having, and describe in detail the fantasy he associates with the name.

2. Choose one physical feature of your character—hair, eyes, hands, etc.—and describe it metaphorically. (Remember Emily Dickinson's eyes, the "color of the sherry the guests leave in the glasses"?) If you wish to take the metaphor further, describe the feature in terms of a setting you associate with your character.

3. Write a long description of a character, or locate one in a story or essay you've written. Break the description into three sections and place each section in a different part of the story. You might wish to start with the most obvious details and save the more intimate or evocative details for later, so that the character is revealed a little at a time.

4. Describe a photograph (or video) of your character that reveals something about him that your story does not yet reveal. If the photograph was taken during a time period not covered

in the story, your description might serve as a flashback.

5. Write a description of your character as he might appear in the future. The description could be from the character's own imagination ("Elaine saw herself years from today . . .") or from another character's viewpoint (see the passage from *Ingenious Pain* quoted in this chapter).

6. Describe a character as a blind person might describe him; use every sense *except* sight.

7. Describe the same character in three different environments—say, the grocery store, a hockey game and the locker room. Notice how the setting affects your character's appearance, posture, mannerisms, speech and thoughts. In which place does your character seem most relaxed, youthful, worried or lighthearted?

8. Write down a particular trait, emotion or attitude your character possesses. Then list at least three "actable actions" that might reveal that quality. For instance, if you wish to show Darla's vanity, your list might include glancing at her reflection in storefronts, wearing turtlenecks and scarves to hide the wrinkles in her neck, undergoing liposuction on her thighs. Expand one of these actions into a full description that *reveals* Darla's vanity rather than merely *tells* the reader about it.

9. If you want to learn more about your characters' inner lives, write a description of how each would react given the same situation. Choose a situation that will reveal the characters' values, attitudes or other qualities of their inner landscape: being accosted by a panhandler, being given too much change by a cashier, being seduced by a beautiful stranger. Which of your characters would fail to report cash earnings to the I.R.S.? Which ones would refuse to have an affair, even if their spouse couldn't possibly find out?

10. Write a description of a person, place, object or event in the language of one of your characters. Use his vocabulary, his grammar and syntax, the rhythms of his sentences. (For an example, study the passage quoted from *Praying for Sheetrock.*)

THE EYE OF THE TELLER: HOW POINT OF VIEW AFFECTS DESCRIPTION

Throughout this book, we've discussed the importance of writers paying attention, of giving full and thoughtful consideration to three components of descriptive writing: eye, word and story. First we attend to the images in the sensory world and the world of the imagination; then, we attempt a precise, vivid and fresh description of these images; finally, we consider how our description serves the overall story, poem or essay.

Attention also refers to a position taken and held. Each time we put pen to paper, we assume a position—call it our posture, angle, persona or point of view. Point of view, in this case, does not mean *opinion* but rather the literary position from which we describe the details of our story. It also concerns how a story is narrated, its journey from author to reader.

If we're writing nonfiction or autobiographical poetry, our stance probably differs little, if any, from the stance of the narrator or speaker. The path from author to reader is fairly straightforward: author speaks to reader. In narrative nonfiction told in first person, the narrator is usually the author himself, or as close to himself as any author can be. (Since literature is not life, but a representation of life, all writers, even writers of nonfiction, can be said to employ literary masks.)

If we're writing fiction, the issue of point of view becomes more complex. Our narrator's position may differ widely from our own, making the route from author to reader a more circuitous one. To get to the reader, we must first go through our narrator. If that narrator also happens to be a character in the story, the path gets even more complicated.

Point of view is arguably the most complex of literary conventions. Countless dissertations have been written on the subject, and almost every writing text devotes a chapter or two to point-of-view issues, including how point of view affects a story's form, content, plot, voice, tone and reliability. For our purposes, we'll focus mainly on those point-of-view issues that directly affect description. We'll show how description frames the narrator's point of view, how shifts in the descriptive frame (or eye) signal viewpoint shifts, and how point-of-view description can organize our stories. Finally, we'll discuss the strengths and limitations of each point-of-view method as it relates to description. But first we'll depart briefly from our discussion of description to review some basic issues concerning point of view. We'll define each method, then show how to establish a story's point of view and how to avoid troubling viewpoint shifts.

POINT-OF-VIEW BASICS

There are three main point-of-view methods: first-person narration, second-person narration and third-person narration.

In first-person point of view, the story is told by an "I" who is a character in the story. The "I" may be the main character around which the story revolves, or he may be a minor character. Everything in a first-person narration is filtered through the consciousness of the "I."

In second-person narration, a character in the story is referred to as "you." Second-person narration goes beyond merely addressing your reader as "you," a technique I've used throughout this book; it actually places the "you" within the events of the story. In chapter four I briefly addressed the reader in second person:

> And what about the hot crusty roll the waiter just placed with a tong on your bread plate? It looks hot, it looks crusty, but how will you know unless you pick it up with

your bare hands, feel its weight and shellacked surface, break it open and feel the steam escaping from the soft center? You swirl the butter knife in the small white crock, spread a smear of herb-speckled butter on the bread, lift it to your mouth.

If I had continued in this manner, and if the "you" had actually become a character rather than merely a grammatical construct, I would have been writing in second person. Second-person narration is such a rare and idiosyncratic form that, for the purposes of this book, we will dispense with it entirely and turn our attention to first- and third-person narration, with variations on each.

In third-person narration, the speaker is not a character in the story. A third-person narrator uses third-person pronouns—he, she, it or they—to tell a story about someone else. (A first-person narrator also uses third-person pronouns, but only to refer to other characters in his own story.)

There are three main variations on third-person narration. The *objective narrator* relates a story solely through outward signs—dialogue, action and description. The *omniscient or god-like narrator* knows everything that a god might know. He not only sees and describes outward signs; he can also see into the minds of all his characters, move freely through time and space, and insert authorial comments. The *limited omniscient narrator* can do everything an objective narrator can do, but less than an omniscient narrator. He can describe outward signs—actions, dialogue, setting—but usually inhabits only one character's mind.

ESTABLISHING POINT OF VIEW

An effective story or novel usually reveals its point of view early on, positioning the reader in the appropriate seat from which to view the show. The eye of the describer focuses the telling, often within the first sentence:

We get married in two days: Charles and me.

—from *Raney* by Clyde Edgerton

The day after Thanksgiving my mother was arrested outside the doors of JC Penney's, Los Angeles, and when I went to get her I considered leaving her at the security desk.

—from "Pitch Memory" by Ethan Canin

Lloyd Abbott wasn't the richest man in our town, but he had, in his daughters, a vehicle for displaying his wealth that some of the richer men didn't have.

—from "The Lover of Women" by Sue Miller

With all three of these opening sentences, we learn right off (from the first-person pronouns "me," "my," "I" and "our") that we'll be viewing the story through the eyes of a first person narrator who is a character in the story. We don't yet know whether the speaker will be the main character or a peripheral character, but we do know the speaker will place himself, to some degree, *within* the story rather than outside it.

Sometimes it takes longer than one paragraph to establish point of view, but in most cases the reader knows by the end of a story's first page who will be narrating the tale, and whether the speaker will be a character in the story or a third-person narrator:

"Yes, of course, if it's fine tomorrow," said Mrs. Ramsay. "But you'll have to be up with the lark," she added.

To her son these words conveyed an extraordinary joy, as if it were settled, the expedition were bound to take place, and the wonder to which he had looked forward, for years and years it seemed, was, after a night's darkness and a day's sail, within touch.

—from *To the Lighthouse* by Virginia Woolf

The first sentence of Woolf's novel suggests a third-person narrator; Mrs. Ramsay is named as a third party. But the point of view isn't firmly established at this point. The narrator might be a first person "I," a character in the story who is telling us about Mrs. Ramsay. It's only when the narrator enters the son's mind that we know for sure this is third-person narration rather than first. A first-person narrator cannot inhabit another character's mind, only his own.

Most contemporary stories are told either from the first-person point of view or from third-person limited omniscient. Since there usually isn't space within a short work for multiple viewpoints to be shown well, very few short stories use a third person narrator who is totally omniscient, capable of entering all characters' minds. Novelists, however, often use this technique, dipping in and out of several characters' minds. Multiple viewpoints can also be accomplished through several first-person narrators, as in Faulkner's *As I Lay Dying.*

In the case of multiple narrators (in third-person narration as well as first) we may not know for several pages, or even several chapters, how many minds we'll be inhabiting. Faulkner's opening sentence—"Jewel and I come up from the field, following the path in single file"—announces a first-person narrator, Darl. We don't know until the next chapter, when another first-person narrator speaks, that we'll be entering the mind of more than one character. Thankfully, Faulkner's opening chapters are quite short, so it doesn't take us long to recognize Faulkner's pattern. In addition, his chapter headings ("Darl," "Cora," "Darl," "Jewel," etc.) provide early hints to his viewpoint structure. Simply by skimming the novel's pages, we can surmise that more than one teller will be relating the tale.

Like most novels and short stories, essays and poems also announce their point of view early on. With some poems, the clues come even before the first line, with titles like W.S. Merwin's "Grandmother Watching at Her Window" or Patricia Hubbell's "The Streetcleaner's Lament." And by the end of the first paragraph of an essay, we usually know whether the writer will be using the first-person narration characteristic of personal essays, opinion pieces and memoirs, or the third-person narration that shapes most biographies, profiles and journalistic investigations.

Through effective use of pronouns and names, you can reveal early on whether your speaker is a first-person narrator or a third-person narrator. It may take a bit longer to establish whether your first-person narrator is a main character or a peripheral character, or whether your third-person narrator is objective, omniscient or limited omniscient. Even so, establishing your narrator's point of view is a fairly straightforward procedure. Maintaining your point of view, however, is more difficult, as is sensing when to subtly shift viewpoints to achieve literary effects. Shift in points of view can be likened to the nursery rhyme girl with the curl in the middle of her forehead. When they are good, they can be very, very good. But when they are bad, they are horrid.

TROUBLING SHIFTS IN POINT OF VIEW

The reader needs time to position himself in a story and to focus his imaginative eye. If that focus changes abruptly, for no apparent reason, his energies are diverted. Radical, awkward or inappropriate shifts confuse and frustrate the reader, making him unsure of whose story he's reading.

One of the most common ways to frustrate your reader is to abruptly switch point of view from one character to another. Let's say that for the first several pages of your story, you've been situated inside Linda's mind, looking out.

> Linda lit a cigarette and watched her mother cram another forkful of chocolate cake into her mouth. I'll never let myself get that fat, Linda thought. Never. I'll starve myself first. Linda inhaled deeply, holding the cigarette between two thin fingers.

Linda's mother has been present in the scene also, but only as described through Linda's eyes. Since the reader has been living solely within Linda's consciousness, he's made an intellectual and emotional investment in Linda; as the writer, you've given no clue that the story belongs to anyone else.

Then suddenly, you ask the reader to slip inside the mother's mind, to feel her emotions.

> Linda's mother looked up from her plate and smiled, hoping that Linda hadn't noticed how big a bite she'd taken.

Until the point of view shifted, the reader had been happily immersed in your fictional dream. One small word—"hoping"—was all it took to distract him. "Hoping" betrays emotion and thought on the part of the mother. It moves the reader inside another character's mind, violating the limited omniscient point of view you'd established.

Luckily, this kind of viewpoint shift is easy to correct. Simply remove the subjective, internalized word or phrase (*"hoping that Linda hadn't noticed . . ."*) and replace it with with an objective, actable action Linda could witness ("Her mother lowered her eyes," perhaps, or "Her mother laid the fork down quickly and wiped the crumbs of chocolate from her mouth.") We'll still get a notion of what the mother is feeling, but the evidence will be filtered through Linda's consciousness. We'll remain inside her mind, securely centered in Linda's story.

Another way to distract or confuse your reader is to switch visual points of reference too often or too quickly. This can happen even when you're firmly centered in one consciousness and don't stray from it. Let's say you open your story with a phrase like "From where he lay, Simon could see the flat Illinois sky, stretched between two silos." So far, so good. The reader mentally lies on his back next to Simon, peering up into the sky.

In the next sentence, Simon watches an ant crawl over his big toe. The reader's still with you. Granted, the reader might have enjoyed dwelling a while longer on sky images, experiencing more detailed proofs, but one abrupt switch won't hurt your description too much. The reader can shift vantage points from the Illinois sky to the ant without suffering a whiplash.

Sentence three: "Simon stared at the ant, then stretched and sighed, remembering the last time he'd seen Flora, her long lean legs pedaling away from him as she disappeared down the country road." By now the reader is dizzy. It's like those three manic minutes on your sister's wedding video. (Remember? You'd set the camera down for a minute, just long enough to get another glass of champagne, and your four-year-old grabbed the camera. Now you've got three minutes of spinning linoleum tiles, stiletto heels, then swoop! a quick pan of the ceiling, your uncle's mouth, an unidentified hand reaching for the punch bowl.) By the time Simon rises to his feet in sentence four, your reader is grabbing a chair for balance. You've shifted visual viewpoints so abruptly that the reader has lost all sense of perspective.

More often, shifts in perspective are not visual, but rather what novelist John Gardner calls shifts in "psychic distance." Psychic shifts are harder to pinpoint than visual shifts, but they are even more disturbing to the reader because they erode the emotional ground of the story. Here's a sentence from Ivan Turgenev's "The Tryst," followed in italics by two sentences which, had they appeared in the story (they didn't—I invented them) would have eroded the psychic ground Turgenev had established:

> I cannot tell how long I slept, but when I opened my eyes, the whole interior of the forest was filled with sunlight, and in all directions, athwart the joyously rustling foliage, the bright blue sky seemed to be sparkling. *The weather report had been accurate after all, I thought. It was indeed a mild day to venture outdoors.*

Turgenev's description is intimate and highly charged with emotion. The speaker is psychically close to the scene and pulls the reader in with him. It's as if the forest is alive, wrapping itself around both speaker and reader. The two sentences that follow, on the other hand, are objectively reported, as if spoken by someone totally removed from the scene. The psychic distance between the two voices is staggering. Any shift in point of view—in visual perspective, psychic distance or a shift from the vantage point of one character to another—must be carefully executed.

USING DESCRIPTION TO SETTLE
INTO POINT OF VIEW

Sometimes what seems to be a shift in viewpoint is actually a kind of settling, a gradual descent into the story, like a hawk circling before moving in for the kill. In this technique, the author brings the story into focus slowly through description. This gradual settling can be likened to the opening of a movie—the camera taking in the large view, its eye sweeping over the terrain. Joan Chase's *During the Reign of the Queen of Persia* begins in this cinematic manner:

> In northern Ohio there is a county of some hundred thousand arable acres which breaks with the lake region flatland and begins to roll and climb, and to change into rural settings . . .

Chase's description continues in this way, a luxurious rendering of the countryside, complete with concrete and sensory details like "water shoots that rapidly lose themselves in gladed ravines," "the hump of railroad lines," and "the jeweled dust of crushed quartz." Chase describes the setting first—the time and place in which the story will take place. Only after the setting is established do we begin to settle into the teller's voice, her visual and psychological point of view.

Another way to settle gradually into point of view is to describe the opening scene from the eye of a removed or objective first-person narrator who stands on the outskirts, visually or psychologically. This technique is especially effective in certain nonfiction forms where you wish to establish yourself as a witness to the events, a presence with the "I" of authority. Once this authority is established, you can slip from the scene so the reader can focus on a character or subject other than yourself.

In fiction, too, beginning with an objective first-person narrator is a way to lend autobiographical authority to a story. Flaubert uses this technique in *Madame Bovary*. Although the bulk of the novel is told from the third-person limited omniscient point of view, it actually opens with first-person narration.

145

"We were at preparation," the novel begins. The narrator is a schoolboy speaking in first-person plural, as if through the communal voice of all the schoolboys present when the new boy, Charles Bovary, arrives on the scene. First-person narration continues for a few pages, but once Charles Bovary is described in detail, the first-person narrator slips from the scene and the third-person narrator takes over. The novel never returns to first-person point of view, for, in fact, it was never firmly situated there. The novelist was simply circling the scene, fluttering briefly but not landing: the permanent nest was third-person narration.

Flaubert's technique—shifting from first person to third—is relatively rare in fiction. More often, subtle shifts in opening points of view occur when a third-person narrator circles the scene objectively, lighting briefly here and there—on setting, minor characters, scenes—before settling into one character's consciousness. Truman Capote's "A Tree of Night" opens with a description of a depot. We're not yet sure who is telling the tale, or whose story it is. The narrator seems removed both physically and psychically, positioned far enough from the scene, in space and time, to describe the large picture.

> It was winter. A string of naked light bulbs, from which it seemed all warmth had been drained, illuminated the little depot's cold, windy platform. Earlier in the evening it had rained, and now icicles hung along the station-house eaves like some crystal monster's vicious teeth. Except for a girl, young and rather tall, the platform was deserted.

Up to this point, the eye of the narrator is objective. We've not entered any character's mind. The girl on the platform may not be a character at all; at this point, she's merely part of the still life the narrator has painted. As the paragraph continues, the eye of the narrator moves closer to the girl. He describes her clothing and belongings, proceeding from the most obvious and generic details (a gray flannel suit, a raincoat) to the particular and telling (a green Western guitar and "a gray suede purse on which elaborate brass letters spelled Kay"). He also describes her hair and face. With each detail, the narrator moves closer to the girl, bringing us with him. Through the description of the purse, we even learn her name.

In the second paragraph, the train enters the depot and the girl springs into action. No longer merely part of the still life, she's an actor in the drama—thus far, the only actor. We get the feeling that something is going to happen on that train, and the girl will be a part of it: "Kay assembled her paraphernalia and climbed up into the last coach."

In the third paragraph, the narrator once again refocuses his descriptive lens. It's no longer trained, close up, on Kay; it's moved into the coach. The next four or five sentences describe in detail the coach's interior, including its balding velvet seats, litter-strewn aisles and leaky water cooler. Coach passengers are mentioned briefly, but they remain in the background, generic and unnamed, seeming to exist only to provide a backdrop for Kay's entrance into the car.

In the fourth paragraph, the narrator moves from an external description of Kay to an internal one. In a few words, he settles into the limited omniscient point of view that will frame the rest of the story:

Kay resisted a temptation to hold her nose . . .

We're now inside Kay's mind, looking out. "Resisted a temptation" is not an external action. It reveals an internal thought process. This kind of phrase will pepper the story from this point on, keeping us centered in Kay's consciousness. Although much of the story will be told through objective action, dialogue, and description, every now and then the narrator will move back into Kay's mind, revealing her thoughts or emotions:

. . . she wished she had a pillow for her back.

. . . the way he was looking at her made her squeamish . . .

She wondered if there might be a seat in a car up ahead.

As the story progresses, other characters move into action. The narrator describes them fully, sometimes objectively and sometimes through Kay's eyes. But he never enters their minds. Every detail of description or action is filtered through either the narrator's point of view or through Kay's. When another character's thought process or feelings are suggested, the suggestion is qualified through objective phrases such as "it seemed" or "as if" (I've used italics to mark the qualifying phrases).

> [The woman] began to unscrew the cap but, *seeming to think* better of this, handed the bottle to Kay.
>
> *As if to deny it,* the man made a queer, furry sound deep in his throat . . .

Capote, having chosen the limited-omniscient point of view and established residence in only one character's mind, does not deviate from that viewpoint. He may take his time circling the scene, but once he settles into Kay's mind, he does not violate his point-of-view method by entering another character's mind, or by radically altering visual or psychic perspectives.

HOW POINT-OF-VIEW METHOD AFFECTS DESCRIPTION

First-Person Narrator

The advantages of describing through the eyes of a first-person narrator are clear. First-person narration narrows your field of vision, providing a single focal point for your descriptions. Descriptions from a single viewpoint can also unify your story's theme and tighten the story line, especially if your story is loosely plotted or episodic. And limiting yourself to one consciousness has the added benefit of creating instant intimacy between narrator and reader, thus intensifying your story's emotional effects.

When my students begin writing stories, most of them choose the "I" point of view. It's easier, they tell me—and more freeing. To a point, I agree. The "I" voice, because it is often so close to our own voice, feels natural. We relax into our narrator's descriptions because they are so closely aligned with our own personal view of the world. We are in control of our descriptions—or so it appears on the surface. In truth, first person narration presents challenges that no other point-of-view method presents, and before we choose to write a story in first person, we need to consider these challenges.

Since everything in first-person narration must be filtered through the "I," every description in our story must be something the "I" has either witnessed firsthand or learned through some other source. If you choose a first-person narrator, he must be present in every scene in the story or if he describes a scene in which he wasn't present, he must rely on secondhand information. A first-person narrator cannot describe what another character is thinking or feeling unless this information is reported to him; he cannot enter another character's consciousness, except through fantasy, conjecture or extrasensory perception. For these reasons, descriptions filtered through the eye of a first-person narrator often feel more limited, fragmented and subjective than those of a third-person narrator.

Although it may appear on the surface that first-person narration gives us supreme control over our descriptions, in reality when we choose a first-person narrator, we relinquish much of our control. We relinquish our right to inhabit more than one mind, to describe places and events outside the narrator's experience, and to voice our own authorial opinions and reflections.

If we choose a first-person narrator, we may also have to set aside concrete, sensory and significant descriptive passages— those passages we've labored so hard to achieve—to make way for our narrator's descriptions. If our point-of-view narrator is less articulate or educated or ironic or sympathetic than we are, we may also have to give up our writerly egos, muting our own voice in order to speak through the voice of our narrator. When Daniel Keyes chose to speak through the voice of a retarded man in *Flowers for Algernon*, he gave up the right to speak as the highly intelligent, articulate writer he is. Whereas the *writer* Daniel Keyes might describe a Rorschach test in stunning, brilliant prose, his first-person *narrator* can describe the test (misspellings and all) only as "some white cards with ink spilled all over them."

The costs of using a first-person describer may be even higher if your narrator is someone whose values are quite different from your own. Not only must you relinquish your own prose style; you must also set aside, for the moment at least, the moral landscape that shapes your life so your narrator can describe the world through his own lens. Here's the narrator of Tom McAfee's story "This Is My Living Room" describing his wife and mistress, his daughter and one of the customers in his store:

> Rosie ain't exactly good-looking. She got to be dried-up but once was on the fat side. She makes a good wife . . . Sometimes I get fed up with her and go to my woman in South Town. I take her a couple of cans of beans and some hose or a pair of bloomers. There ain't nothing much a woman won't do for food or clothes . . .
>
> Ellen Jean, the oldest, is a right good-looking girl but sassy and you can't hardly do anything with her . . . Like as not she's got a baby starting in her belly right now. She's a sassy bitch-girl and don't take after her ma or me. Sometimes I wonder if she's mine . . .
>
> Old Ezmo was what you'd call a low class of nigger . . . You're a crooked, low-down nigger, I told him, and they ain't nothing much worse than that. You ain't fit for making side meat out of . . .

If you're considering using a first-person narrator, or if you've written a story in first-person narration and wish to reconsider your choice, here are some questions to ask yourself:

How will the character's limitations (age, sex, intelligence, ability to perceive irony or humor, etc.) affect his descriptions?

Am I capable of telling the character's story solely through his words? (His voice, including his descriptions, must sound authentic.)

Is the character interesting enough to warrant the time the reader will spend in his presence? (First-person narrators can't be boring. Theirs is the only voice our reader will hear. Who wants to listen to a boring storyteller?)

How will I include important information that the narrator cannot possibly know?

Am I willing to give up my own voice in exchange for the narrator's voice? What if I can describe a river in liquid, brilliant prose, but my narrator can say only, "Wow, what a—I mean, it's like, well, really cool, huh?" Whose voice will win out?

After considering these questions, you may decide that despite its inherent difficulties and limitations, first person is the most appropriate viewpoint for your story. Whereas an omniscient narrator is expected to know everything God knows (a daunting challenge, since God is seldom wrong) and an objective narrator is expected to report events with computer accuracy, a first-person narrator is allowed to be human. As such, we accept that his descriptions are colored by his ignorance, prejudices, misconceptions and all those other warty inadequacies that make human beings so fascinating. If you decide on first-person narration, you'll be in good company. Many of the world's most brilliant and moving literary pieces—novels, short stories, essays and poems—are written in first person.

Special Challenges of Main-Character Description

Think of first-person description as a convertible camera lens attached to the eyes of your character. The lens can do two things, and only two things. Flipped one way, the lens can focus inside the character's head. We see what he is thinking, feeling, remembering, dreaming. Flipped the other way, the lens records everything the character sees through his own eyes.

That's it. That's all a first-person lens can do. It can't focus on the character's whole body or view his actions, unless he's looking in a mirror or at a photograph or video of himself. That's one reason why first-person narrators are usually the most thinly described characters in the story. The "I" is the camera lens, the inside-looking-out.

One of the hardest challenges you'll face if you choose a main character as your teller is how to physically describe him. This is true with peripheral narrators, also, but since a peripheral narrator is not the center of the action, readers aren't usually as eager to "see" him as they are to see the main character. Some highly imaginative readers require no bodily description of the narrator; they climb right inside his skin without stopping to wonder what he looks like on the outside. Most readers, however, need descriptive clues to help visualize the narrator, especially if he's the main character in the story.

If you're using a first-person narrator and wish to describe him visually, how will you do it? We've already mentioned one way: having your narrator describe himself while looking in a mirror or while studying a photograph, sketch, painting, video or home movie of himself. The mirror technique has been used so much in literature that it's become hackneyed; it also limits your description to the present time period. A photograph, however, can reveal how your character looked in the past, and a moving picture (a video or home movie, for instance) can show your character in action. You might even travel into the future by having your character view a computer-generated image of himself, like those age-progression images the FBI uses to track missing persons.

Sometimes a first-person narrator, rather than revealing himself visually through a scene in the story, simply tells us about himself. (First-person narration lends itself to telling rather than showing—another challenge for the "I" point of view.) In Reynolds Price's *Kate Vaiden*, the title character starts talking in the first sentence; by the second sentence, we begin to visualize her through the details she supplies:

> The best thing about my life up to here is, nobody believes it. I stopped trying to make people hear it long ago, and I'm nothing but a real middle-sized white

woman that has kept on going with strong eyes and teeth
for fifty-seven years. You can touch me; I answer.

Price's details aren't intended to be visually specific but
rather to reveal Kate's sense of being "nothing but" an ordinary
woman. The two distinguishing characteristics she mentions—
her strong eyes and teeth—are not details an outside observer
would notice. Instead, they're what a woman might *feel* about
herself from the inside-out. She tells us not that her eyes are
blue or her teeth crooked, yellow or gleaming white (visual
details a third-person narrator might mention) but that they
are *strong*, something she knows from living within her own skin.
"You can touch me," she says. "I answer." Though first-person
narrators cannot *see* themselves, they can *experience* themselves as
physical bodies and describe the sensations of moving physically
through their world.

Some first-person narrators are more concerned with their
appearance than Kate is—very beautiful or homely people, for
instance, or self-conscious adolescents. This concern is heightened when other characters in the story refer to the narrator's
physical characteristics. When I wrote "The Freemartin," I
wanted the reader to visualize Regina, since her body image
was an important element in the story. I didn't want a traditional
mirror scene, but I did want to suggest how Regina felt about
her body. I decided to use her aunt's dialogue to jump-start
Regina's self description:

> "Gina, quit frowning like that. You look like an old
> woman," Aunt Mag says from behind her reading
> glasses, which should be called knitting glasses because
> she never reads. I don't look old to me—bony knees,
> flat chest, a gap between my teeth that I might get fixed
> someday, although Miss Kitrick says a lot of beautiful
> women have gaps in their teeth . . . Miss Kitrick says that
> girls like me usually fill out real fast as soon as they start
> their periods . . .

It's obvious from the description that Regina has studied her image in the mirror at some point. However, much of her self-knowledge comes from what others say to her. Through Aunt Mag's direct dialogue, we visualize Regina's furrowed brow, her worried look; through Miss Kitrick's indirect dialogue, we picture Regina's slight, girlish frame.

If you don't want your first-person narrator to study himself through mirrors, photographs or other graphic images, you can give the reader a physical sense of the character through what other characters say about him. It's not necessary to supply a blow-by-blow description of your character's every physical feature. As in other kinds of description, a few telling details go a long way.

Description by a First-Person Peripheral Narrator

Not all first-person narrators are main characters. Some stand off to one side, relating someone else's story. Willa Cather employs this form of narration in *My Antonia*, as does F. Scott Fitzgerald in *The Great Gatsby*. Using a first-person peripheral narrator allows you many of the benefits of first-person narration while avoiding some of its limitations. Because the telling is centered in a single consciousness, you can engage the reader emotionally, relate events efficiently, and focus your descriptions through a single lens. At the same time, a peripheral narrator can lend an air of objectivity and psychic distance that a main character cannot. Because the peripheral narrator is not the center of the action, he is free to observe events from his box seat. An added benefit is that a peripheral narrator can describe the main character's physical attributes and actions as viewed from the outside, something that a first-person main character can't accomplish for himself.

Although all successful descriptions require some knowledge of the things of this world—its places, persons and things— first-person narrators, especially peripheral narrators, can be forgiven for not knowing everything. This is a great relief for most of us. Let's say I want to write a story about an Italian chef, but my knowledge of sauces is limited to sauteing onions and garlic in a skillet, then dumping in a can of Ragú. Well sure, I could do the research, and I probably would—I'd go to the library a few times, visit my neighborhood restaurant and quiz the chef, maybe even take a six-week course in Italian cooking. Even so, my knowledge would be too limited to justify telling the story from the chef's point of view. However, I could tell the chef's story through another character's point of view, someone standing in the doorway of the kitchen, a character whose knowledge of Italian cooking is as limited as my own.

As a peripheral narrator, my descriptions of pasta primavera might not be as thorough or accurate or gastronomically enticing as those by a trained chef, but they would at least sound authentic. And my ignorance might lend just the amount of interest, humor, or mystery my story requires. A first-person peripheral narrator is like a student learning a difficult subject, putting the puzzle together piece by piece. He catches glimpses of the central character and events, then reveals them to the reader little by little. Psychologically this puts him in cahoots with the reader, who may know even less, and who enjoys unraveling the mystery bit by bit. I can't speak for all readers, but I hate to be lectured to by a know-it-all. I prefer to be taken by the hand and led, step by stumbling step, through the story's terrain.

Reading a story that employs a peripheral narrator allows me this privilege. And writing a story, narrative essay or poem from this point of view allows me to use my partial ignorance as a helpful guide for my reader. When I began writing "With My Father in Space-Time," a narrative essay that alternates between autobiographical episodes and meditations on the nature of space-time, I was nervous about my paltry knowledge of physics. Though I'd spent dozens of hours in the library and many more hours interviewing physicists, I was still painfully inadequate in the subject area. My descriptions were laughable, my explanations sophomoric.

After several months of drafting and redrafting, I was about to give up, when it occurred to me that my ignorance of physics was the key to the essay. My ignorance mirrored the human mystery—my relationship with my father—which had prompted me to begin the essay in the first place. And since the essay would be published in a literary magazine, most likely my readers would be laypersons rather than physicists; they might need a beginner's guide through the mystery as much as I had. In descriptions by a peripheral narrator, a certain amount of ignorance can be bliss—for the writer as well as for the reader.

A peripheral narrator is, by definition, an outsider—a stance that comes naturally to most writers. Many of my students tell me they often feel like they're standing outside their own lives, looking in. Some can remember feeling this way since childhood. "Of course," I tell them. "That's the way writers are. That's how we make stories out of our lives." Perhaps that's why first-person peripheral narration is a natural choice for many of us. The problem comes when the peripheral narrator remains only an observer, without becoming emotionally involved in the story's outcome.

Although the first-person peripheral narrator is not the center of the action, he *is* the center of the telling. He witnesses the main events of the story, and through his eyes we watch the drama unfold. Cather's title, *My Antonia*, illustrates the double-sided equation that governs a story told by a first person peripheral narrator. "Antonia" tells us that this is a story centered on someone else, in this case a girl named Antonia; "my" stakes the narrator's claim to the telling. Both of these elements must be present in any successful narration employing a peripheral narrator. As Rust Hills points out in *Writing in General and the Short Story in Particular,* when point of view fails, it is often because the point-of-view character is not the character moved by the action.

A peripheral narrator must do more than merely report objectively (or subjectively) the story's events. He must also be changed, in some degree, by what he witnesses, and his descriptions should reveal this change. Why else employ a peripheral narrator? Why spend time and effort setting up housekeeping in your narrator's head, seeing through his eyes and hearing with his ears, if you don't also reveal the narrator's stake in the story? The choice of a first-person peripheral narrator is also a choice to explore the impact of the story's events, however slight, on that narrator. If you want "just the facts, ma'am," a straightforward telling by a witness who is not moved by the events, an objective narrator would be a better choice.

Third-Person Objective Narrator

Although no writer living inside human skin can be totally objective, if she wishes to create a fictional dream that appears strictly reportorial, she can employ an objective narrator to tell her tale. The objective point of view is also referred to as "dramatic" or "scenic," suggesting that a story told by an objective narrator unfolds like a stage play. Most stage plays—*Our Town* is a notable exception—do not use a narrator or other authorial presence. The story is told solely through onstage dialogue and action.

With a third-person objective narrator, what you see is what you get. An objective narrator cannot intrude on the story by giving his opinion or lapsing into reverie. He is also banned from entering characters' minds or commenting on characters' thoughts or motives. He can't write phrases like "he thought" or "she wishes." All descriptions must be based on concrete, external evidence.

At first glance this point-of-view method seems overly restrictive. In truth, it's a flexible form that allows for much freedom, especially in matters of description. An objective narrator is free to relate any external information, including knowledge about observable events happening to anyone, anywhere. Objective narration is like having an unlimited number of cameras available, each one taking pictures for the reader. An objective narrator can also move freely into the past, supplying information about the histories of places, people and actions. He can describe—people, places, objects, actions—to his heart's content. There are only two things an objective narrator cannot do: enter any character's consciousness, and reveal what he (as a writer) thinks or feels.

The third-person objective point of view is especially suited to stories in which the event itself is unusual, suspenseful or otherwise intriguing, an event such as a hostage standoff, suicide attempt, rock-climbing expedition or a dangerous surgical procedure. The power of the action, coupled with the author's skillful use of description and dialogue, is often enough to propel such a story; the reader won't miss authorial comment or access to the character's inner world.

External event alone, however, can't hold our attention forever, and physical action alone doesn't guarantee a forward-moving story. Some of the most successful objectively reported stories—Hemingway's "The Killers" or "Hills Like White Elephants," for example—rely more on psychological action than on physical activity. The impersonal, reportorial quality of the third-person objective point of view works well to suggest ironies of situations and speech, those understated subtleties of discovery and reversal that make for psychological suspense.

Shirley Jackson's "The Lottery" is fundamentally an objective description of an event that appears at first to be nothing more than an ordinary town gathering. The narrator reports the event in detached, understated prose, thereby creating psychic distance between reader and story; we feel we're watching the scene from afar. As the story progresses, Jackson begins dropping hints—a stone in a boy's hand, nervous laughter—suggesting that perhaps this event is not so ordinary after all. Each detail is described with clinical precision, and with each description the tension mounts, the very ordinariness of the details belying the horror unfolding sentence by sentence. As each townsperson draws a slip of paper from the wooden box, we watch breathlessly. Who will draw the paper with the black mark? We don't yet know what the mark signifies, but by now we're fearing the worst.

Yet however suspenseful Jackson's tale-telling and however sharp her use of ironic dialogue, "The Lottery" could not succeed without her precisely rendered descriptions of people, place, objects and action. Although all descriptions should pass the tests of precision and significance, descriptions written from the objective point of view must fairly *sing* with clarity and truth. An author using objective narration can't divert our attention with a character's musings or with authorial flights of existential angst; our attention must remain focused on the scene at hand. Because an objective narrator's tale is built solely on externals, she must give her utmost attention to the objects, people and places that make up this external reality. The characters are the actors in her drama; the objects and places are the set pieces. All elements of the outward scene must be chosen carefully, rendered with clarity and precision, and directed with a firm, even hand.

Jackson selects only those details that contribute to the mounting horror, and reports those details in spare, unemotional language. In the following selection from "The Lottery," we are introduced to the black box, carried into the town square by Mr. Summers:

> . . . When he arrived in the square, carrying the black wooden box, there was a murmur of conversation among the villagers, and he waved and called, "Little late today, folks." The postmaster, Mr. Graves, followed him, carrying a three-legged stool, and the stool was put in the center of the square and Mr. Summers set the black box down on it.

Jackson follows this no-nonsense description with a paragraph detailing the history of the black box. (That's the prerogative of the objective narrator, remember? She can fill us in on all external events, even those in the past.) When we return to the present-day box, we're given another clearly stated, unemotional description of the box:

> The black box grew shabbier each year; by now it was no longer completely black but splintered badly along one side to show the original wood color, and in some places faded or stained.

In objective narration, descriptions of actions must be as functional and significant as descriptions of objects, places and people. Since we as readers aren't allowed access into characters' minds, we must surmise everything about their inner motives, fears and joys through outward signs. We can't overhear their unspoken language; we can hear only what they say through body language or dialogue. At the climax of Jackson's story the lottery has been narrowed to the Hutchinson family and five slips of paper have been placed in the box, one for each family member to draw. Through precise descriptions of the family's gestures and speech, Jackson succeeds in revealing the powerful emotions roiling beneath the surface.

First to draw is the youngest son, Davy, who holds the folded paper tightly in his fist, then looks "wonderingly" up to Mr. Summers. Next is twelve-year-old Nancy, who "breathed heavily as she went forward, switching her skirt, and took a slip daintily from the box." Bill Jr. lunges clumsily for the box, "his face red and his feet over-large." Mr. Hutchinson is silent and calm as he reaches for his slip. Only Mrs. Hutchinson hesitates, studying the crowd with defiance. Then, we are told, she "set her lips and went up to the box . . . snatched a paper out and held it behind her."

By this point, we are fairly certain whose slip is marked with an x. We've not looked into any character's mind, nor has the author supplied us with her own suspicions. Relying solely on descriptions of external action, people and setting, Jackson has provided all the clues we need to enter her fictional dream.

Description by an Omniscient Narrator

To know everything; to move freely in time and space; to look into the heart of every person, tree and insect; to opine or praise or condemn with impunity. What power! It's no wonder so many authors have chosen, and still choose, to speak through an omniscient narrator. Omniscience was the point-of-view choice for classic writers like Chekhov, Tolstoy, Dickens and Dreiser, and though omniscient narration is much less popular today, some modern writers (Joyce Carol Oates and William Gass come to mind) continue to explore its boundaries.

Omniscient narration provides for ease of exposition, panoramic views of time and space, and psychological complexities. Since it allows access into any and all characters' minds, it also helps guard against the creation of one-dimensional characters. Once we've glimpsed a character's individual dreams, fears, memories and joys, it's hard to think of her in stereotypes; the omniscient method can round her out.

When we read a novel with an omniscient narrator, we can relax and enjoy the descriptive scenery, secure that a godlike presence is leading us, someone more knowledgeable and reliable than any one character might be. After all, the omniscient author knows everything all his characters know, and more. If our narrator is also brilliant, witty, wise or otherwise fascinating, and if he chooses to share his opinions, feelings, judgments and personal memories, we are doubly blessed. Besides immersing ourselves in the novel's plot and characterization, we also get the pleasure of the author's company—or more precisely, the company of the persona created by the author.

Notice that I said "novel." It is difficult, though perhaps not impossible, to write a successful short work that employs the omniscient point of view. It takes time to travel everywhere, to learn everything there is to know, to set up housekeeping in multiple heads, and to describe it all to the reader. And each time the author changes positions, which is what omniscient narrators must constantly do, the reader needs time to adjust to the change. An author using the omniscient viewpoint must be adept at making these transitions. Within the first few pages of *Pride and Prejudice*, Jane Austen accomplishes no fewer than six such switches, alternating vantage points from omniscient narrator to character and back again, then from one character to another, finally circling back to the narrator.

The complexity of the switches inherent in omniscient narration affects the quantity and quality of descriptive passages. We've already said that omniscience provides for ease of exposition. Since a godlike narrator is capable of infinite knowledge, it seems natural that he would want to impart this knowledge to his readers. Exposition appeals more to the mind than to the senses; its playing field is the world of ideas, explanation, analysis and meaning. Where most description concerns itself with concrete and sensory details, exposition often involves abstraction. Generally speaking, description *shows*; exposition *tells*.

If your main goal is to describe people, places or objects in specific and concrete detail, omniscient narration may not be your best viewpoint choice. Omniscience invites telling. After all, there's a lot of narrative ground to cover, and taking time to fully describe a tennis shoe, for example, or the bald spot on the back of a character's head, takes time away from all the other tasks you're called upon to perform as an omniscient narrator. This is not to say that evocative descriptions do not appear in third-person omniscient novels. I'm suggesting only that it may be more difficult for you to stop and smell the roses when you're also trying to explain their horticultural origins, comment on their symbolic import, or imagine your way into a rose's thoughts—just a few of the options open to the omniscient narrator.

Another reason the omniscient viewpoint encourages abstraction is because the narrator is capable of dwelling inside his characters' minds. Whereas the objective narrator must describe concretely and specifically the externals of a story, those things that can be witnessed through the senses, the omniscient narrator knows characters, places and events from the inside out. This internal view makes it easy to bypass concrete details on the road to comment or explanation. Thus, in the opening of *Pride and Prejudice* Jane Austen describes the Bennetts not as an outside observer might, in specific bodily detail, but rather as a spirit who dwells inside their heads, which is exactly where omniscient narrators dwell:

> Mr. Bennett was so odd a mixture of quick parts, sarcastic humour, reserve, and caprice, that the experience of three and twenty years had been insufficient to make his wife understand his character. Her mind was less difficult to develop. She was a woman of mean understanding, little information, and uncertain temper. When she was discontented she fancied herself nervous. The business of her life was to get her daughters married; its solace was visiting and news.

Austen's description creates no moving pictures for our imaginations, and stirs no visceral reactions in our bodies. We are given no smells, sounds, tastes, textures or sights to experience.

Although we learn much about the Bennetts, what we learn is what the mind can know rather than what the body can experience. Omniscient narration invites exposition, internalization and the whole realm of ideas, sometimes at the expense of vivid description.

However, when an omniscient narrator takes the time to describe precisely, concretely and with significant detail, the results are often stunning. Since many omniscient narrators are articulate, worldly and literary, their descriptions are often more richly observed and beautifully worded than descriptions by a first-person narrator (who may be intellectually or linguistically limited) or descriptions by an objective narrator bent on revealing "just the facts, ma'am." Here, Charles Dickens takes his time describing the view from Rochester Bridge:

> On the left of the spectator lay the ruined wall, broken in many places, and in some, overhanging the narrow beach below in rude and heavy masses. Huge knots of sea-weed hung upon the jagged and pointed stones, trembling in every breath of wind; and the green ivy climbed mournfully around the dark and ruined battlements.
>
> —from *The Pickwick Papers*

Despite its many challenges, the omniscient viewpoint offers many rewards. Like the starship *Enterprise*, an omniscient narrator can boldly go where no man has gone before. He can describe the emotions of green ivy on one page, the smells emanating from Pluto or Neptune on the next, and conclude the chapter with a dead Napoleon's view of Josephine. He can describe scenes hidden from his characters' views, everything that goes on behind all the doors closed in his characters' faces. An omniscient narrator can remember events his characters have forgotten, and describe these events in detail—the color and texture of the crib blanket Josephine's mother wrapped around her, the aromas of her first cooked meal. Since he can also move forward in time, an omniscient narrator can even describe the world of Josephine's future—the sights and smells and sounds that will fill her last days.

Description From a Limited Omniscient Narrator

Readers like me demand a lot. On one hand, we want to be swept into a character's inner world of dreams, joys and terrors. We want to smell the cologne he splashes on his face, taste his morning coffee, feel the satin sheets he pulls around him as he climbs back into bed. On the other hand, we don't want to be confined too long. After all, there's a big world out there. What's the weather like? Who won the pennant?

It's difficult for a writer to satisfy readers like me. First-person narration can feel too fragmented and subjective, confining the telling to one consciousness and one voice. Third-person objective, which is limited to concrete, external narration, can leave me emotionally cold. And omniscient narration, with its vast freedoms of time, space and consciousness, creates distances of its own. For the reader who craves both psychological intimacy and worldly verisimilitude, stories told from the limited omniscient point of view are the answer.

Baldly stated, when you write in the limited omniscient viewpoint, you limit your omniscience. There are many ways to accomplish this. You can limit your ability to move freely in time and space, to comment on issues arising in the story or to make judgments. The most common method is to limit your access to characters' inner lives. You can still describe externals—people, places, events—much as an objective observer would, while choosing to inhabit only one character's mind. Perhaps two, if your story is long enough to sustain your efforts.

As the story progresses, you move between these two worlds—outer reality as described in concrete detail by an objective observer, and the inner world of a character's feelings and thoughts. In "Still Life With Fruit," Doris Betts uses the limited omniscient point of view, alternating between external details objectively reported and subjective musings by her main character, Gwen, who is preparing to give birth in a Catholic hospital:

The labor room, pale green, was furnished in buffed aluminum. Its single chair was dull metal, straight, uncomfortable. Her clothes had been hung in a green wall locker next to Jesus, including the linen dress with the 24-inch waist she hoped to wear home next week. On her bedside table was a pitcher of water and crushed ice, and a glass with a clear tube in it. She drank water as the sister had ordered. Maybe it went down the sliding ramp where Junior, like some battleship, would be launched to the open sea. He felt to her like a battleship, plated turrets and stacks and projections, each pricking her own organs until they withdrew and gave him room. . . .

The first two sentences of Betts's description include details any observer might notice. The third sentence begins objectively, then moves into Gwen's mind, revealing her wish to wear the dress with the twenty-four-inch waist. The next two sentences switch back into objective reporting, and then we're again into Gwen's mind, inside her wild imaginings and her physical pain. Betts includes markers—phrases like "she hoped" and "he felt to her like"—to alert us to subtle transitions that move us into Gwen's mind.

Some authors omit these markers, steering us seamlessly between the inner and outer worlds. One of the most subtle point-of-view switches occurs within internal monologues when objective description alternates with subjective description. In internal monologue, the reader overhears the narrator's or character's thoughts, his *stream of consciousness*, a stream that may appear to have little order or coherence. The author seems absent: is anyone steering this boat? If we look closer, we see, yes, someone is steering. Objective description is surfacing, here and there, in the stream. In this section from James Joyce's *Ulysses*, Leopold Bloom is preparing to go to the market for breakfast supplies, but first he goes upstairs to check on his sleeping wife:

On quietly creaky boots he went up the staircase to the hall, paused by the bedroom door. She might like something tasty. Thin bread and butter she likes in the morning. . . .

He said softly in the bare hall: . . .

—You don't want anything for breakfast? . . .

No. She did not want anything. He heard then a warm heavy sigh, softer, as she turned over and the loose brass quoits on the bedstead jingled. Must get those settled really. Pity. All the way from Gibraltar. Forgotten any little Spanish she knew. Wonder what her father gave for it. Old style. . . .

On the doorstep he felt in his hip pocket for the latchkey. Not there. In the trousers I left off. Must get it. Potato I have. Creaky wardrobe. No use disturbing her. She turned over sleepily that time. He pulled the halldoor to after him very quietly, more, till the footleaf dropped gently over the threshold, a limp lid. Looked shut. All right till I come back anyhow.

Some of Joyce's details are reportorial in nature, things an outside observer might note—creaky boots, the jingling quoits, a soft sigh. Others are extremely idiosyncratic, colored with Bloom's emotion, thoughts and personal history. These two perceptions alternate freely without any mechanical markers provided by the author (except for the switch from "he" to "I"). It's like a duet between two voices: one, removed and factual; the other, psychically connected. Both voices describe, but it's the combination of the two that completes the description of the scene.

POINT-OF-VIEW DESCRIPTION AS AN ORGANIZING DEVICE

Point of view is an automatic focusing device, a selector of detail. Once situated inside a particular point of view, you don't have to worry about including every sensory detail—only the ones your narrator or character would most likely notice. Once you've established the perspective, the eye from which scenes will be observed, you can use that eye to organize and unify your descriptions. And as your character moves physically and psychologically through the story, subtle shifts in his point of view will lead your reader through the descriptive terrain of the story.

Jessamyn West opens "Love, Death, and the Ladies' Drill Team" with a series of descriptive snapshots. The point of view is third-person limited omniscient, and though the narrator supplies some objective description and information, most of the descriptive snapshots are focused through the eye of Emily Cooper, the main character. As Emily moves physically through the story, we move with her, experiencing the sights, sounds and feelings she experiences from each vantage point. When Emily arrives for the drill team practice session, she stands "for a while enjoying the wind—California's warm, dry September wind—before starting up the stairs to Burnham Hall."

As she begins her climb up the stairs, we follow her. Emily's eyes become our eyes, our way of organizing the scenes passing before us.

> Emily was halfway up the stairs when she was hailed from the sidewalk below by Mr. Burnham himself, holding a key aloft. "You one of the Pocohontas girls?" he called.
>
> Emily turned about on the stairs and gazed down at the wide-shouldered old man. The wind was lifting his coattails and tossing his white hair about in tufts, like those of the bunch grass she had known as a girl in the Dakotas.

In these brief paragraphs, West centers us securely within Emily's consciousness. As the story continues, we will leave Emily's mind for brief interludes, long enough for the narrator to insert necessary information, but mostly we'll be viewing the scenes through her eyes. Soon Emily will be leaning out a window "to watch a tumbleweed, blown into town from one of the surrounding barley fields," and we'll lean out the window with her. Emily is our guide, so to speak, and we take her hand, looking over our shoulder when she looks over hers, peering down at the sidewalk when she peers down.

Each subtle shift in Emily's perspective is like a trail marker. As readers, we don't have to take a dozen wrong turns, ending up in some blind alley. The author provides a descriptive map for us to follow. West's effective choice of point of view, and her subtle shifts of perspective within that point of view, create an ordered, organized fictional universe.

EXERCISES

1. Choose a story—one of your own or someone else's—and rewrite the opening paragraphs in a different point of view. Change first person to third, omniscient to objective, objective to first person, etc. Then experiment with other subtle changes. If the story opens with a character's name, remove the name and substitute "he" or "she"; if the characters are known only as "he" or "she," insert names. Notice how even slight changes in point of view affect the story.

2. Check your story draft for point-of-view switches by using a colored highlighter. Whenever the point of view changes, even slightly, mark the transition. Then decide whether the switch is effective or merely troublesome. Using the techniques detailed in this chapter, revise any troublesome switches.

3. If you're using the limited omniscient method in which you have access to only one character's thoughts, check your story to see if you've inadvertently entered a second character's thoughts. If you have, revise the section to remove the internalized phrase, then replace it with an "actable" action that an objective reporter could witness.

4. Using your own natural voice, write the most detailed, sensory and articulate description of a place or object you can manage. Then write a description of the same place or object in the words of a first-person narrator who is less articulate than you— a young child, an Alzheimer's patient, a Valley girl, an uneducated peasant. What differences do you see between the two descriptions? Did you have to give up any of your own descriptive details to allow your narrator to have his say?

5. Write a physical description in which a first-person main character describes himself so the reader can visualize him. You might want to use a photograph, video or other graphic representation as your vehicle for relating physical attributes. Your character could also describe himself by relating what others say about him.

6. Write a description of a first-person narrator that reveals his experience of living inside his body and moving physically through the world. Rather than describing how the character looks on the outside, use sensory details to show us how it feels to live *inside* his skin. (Refer to the *Kate Vaiden* selection for an example.)

7. Using third-person peripheral narration, describe a place, person or event your narrator knows little about. Position the narrator on the outside, looking in. How does he view his subject? What language does he use to describe something he doesn't really understand? To get you started, think of a subject you know little about. Describe it to the reader in your own words, with all the limitations and challenges that partial ignorance requires.

8. Write a description of an object, person or scene that combines objective reporting with internalized thought. (See "Still Life With Fruit" passage for an example.) Alternate between the two kinds of description, marking your transitions with phrases like "she thought" or "it seemed to him that . . ."

Then remove the transitional markers so your description alternates freely between objectively reported statements and highly personal stream of consciousness. (See *Ulysses* passage.)

9. Describe a scene or event from the third-person objective viewpoint. Report only what can be known through the five senses; this can include characters' concrete actions or dialogue. You may move in time and space as long as you report only what can be witnessed externally. Do not give your opinion about the event or enter any characters' thoughts.

10. Using the omniscient point of view, describe something no character in your story could possibly know. You might travel behind the scenes, describing a place your characters could never visit. You might time travel into the distant past or future

and describe what you see. You might even enter the consciousness of an animal, a force of nature or an inanimate object.
What does the dog in your story dream of? What is the ocean's
memory of your character? What secret is a young girl in India
(the girl who will one day become your character's wife) already
storing up to keep from him?

THE STORY TAKES ITS PLACE: DESCRIPTIONS OF SETTING

When I hear *setting*, I immediately think of the physical space in which the events of a story occur, but in truth, place is only one element of setting. The common phrase "the story takes place" refers not only to the *where* of the story but to the *when*. Setting grounds us, literally, in the fictional dream. And descriptions of setting provide the foothold, the physical and temporal vantage point from which to view the events of the story. "You couldn't write a story that happened nowhere," Eudora Welty once told an interviewer. "Time and place make the framework that any story's built on . . . a fiction writer's honesty begins right there, in being true to those two facts of time and place."

But to describe a setting effectively, we must go beyond merely situating the reader in a particular locale and time period. Every detail that contributes to a feeling of time and place is an element of setting. Details of place include the set pieces of a location (its props, furniture, flora and fauna) as well as surrounding elements (the storm hammering outside the door, sunlight ricocheting off the curtains). Time-wise, a story may be said to "take place" not just sometime in the 1850s but, say, on the opening day of summer or the last day of autumn, or more particularly, at twilight, high noon or in the first sleepy moments of morning.

The importance of setting varies greatly from story to story. In some stories, setting is primarily functional, serving as little more than a backdrop for elements such as characterization, language or plot development. In other stories, setting is the most important ingredient, the main character whose personality and eccentricities shape the story's outcome. Between these two extremes lie many variations. Some literary works, such as *Madame Bovary* and Caleb Carr's *The Alienist*, are almost documentary in descriptions of time and place. In other works, settings function symbolically to mirror the events of a story, as in Poe's "The Fall of the House of Usher." Sometimes the setting, including the weather, is a benign, even sympathetic force; other times it acts as antagonist, challenging the human protagonists in a struggle for survival. Settings can be natural or man-made, realistic or surreal, ancient or modern, beautiful or ugly or anything in between.

Few stories contain only one setting. In most stories our characters move from place to place, requiring us to describe several locales. Even if a character remains stationary, never moving from his easy chair, we may still need to describe more than one setting. Our character's thoughts and daydreams transport him to a different place or time, perhaps, or we find we need to supply background information about the places and times that have shaped our character's life.

Strictly speaking, even the most static story—one in which the character remains in the same location physically and mentally—requires us to describe more than one setting. Stories, by definition, occur not only in space but in *time*, and the passing of time influences how a setting is described. Yes, Zack may remain in his easy chair throughout the story, staring at the television screen. Yet minute by minute the scene is changing. A different soap opera comes on, sunlight through the venetian blind changes from yellow to pink, the spring-loaded sofa cushion that had felt so comfortable three hours ago begins to assert itself. As Heraclitus said, "You can't step into the same river twice." The settings in our stories are constantly shifting. Even if our characters never move an inch, time has its way with their world. And our descriptions must evoke those changes.

A WRITER'S SENSE OF PLACE

For many writers, setting is the primary element that births the creative process. Historical novelists seem drawn to the *when* of the story; mystery writers seem more intrigued by the *where*. Margaret Maron says most of her mystery books begin with a sense of place. Once place is established, she inserts a character into that place and waits to see what will happen. Other mystery writers, asserting that danger is closely related to physical location, look for places where things can go wrong, then set their stories in those places. Maron echoes this sentiment, adding that her own fear of heights often takes her, in her writing, to stairways and cliffs.

"A sense of place" is a popular phrase in literary circles. Good writers, so the theory goes, have a strong sense of place that defines their work. Thus, when we think of Pat Conroy, we think Carolina beaches; when we think of Ivan Doig, we think Montana; when we think of Updike, we think New England. When I first began writing I thought "a sense of place" meant a writer had to live in one place all his life. This assumption, coupled with comments from a literature professor that I could never be a writer because I lacked a sense of place, almost kept me from pursuing my writing goals. "Where are your roots?" the professor asked. I was a Marine brat, and had at one time or another claimed allegiance to Texas, Virginia, California, Illinois and Maryland. I'd spent childhood summers at my grandparents' Indiana farm, but I'd never actually lived there.

And now here I was in a South Carolina university, being questioned by a man whose southern accent I could never replicate, on the page or elsewhere. I decided I had no roots. Or if I did have roots, they were shallow, planted just deep enough to survive a few years here, a few years there. If a sense of place was a crucial source of a writer's power, then I guessed I'd never be a Writer (a vocation I now thought of as an uppercase, proper noun).

This didn't mean, however, than I would stop *writing*, a lowercase, menial activity I seemed quite able to accomplish. My poems, stories and essays didn't seem to care that I had no roots; they just kept coming. After a few years I started sending my work to editors, and I was amazed not only that they began publishing my work, but that almost every editor commented on my descriptions of settings, my strong "sense of place." It was a riddle so delightful I didn't wish to solve it.

Many years later, I was sitting in the lecture hall at the Bread Loaf Writers' Conference listening to Tim O'Brien respond to a question about how the brief time he'd spent in Vietnam had shaped his novels and stories. As O'Brien spoke, I suddenly realized why those editors had commented on my "sense of place." And why the essay I'd written about the South Carolina garage apartment where I'd spent four damp, cockroach-infested *weeks* was more vibrant than my story of four *years* of suburban ennui in California.

"It's not the *amount* of time you spend in a place that matters," O'Brien answered. "It's the *intensity* of the time."

Click: my riddle was solved. When it comes to evoking a sense of place, the intensity of a writer's involvement—based in real-life experience or in the imagination—is more important than the amount of time spent in any one place. Perhaps you've lived in the same town all your life and your window opens to the same herb garden your father worked, on his knees, forty years ago. Or maybe you've moved nineteen times, a Marine brat like me, and the window to your father's garden opens only inside your head. Either way, you possess a sense of place. And each time you put pen to paper, describing the smells and sounds and textures of that garden—whether real or imagined, present or past—you are planting roots that will feed your stories, essays and poems.

THE CHALLENGES AND REWARDS
OF REAL-LIFE SETTINGS

Real-life settings form the bases of many writers' work. I think of the family apple orchards in Jane Brox's essays, the New England fishing village that animates Frank Gaspar's poems, and the San Francisco streets of Amy Tan's novels. As writers, we naturally focus on the places and times we know best. Our firsthand experience provides us with the sensory details that render a work, in E.M. Forster's words, "spasmodically realistic." And our passionate attachment to the places and times of our lives can infuse our descriptions with emotion no outsider could provide.

One place we have lived or one period of time, if mined deeply enough, can yield up treasures. Several years ago during an unusually dry spell in my writing life, I drew a map of my grandparents' farm the way I remembered it from childhood—in particular, my twelfth summer, which was a particularly memorable one. I drew the twin barns, the chicken coop and outhouse, the trail to the creek, the apple tree, the lopsided garage and the small building off the garage my grandmother called her "loom room." I drew a breakaway version of the house itself, revealing each room, window, door, bed, table and chair I could recall.

Then, as if marking sites of buried treasure, I placed an x at every location I associated with a particular person or event. The milking barn: my grandfather in rubber boots, whistling. The trail to the creek: my little brother, shivering and hysterical after having fallen through the ice. The double-seater outhouse: Great Aunt Bessie crouched beside me, telling ghost tales. I was astounded at the stories that rose from the map, begging to be told. By the time I finished drawing my treasure map, I had the beginnings of several poems and a dozen essays. Not every beginning would yield up riches, but some would. Many more remain to be unearthed.

Try drawing a map of a place in your memory (or a place that exists only in your imagination). Mark entrances and exits, furniture and props, flora and fauna. Place an x where certain characters might show up or where particular events might take place. Remember the mystery writers' advice on setting? Look for a place where things can go wrong, and position your character there. The place might be physically threatening—an icy creek, a steep cliff, a deserted road. Or it might be a setting that invites psychological danger—the principal's office, the monthly weigh-in at the diet center, your mother-in-law's kitchen. Dangerous places suggest trouble. And trouble is one of the keys to compelling stories.

If you decide to use a real-life setting rather than a fictional one, you will face many challenges. Descriptions of actual settings, especially those identified by place names and particular time periods, must be unfailingly accurate. Nonfiction writers must pass the toughest tests for accuracy, but fiction writers and poets who choose real-life settings must also render their settings accurately if they wish for their work to be believed. If you set your story in an actual place—say, San Francisco or Savannah or Chicago—your readers will expect you to know the correct names of streets, restaurants, bars, colleges and parks. You can't just make them up, and you might not be able to rely on memory. You may have to consult a city map or take a drive through the streets your character is supposed to be familiar with.

And if your story is set a hundred years ago, or even thirty, you'll probably need to do additional research. Maybe that restaurant you name and describe, the smoky lounge where your two main characters first met, wasn't even built in 1969. Maybe the parking lot at Edgewater and Fourth wasn't a parking lot at all, but a tobacco field. Be assured, someone who reads your story will *know* it was a tobacco field. And though she might not slam your book to the floor, she'll at least pause, scratch her head and reconsider spending time in a dream that, though fictional, is set in a real place, a place she no longer believes in.

Even if we don't identify our settings with recognizable names and time periods, we still face challenges in describing real-life settings effectively, especially if the settings are autobiographically based. We may be so closely connected to the times and places of our lives, so busy living *within* the details, that we find ourselves unable, or unwilling, to supply the sensory proofs the story demands. We may be too close to the bare facts of the description—say, every detail of what our backyard looks like at this time of morning—to select the telling detail that will sustain the fictional dream (the old can't-see-the-forest-for-the-trees dilemma).

If we're describing the setting of our present-day life, we may not yet have enough artistic distance to order the description effectively. And if we're writing about the settings in our past, we may have forgotten so many details that our descriptions do not ring true. On the other hand, we may have forgotten just enough. Over time, our memories of a particular place and time may have distilled, our minds culling out unnecessary details so that only the most sensory, telling and emotionally colored proofs remain.

REALISTIC DETAIL IN NONREALISTIC STORIES

Sensory proofs are necessary ingredients in almost all forms of literature, providing what E.M. Forster, in *Aspects of the Novel*, calls "intermittent realism." Ironically, these sensory proofs are perhaps most important to the writer of nonrealistic fiction. Before the fantasy writer can pull the reader into her story, she must first convince the reader that the events of the story could actually take place within the setting she creates.

Forster uses the metaphor of the carnival sideshow to explain the importance of realistic detail to the fantasy writer. The reader of any novel, he says, must "pay the entrance fee to the exhibition"; that is, he must suspend disbelief in order to enter the fiction. For the reader of fantasy, however, the cost is even higher. Not only must he pay the entrance fee for the main exhibition (the novel) but, once inside its gates, he must "pay something extra" before he can be admitted into the sideshow (the fantasy).

When I read the back cover of Rachel Ingalls's *Mrs. Caliban*, I thought *No way, this is not for me. A housewife who has an affair with a six-foot-seven green monster named Larry? Give me a break.* But the novel had been highly recommended by several readers whose tastes I admired, so I decided to give it a try. After a few pages, I was hooked. Not only was the main character sympathetic, the prose lucid and witty, and the plot intriguing, but to my surprise, Ingalls's setting was so filled with realistic detail that I felt as if I had stepped directly into the story. When Dorothy started hearing strange voices from her kitchen radio,

I accepted them as wholeheartedly as Dorothy did. After all, the radio was described as "a large, dark brown old-fashioned set, the kind that looked like a 1930s Gothic cathedral." That was good enough for me.

For twenty-four pages I followed Dorothy through the physical world of the story. Together we rinsed her sweat-soaked leotards and hung them over a very real shower rod, fended off the advances of a supermarket salesgirl in a majorette's uniform who was trying to force a parmesan square down Dorothy's throat, and tied a kitchen scarf over Dorothy's head "to keep her hair from picking up the garlic and onion smells." So on page twenty-five, when the screen door opened and Larry entered the kitchen, I barely blinked.

Oh, I was surprised, of course, as Dorothy was, caught up as we were in hurrying across the checked linoleum, trying to reach the cheese toast before it burned. I was *surprised*. But I wasn't *unconvinced*. I accepted the six-foot-seven green monster because the setting in which he was placed had been delineated with such care.

Writers, says Forster, must be "spasmodically realistic." Whether our writing is centered on the real or the surreal, we must pay a servant-like attention to the settings of our stories. Without attention to minute details of time and place—those sights, smells, sounds and textures of our fictional world—the reader will simply not believe that world exists (or might exist, in some other realm). And even if the reader *does* believe, even if he pays admission and enters our story or poem, he will leave as soon as we cease to render that world in all its sensory detail. As writers, we must be vigilant in maintaining the illusion of our fictional dream. "Whenever its world of outside appearance grows dim and false to the eye," wrote Eudora Welty, "the novel has expired."

INTRODUCING AND ORGANIZING DESCRIPTIONS OF SETTING

When to introduce a story's setting, how to organize our descriptions, and how to weave descriptions of setting into narrative and expository passages are questions we must consider if setting is to be an integral part of our story. Some writers front-load their works with descriptions of setting, much like stage hands bringing on set pieces at the beginning of a play. Gail Peck uses this technique in her poem "Flood," which opens with a description evoking both place and time:

> That year spring came early
> even for New Orleans, the buds
> unpuckering only to be sheathed in ice,
> then warm again and rain for days,
> the water crawling up our street . . .

With the front-loading method, setting acts almost as a character, the first character arriving onstage. If you use this method, it's important that your description be lively and evocative enough to hold the reader's attention. Peck's lines contain images that engage our imaginative eye. We witness the buds "unpuckering," the slick coverings of ice, and the water "crawling." Because the setting is described imagistically, as a vivid, active force in its own right, we do not become impatient for the human drama to begin. The reader of a novel, settling in for the long haul, will probably be more patient with front-loaded description of setting than will the readers of short fiction or poetry, who expect to be plummeted more quickly into the story's central conflict.

A more common technique than front-loading is to introduce your character or narrator first, then describe the setting through the teller's eyes. Joseph Conrad's "The Secret Sharer" opens with a young captain standing on the deck of his ship before it is about to leave port:

> On my right hand there were lines of fishing-stakes resembling a mysterious system of half-submerged bamboo fences. . . . To the left a group of barren islets, suggesting ruins of stone walls, towers, and blockhouses, had its foundation set in a blue sea. . . . And when I turned my head to take a parting glance at the tug which

had just left us anchored outside the bar, I saw the straight line of the flat shore joined to the stable sea, edge to edge. . . . Here and there gleams of a few scattered pieces of silver marked the windings of the river; and on the nearest of them, just within the bar, the tug steaming right into the land became lost to my sight. . . . My eye followed the light cloud of her smoke, now here, now there, above the plain, according to the devious curves of the stream, but always fainter and farther away, till I lost it at last behind the mitre-shaped hill of the great pagoda.

Notice how Conrad organizes the description. First he positions the captain in a stationary place. Then, through the use of positional markers—"on my right," "to the left," "when I turned my head," "here and there," "my eye followed"—he guides the reader through an ordered landscape. In this way, Conrad succeeds not only in describing the panoramic view but also in tracing the visual journey of the captain's eyes. This technique lends a feeling of movement to a scene that might otherwise feel static. James Wright's poem "Lying in a Hammock at William Duffy's Farm in Pine Island, Minnesota" also employs positional markers, using phrases like "over my head," "to my right," and "down the ravine" to lead the reader through a guided tour of the farm.

Another organizational method is to describe a place that will not hold still for the viewer. The viewer remains stationary while the scene rushes past his eyes. Perhaps he's staring through a train window, or watching from the sidelines at a carnival where the attractions—tilt-o-whirls, spinning teacups, ferris wheels—are in full swing.

An alternative method is to describe a stationary setting that only appears to be moving because the viewer is in motion. While he's skiing down a steep slope or holding fast to a horse's mane, the scene unfolds swiftly, in a blur of colors and shapes. The position of the viewer, which is constantly changing, organizes his view as well as the view of the reader.

You can also organize a description of place by emphasizing one detail, allowing it to stand out from other details by virtue of its color, shape, size or movement. Remember the red coat on the little girl in the film *Schindler's List?* It caught our eye because everything else in the scene was in muted shades of black and white. James Baldwin uses a similar technique in *Go Tell It on the Mountain* when he describes the street outside the narrator's window. Every detail is heading toward revelation of the visual focal point, the red stocking cap:

> . . . It was the end of winter, and the garbage-filled snow that had been banked along the edges of sidewalks was melting now and filling the gutters. Boys were playing stickball in the damp, cold streets; dressed in heavy woolen sweaters and heavy pants, they danced and shouted. . . . One of them wore a bright-red stocking cap with a great ball of wool hanging down behind that bounced as he jumped, like a bright omen above his head.

The stocking cap grabs our attention partly because of its color (it's the only bright swatch in a gray, bleak scene) and partly because of its movement. As in all kinds of description, description of setting comes alive when shown in a state of activity.

We've been speaking of organizing description through the teller's *eyes,* but details of setting need not be visual. As we've noted earlier in this book, descriptions employing the other four senses often engage the reader quicker, and more viscerally, than descriptions that rely solely on visual clues. Try describing a place (a school cafeteria, the indoor swimming pool at the Y, a rain forest) using only the sense of smell. Then describe a few visual details. Next, shift your attention to tactile details. What does your hand light upon in this place? Describe the textures you encounter. Then move back to visual details, describing in detail what your eye sees. This particular pattern—moving from smells to sights to textures to sights—is how the following description, taken from *Dodsworth* by Sinclair Lewis, is organized:

> The smell of London is a foggy smell, a sooty smell, a coal-fire smell, yet to certain wanderers it is more exhilarating, more suggestive of greatness and of stirring life, than spring-time hillsides or the chill sweetness of autumnal nights; and that unmistakable smell, which men long for in rotting perfumes along the Orinoco, in the greasy reek of South Chicago, in the hot odor of dusty earth among locust-buzzing Alberta wheatfields, that luring breath of the dark giant among cities, reaches halfway to Southampton to greet the traveler. Sam sniffed at it, uneasily, restlessly, while he considered how strange was the British fashion of having railway compartments instead of an undivided car with a nice long aisle along which you could observe ankles, magazines, Rotary buttons, clerical collars, and all the details that made travel interesting.
>
> And the strangeness of having framed pictures of scenery behind the seats; of having hand straps—the embroidered silk covering so rough to the finger tips, the leather inside so smooth and cool—beside the doors. And the greater strangeness of admitting that these seats were more comfortable than the flinty Pullman chairs of America. And of seeing outside, in the watery February sunshine, not snow-curdled fields but springtime greenness; pollarded willows and thatched roofs and half-timbered facades—
>
> Just like in the pictures! England!

As readers, we enter Lewis's fictional dream with our whole bodies, not just our eyes. Along with Sam, we sniff the London air, walk to our train compartment, touch the embroidered hand straps, settle into a comfortable seat, and open our eyes to the scene outside our window. We settle not only into the place—a British rail car—but also the time period of the story. Reading Lewis's description, we sink back into the past, an era when coal-fire, Pullman chairs, and Rotary buttons defined the scenery. But Lewis evokes more than a vague time period, the late 1920s. More particularly, it's a February day filled with "watery" sunshine and "pollarded" trees. Through Lewis's sensory proofs and well-organized description, we enter a time and place that, for most of us, never was.

RENDERING HISTORICAL SETTINGS

When we write a contemporary story, especially one set in a recognizable place filled with modern-day props, we assume our reader will meet us, if not halfway, at least part of the way. We supply a few concrete and telling strokes—of a strip mall, a telephone answering machine, faded jeans, Disneyland—and the reader completes the word painting for us. After all, he's been in enough strip malls to last him a lifetime, he owns an answering machine or is forced to leave messages on one, he wears faded jeans or knows someone who does, and he's been to Disneyland or has at least seen the brochures.

But when we set our stories in another time, an era removed from us, we face some of the same challenges the writer of nonrealistic fiction faces. Like the fantasy writer, we're trying to render and maintain a "world of outside appearance" that we've not experienced firsthand. Our reader is equally new to this landscape, and we can't assume that he will enter our fictional dream as easily as the reader of a contemporary realistic novel would.

If our story takes place, say, at the turn of the century, in medieval times, or even, as Jim Crace's novel does, in the Stone Age, we have to go beyond merely researching our subject. We have to lead the reader through the world of the story, the way a costumed guide at Williamsburg points to a rusted plow that's outlived its function. Or the way a museum docent calls our attention to the hidden layers of a Rembrandt oil. We must peel back the layers of time to render our setting not only accurately but concretely, returning again and again to the sensory proofs that ground the reader in our story.

First we position our reader in time and space. We can announce the information directly—for instance, with a sentence that begins "The London of 1620 was . . ." or with a chapter title like "San Francisco, 1890." Or we can evoke the setting indirectly through description, action, dialogue and prose style. In *The Gift of Stones*, Jim Crace uses the indirect method, yet it doesn't take him long to ground us in his story. Horseback riders arrive at a village in search of arrowheads and spear-stones. A bowman wounds a boy with a spear poisoned with "goat's purge" or "urchin milk" or "silverdew," but rather than finishing off his victim, he goes in search of the arrow because "an arrow can stop a deer, a seal, a hen" and can be bartered for "some honey, say, or skin." After only a few pages, we are situated in a village of stonecutters in a time before written history.

One of the most basic ways to set the time-stage for a story is to load the stage with set pieces, the furnishings of the era. By furnishings I don't mean only chairs, tables and drapes, but all the physical elements—indoor and outdoor, natural and man-made—that make up the historical environment. You may need to conjure up a steam locomotive or an omnibus, a Conestoga wagon or a '37 Ford. Depending on the subject and scope of your story, you might also need to describe the flora, fauna, housing, clothing, food, tools and other accoutrements of the era you're portraying.

Setting the stage and filling it with set pieces may position your reader in time and space, but it won't keep him there unless you continue, throughout the story, to supply sensory proofs. Thus, several pages into the story, after the main character has been fleshed out and dramatic tension established, Crace reminds us of where we are:

> . . . the workshops busy with the rhythm of bone and wood and stone, the causeways quiet and empty except for children delivering new flints, the market-place a murmur of transaction as wheat and skin and pots changed sides with axes, spears and knives.

In chapter three we discussed the importance of supplying, in Aristotle's words, "the proper and special name of a thing." Precise naming is especially important when we're rendering historical settings. No one who reads Crace's novel has lived during the Stone Age (except perhaps Shirley MacLaine, in one of her former lives), and few readers have fashioned primitive implements from stone. Crace has to convince us that the stone-cutter's way of life actually existed, at least for the purposes of his story. So he provides the proper and special names of things. The villagers trade not just tools but "borers, burins, sharpeners, harpoons, stone wrist-guards, sickles, fire-flints, sling-stones, scrapers, hand-axes, arrow-heads and tangs and barbs."

But a mere list of set pieces won't convince the reader. Anyone can scan a reference book and supply technical terms; only a good writer can expand these terms into description rich enough to create a fictional dream. When one of the artisans, Leaf, is chosen to fashion the blade that will amputate a boy's poisoned arm, Crace describes the process in painstaking detail. We are shown the flint, the anvil, the antler tines and wooden mallet. We watch every step of his preparation, up to and past the moment when:

> . . . the blade blank broke loose, spiraled for an instant on the anvil and fell on Leaf's lap. There, on its underside at the point of impact, was the distinctive raised tump of stone, like a tiny bulb or a wrinkle shell. Beyond, in the foothills of the tump, the flint feathered and radiated like a slow tide on a flat beach. It was a good, long blade, still warm from the fire.

In the midst of the description, Crace inserts a disclaimer that begins "There is no need to detail the patience and the expertise with which Leaf etched a pattern of shallow facets . . ." and continues with yet another paragraph filled with precise description of Leaf's process. Crace's disclaimer is, of course, ironic. The need to describe every significant detail is strong. Without a vivid and believable description, we will not be able to participate in Leaf's dramatic moment, the shaping of the blade that will soon sever a boy's arm.

If you're a reader who notes every minute detail and files it away for future reference (a Virgo, like me), you may have noticed that Crace's disclaimer begins with a grammatical construction you were cautioned against in our discussion of "filler phrases" in chapter three. Sentences beginning with *there is* or *it was*, you were warned, can deflate the energy of your prose. More often than not, this warning rings true; usually these phrases are no more than fillers. But sometimes they serve important functions. *The Gift of Stones*, though written in vivid lively prose, is sprinkled with passages like:

> It was his misfortune to be walking . . .
> It was his seventh year . . .
> There was a moment when . . .
> But there was some sense of triumph there . . .

A writer as skillful as Crace knows what he's doing; these phrases are not fillers. They are necessary ingredients in his descriptions, serving not only to sustain dramatic tension but also to suggest the rhythms of an ancient storyteller's prose. Although the most common way to describe a historical setting is by means of accurate word choice and sensory detail, the style of our prose—whether short and clipped or elegantly long-winded—also plays its part in creating and sustaining the fictional dream.

COMBINING DESCRIPTIONS OF SETTING WITH NARRATION AND EXPOSITION

In chapter one we discussed how description works alongside narration and exposition to create the world of the story. Although we sometimes have our reasons for inserting isolated blocks of description, more often we wish to weave descriptions into the narrative arc or into passages of exposition. Skilled writers are so successful at combining description of settings with other story elements that we hardly notice the seams. But if we look closely, we can see how the weaving is accomplished.

One effective method is to use descriptions of setting to introduce, or reintroduce, the characters in our story. In *The Joy Luck Club*, Amy Tan describes the narrator's home street, Waverly Place. She begins with the early morning smells that float up from the street and fill Meimei's bedroom, and her description proceeds spatially, by way of positional markers like "from my bed" and "at the end of our two block alley," a technique we've detailed earlier. Then, in the midst of Tan's tour through Waverly Place—a guided tour from her house to the end of the alley, then to the sandlot playground, and back into the alley itself "crammed with daily mysteries and adventures"—she embeds a section of exposition, which I've noted with italics:

> My brothers and I would peer into the medicinal herb shop, watching old Li dole out onto a stiff sheet of white paper the right amount of insect shells, saffron-colored seeds, and pungent leaves for his ailing customers. *It was said that he once cured a woman dying of an ancestral curse that had eluded the best of American doctors.* Next to the pharmacy was a printer . . .

As swiftly as Tan slides from description of setting into exposition, she slides back into setting. In this way, her tour continues briskly as we are introduced to minor characters and reintroduced to major ones. At the same time, we learn some of the stories hidden behind the doors on Waverly Place, stories that will shape the psychological terrain of the story.

Tan's description of the alley continues for two more pages, during which she again slides briefly out of the purely descriptive mode to provide bits of exposition and narration, including dialogue, which move the plot along and round out her characters. For instance, after Meimei describes in detail the Ping Yuen Fish Market, she tells us that the sanddabs in the tank had eyes that "lay on one flattened side and reminded me of my mother's story of a careless girl who ran into a crowded street and was crushed by a cab. 'Was smash flat,' reported my mother."

Then Tan moves out of the fish market and to the corner of the alley to Hong Sing's, an authentic Chinese cafe that tourists rarely visit. Once, though, as Meimei recalls, a Caucasian tourist asked her and her friends to pose in front of Hong Sing's so he could take a picture of them. Here's what happened, in Meimei's words:

> . . . He had us move to the side of the picture window so the photo would capture the roasted duck with its head dangling from a juice-covered rope. After he took the picture, I told him he should go into Hong Sing's and eat dinner. When he smiled and asked me what they served, I shouted, "Guts and duck's feet and octopus gizzards!" Then I ran off with my friends, shrieking with laughter as we scampered across the alley and hid in the entryway grotto of the China Gem Company, my heart pounding with hope that he would chase us.

Look at how much we've learned not only about Waverly Place but also about the characters who people the story. What kind of mother would tell her young daughter the fate of a girl who "was smash flat" by a car? A cruel mother, or a mother who loved her daughter so much that she wanted to save her from harm? And what do we learn from Meimei's actions? Are her antics toward the tourist merely that—childish antics—or do they reveal conflicting emotions of a child already divided between two cultures? As readers, we're being pulled into the mystery of the human drama and we want to know more. More will be revealed, of course. That's the nature of good story-telling. But for now, Meimei is ducking into the entryway of the China Gem Company.

Tan begins the section by describing Waverly Place, and she ends in Waverly Place. Descriptions of setting ground the fictional dream and build a framework from which to proceed. But shining between the seams of the framework are splinters of light, bits of narration and exposition that illuminate the story.

USING SETTING TO ILLUMINATE A STORY'S THEME

Eudora Welty seems to *breathe* setting the way most of us breathe air. From this breath, this seemingly effortless evocation of time and place, her stories are born. In "No Place for You, My Love," setting serves not only to ground us in the sensory proofs of the story but also to reveal the characters' emotions, to move the plot along, and even to suggest the story's theme. As early as the story's title, Welty hints at the importance setting will play, and in the first sentence she introduces us to the place, which shares equal billing with the human characters in the drama:

> They were strangers to each other, both fairly well
> strangers to the place . . .

The place is a New Orleans restaurant where a man and woman meet, through mutual friends, at a luncheon. Both are Northerners, and the man, we are soon to discover, is married. It's a steamy Sunday afternoon, and as the story progresses, the man suggests to the woman that they take a drive south. "South of New Orleans?" she asks. "I didn't know there was any south to *here* . . ."

His car is a rental car, a detail that adds to the feeling of free-floating alienation. Since neither the city nor the car belongs to either of them, the rules of home do not apply, and their homebound identities seem to dissolve in the humid air. A shyness moves between them, an underlying sexual tension that we sense solely through Welty's description of their surroundings as they walk toward the car:

> . . . flaked-off, colored houses were spotted like the hides
> of beasts faded and shy, and were hot as a wall of growth
> that seemed to breathe flower-like down onto them . . .

They drive awhile, mostly in silence. In concrete and sensory detail Welty describes the heat, the mosquitoes, the families walking along the side of the road and fanning themselves with palmetto leaves. She describes the flora and fauna of the place—the terrapins, turtles and other "little jokes of creation" that "persisted and sometimes perished, the more of them the deeper down the road they went."

We get the feeling the man and woman are also "little jokes of creation," that they are compelled, through evolutionary fate, to play out their short-lived time together. The further they drive and the deeper down the road they travel, the more the land reveals its private, vulnerable self. When the land dead-ends into water, they can go no further without, in effect, becoming amphibious, a feat they accomplish by boarding a ferry. Landscape becomes seascape, and they are in the midst of it:

> Ahead of the boat it was like an exposed vein of ore. The river seemed to swell in the vast middle with the curve of the earth . . .

After the ferry ride they continue their car journey, for a brief time traveling on a paved road. Soon, however, the paving changes from asphalt to shells. If they are to continue further south, they must make their way on foot. Which they do, ending their journey in a bar filled with blacks, dogs and children, one of whom wears " a live lizard on his shirt, clinging like a breast pin—like lapis lazuli." They have gone as far as they can, into the unknown landscape of the South and of their lives together.

They drive back to New Orleans in a wordless, dreamlike state, anchored only by Welty's description: "It was a strange land, amphibious—and whether water-covered or grown with jungle or robbed entirely of water and trees . . . it had the same loneliness . . ." In this strange, in-between state the strangers kiss, and the kiss alters, for the moment at least, the landscape surrounding them:

> He had the feeling that they had been riding for a long time across a face—great, wide, and upturned. . . . A whole giant body sprawled downward then, on and on, always, constant as a constellation or an angel . . .

This moment will not last, of course; such is the nature of moments. As the man and woman drive north, back into their grounded lives, the landscape once again returns to its original state, mirroring the loneliness and alienation of strangers who "had ridden down into a strange land together and were getting safely back—by a slight margin, perhaps, but margin enough . . ."

Welty goes beyond merely establishing the setting of her story and providing concrete and sensory proofs to maintain the illusion of time and space. She even goes beyond weaving her descriptions seamlessly into narrative and expository passages. Welty may begin, as she asserts all honest storytellers must, with the bald facts of time and place. But by the end of the story, the *where* becomes more than a place on a map, and the *when*, more than the slice of a time line. The physical setting is transformed into the landscape of her character's inner conflicts, a symbol of the heart's journey to find itself.

EXERCISES

1. Make a series of lists:

   - Places where you've been in the last twenty-four hours; be very specific
   - Places where you habitually find yourself, whether you like it or not
   - Places from your past that are connected to specific events
   - Places from your past that are connected with particular people
   - Places that are threatened with extinction—global, local or only in personal memory
   - Places where you feel uncomfortable, where you feel, literally, "out of place"
   - Places you've never traveled except in imagination

Look over your lists. Circle the place that most interests you at this moment, then write a description of the place using one of the methods suggested in this chapter or one of the following:

- Speak to the place as if it were a character, describing what you see when you look at it, and how you feel about what you see.
- Organize your description around a catalog of objects found within that place. Describe each item in concrete detail.
- Pretend you are looking at the place through a camera lens. Try different angles. Move in for close-ups, pull back for the big view. Describe what you see from each vantage point.

2. Select a place where a character in your story spends much of her time: an office, bedroom, swimming pool, golf course. Then choose three different time periods in your character's story, identifying each period with a phrase that suggests the character's psychic landscape at that moment—for example, the morning of her job interview, the night her father died, the day she received the results of the pregnancy test. Describe the setting in terms of how it appears to your character during each of these time periods. Remember, you're describing the same setting, but you're describing it three different ways, based on your character's inner drama.

3. Move a character to at least three different locations within the same story, three different vantage points from which to view her world. With each move, describe what she sees.

"From the window of her apartment Fran could see . . ."
"Looking across the breakfast table at her husband, Fran saw . . ."
"Every night in her dreams Fran saw . . ."

4. We sometimes refer to a place as having "character," meaning that it has been shaped by the hands of time, people or events. Describe such a place (a beach house, auto salvage yard, abandoned schoolhouse, ancient forest, barn, burned-out

church), revealing the elements that suggest its history. Pay close attention to physical details. What initials are carved in the wooden school desk? Are weeds crawling through the Edsel's broken window? Choose details that evoke both the human touch and the touch of nature.

5. Describe the same neighborhood as viewed by three different people—for instance, a lifelong resident who's so accustomed to the scene he barely notices it anymore, a teenager who can't wait to escape the place, and a dewy-eyed honeymooner moving into her first home.

6. Using Amy Tan's description of Waverly Place as a model, describe a neighborhood as seen by a resident walking its streets and reporting on what she sees, hears, smells and touches. Intersperse your descriptive passages with bits of exposition (including dialogue, if you wish) that introduce minor characters, reveal past neighborhood events and suggest the personality of the teller.

7. Take the characters from one of your stories and move them into a new setting, one that does not appear in your story. Send them into the past or catapult them into the future. Give them a new world in which to live and move. If they've been confined within an office building of steel and glass, send them to the country. If all they've known is the ocean, construct a desert in which they can roam. Describe the setting concretely, then position your characters in it. How does the new setting change the way they look, act and think? Can you learn anything new about your characters by changing their environment?

8. Describe a natural setting—a woodland, beach, park, mountain—as it appears in each different season or at different times of one particular day. Notice which details remain the same and which ones change. How does the language of your description change depending on the season you're evoking, or the time of day?

PLOT AND PACE: HOW DESCRIPTION SHAPES THE NARRATIVE LINE

A ll good writing is mystery writing. And every successful story, poem and narrative essay is a page-turner—or, in the case of a short poem, a line-turner. We may begin reading out of mild curiosity, to pass the time, but we *keep* reading to unravel the mystery. If there is no tension, we stop caring. When suspense dissolves, when the mystery is solved, we stop turning pages.

By mystery, I don't mean only "What's going to happen?" Sometimes the outcome is known from the beginning. We don't read a book about the Titanic, for instance, or the Civil War, or Hiroshima, to find out what will happen. We *know* what will happen: the ship will sink, the South will lose, the bomb will be dropped. Mystery extends beyond revelation of uncertain outcomes. It also involves *how* a story is told—how description is created and controlled, how characters are developed, and how the plot unfolds.

The notion of plot used to terrify me; the word alone was enough to send me into a cold sweat. Plot: what the cemetery salesman kept trying to talk me, literally, into.

Plot, I was certain, would bury me. Or I'd bury myself. Already I was knee-deep in confusion, digging my own grave. Try as I might, I could see no connection between my heartfelt descriptions—of characters, settings and events—and the story's plot. Maybe, I thought, if I can just plan the action, each step of my character's path, if I can just *plot* it all out like points on a grid,

I'll be able to write a successful story. My shovel went deep into diagrams, graphs and outlines until I was over my head in diabolical plans.

Which leads us to another unfortunate connotation of *plot*: a secret, underhanded scheme to accomplish a hostile or illegal act.

In truth, plot doesn't have to be our final resting place. Nor must it stand coldly apart from our descriptions. In the best stories, as in many essays and poems, plot and description not only coexist; they aid one another. Plot helps to focus and sharpen our descriptions of people, places and action. In return, description shapes the narrative line by lending immediacy to scene and summary, controlling the pace of our story, and modulating narrative tension.

DESCRIPTION IN SUMMARY AND SCENE

Few stories are told solely through scene or solely through summary. Most stories combine the two methods. A scene is an episode acted out by characters; it takes place in a particular place at a particular time. Reading a scene, we feel we're witnessing the action firsthand. The characters are on their own, and we watch them move and talk.

Scene is foreground; summary is background. Rather than re-creating a scenic action, summary sweeps over the larger terrain of accumulated action. A summary is not a close-up but a long shot. And where a scene is primarily a *viewing* of an event, a summary is primarily a *telling*. Someone—an author or a narrator—is relating events to us secondhand, filling in information, catching us up on what has gone before and preparing us for the next scene.

In a scene we're thrown into the center of the drama, and the pictures move swiftly before our eyes. (This is especially true of long scenes; a series of short scenes can break our attention span, making us more conscious of time passing.) And though it's true, in general, that scene quickens a story's pace and summary slows it, this explanation oversimplifies the complexities of pacing. A story composed entirely of scenes—dialogue, action and event—can become tiring, even monotonous. If everything is a scene, then how do we ration our attention? When do we lean forward in anticipation, and when do we lean back?

Jerome Stern, in *Making Shapely Fiction*, suggests that the writer, like a child, should make a scene only when he wants your full attention. This makes sense. It takes time and energy to write a fully rendered scene, and it takes time and energy to read one. In a scene, everything is in the foreground and we're asked to look closely at each detail. If everything in the story is vying equally for our up-close, intense scrutiny—which is what scenes demand—we may begin yearning for the relief that summary provides.

When summary begins, we feel a change in the wind. We become conscious of Someone, the Teller, relating the events. During the scene we were on the edge of our seats, so close to the drama we could almost reach out and touch the actors. Now, as the Teller begins to summarize, we ease back into our seats the way we relax into a leisurely tale told by a wise, informed storyteller.

When we write a scene, we place ourselves in a particular place at a particular time, so it's easy to imagine the concrete, sensory details that fill the space. In this passage from James Baldwin's *Go Tell It on the Mountain*, John has just awakened in the room he shares with his brother. It's the morning of John's fourteenth birthday, and Baldwin enters the scene directly, supplying specific sensory details:

> He stared at a yellow stain on the ceiling just above his head. Roy was still smothered in the bedclothes, and his breath came and went with a small, whistling sound.

Scenic description comes naturally to most writers. But once we leave the scene and begin to summarize, description becomes more of a challenge. Summary invites abstraction and explanation; in its attempt to cover lots of ground in the shortest amount of time, summary sometimes fails to describe the real world or the world of the imagination. As the Baldwin passage continues, John begins thinking about his shortcomings—in particular, what he sees as the sins that blot his life, sins that will keep him from following the straight and narrow path of his forefathers.

> He would not be like his father, or his father's fathers. He would have another life.
>
> For John excelled in school, though not, like Elisha, in mathematics or basketball, and it was said that he had a Great Future. He might become a Great Leader of His People. John was not much interested in his people and still less in leading them anywhere, but the phrase so often repeated rose in his mind like a great brass gate, opening outward for him . . .

In this passage, Baldwin leaves the scene for a moment. Not the room itself—John is still lying in bed—but Baldwin departs briefly from the scenic method to give us background information. (His summary actually lasts for several long paragraphs.)

Although we are no longer watching the scene unfold, we nevertheless remain involved in the story. We continue to feel the immediacy of the moment, partly because Baldwin, in the midst of summarizing, inserts a description. A gate rises, we are told, in John's mind, and we visualize it—large and brass—as it opens for him.

If during a passage of summary your story slows, one way to quicken the pace is to insert a concrete and sensory description. This provides the illusion of scene while still allowing you to supply information. As we learned in chapter three, it helps if your description also contains movement. Remember Aristotle's suggestion? *Whenever possible, describe your subject in a state of activity.* If what you're describing isn't capable of independent action, you can create the illusion of movement by using active verbs. Baldwin shows the brass gate in action—it rises, then opens.

Sometimes the action in our descriptions is present but hidden, and a slight rewording is all it takes to bring the motion into view. For instance, "Her hair was black and *curly*" can become "Her black hair *curled* in ringlets around her cheeks." Even a static summary passage can appear active and immediate when it includes an active, immediate image.

Another way to achieve immediacy while you're summarizing is to create the illusion of scenic event. Although a summary is not a dramatic re-creation of an event, it often refers to past or ongoing events. When you're writing a summary passage that mentions such events, you can't stop to reenter particular moments or to render each detail concretely and specifically; that would require employing the scenic method. You can, however, use descriptive techniques to suggest the immediacy of scene while still maintaining a wide, sweeping pace. In the following example, which alternates between scene and summary, Baldwin creates the illusion of scenic events even in the midst of summary:

> Roy stirred again and John pushed him away, listening to the silence. On other mornings he awoke hearing his mother singing in the kitchen, hearing his father in the bedroom behind him grunting and muttering prayers to himself as he put on his clothes; hearing, perhaps, the chatter of Sarah and the squalling of Ruth, and the radios, the clatter of pots and pans, and the voices of all the folk nearby. This morning not even the cry of a bedspring disturbed the silence, and John seemed, therefore, to be listening to his own unspeaking doom.

Baldwin's first sentence uses the scenic method; as in the previous example, we're watching John in bed on the morning of his fourteenth birthday. In the second sentence Baldwin switches to summary, combining information about all the other mornings John has known into one long sentence filled with sensory details—his father's grunting, pots and pans clattering.

Notice that Baldwin does not move us into a new scene. Rather, he suspends the scene in the bedroom just long enough to provide the context, to show how John's emotions on this particular morning have been shaped by his personal history of mornings spent in his parents' house. In one long summary sentence, he combines information gathered from many previous mornings and anchors this information with concrete, sensory description. Finally in the third sentence, through the transitional phrase "this morning," Baldwin throws us back into the scene.

Baldwin begins with the scenic method, moves to summary, then returns to the scenic method, all in three sentences—and we never even feel the bump. His descriptive details create a smooth bridge between the birthday morning and all other mornings. Through sensory description, Baldwin manages to supply important information while still retaining a vigorous prose style that keeps the passage moving briskly.

USING DESCRIPTION TO MODULATE PACE

Readers often maintain that description stops or slows a story's action, and many admit to skimming over descriptive passages in order to "see what happens next." (I confess that Michener's *Hawaii* had this effect on me.) Although sometimes description serves mainly as a transitional device to link scenes of action, description can also create its own vitality. As the gear shift of the narrative vehicle, description can just as easily speed up the action as slow it.

Before we move on to discussing specific ways description can modulate the pace of a story, let's clarify what we mean by action. Action in a story is not the same as activity. Action is motion that is going somewhere, that pushes the story along. It's a forward movement, an outward sign of an inward motive. Motion serves, as the lyrics of a popular song suggests, to "second that emotion." Activity, on the other hand, is mere random movement. Made-for-TV movies often include lots of activity—cars crashing, buildings exploding, bullets flying—with little or no motivated action. When a viewer or a reader turns off the TV or closes the book, complaining that "nothing's happening," he's usually referring not to the lack of activity on the screen or page, but to the lack of forward movement. The difference between activity and action is the difference between running on a treadmill and running in a race.

So if you're concerned with modulating the pace of your story, with speeding up or slowing down your story's action, you first need to be clear about your character's motives (conscious or unconscious). Once you know what your character wants, or what the universe wants for your character, you'll have a better sense of when to vary your story's pace to move the plot along. Both abilities—speeding up and slowing down—are essential to good storytelling. Tension is created not merely by quickening the pace of our story but by varying that pace to achieve certain results. To maintain suspense, we must alternate between scene and summary, showing and telling, and between braking and accelerating.

One of the most effective ways to quicken your story's pace is to move from a static description of an object, place or person to an active scene. The classic method for accomplishing this is to have your character interact with the subject that's been described. For instance, let's say you've just written three paragraphs describing a wedding dress in a shop window. You've detailed the Belgian lace veil, the beaded bodice, the twelve-foot train, even the row of satin buttons down the sleeves. Instinctively you feel it's time to move into an action scene, but how do you do it without making your transition obvious?

A simple, almost seamless way is to initiate an action between your character (let's call her Miranda) and the dress you've just described. Perhaps Miranda could be passing by on the sidewalk when the dress in the window catches her attention. Or she could walk into the shop and ask the shopkeeper how much the dress costs. This method works well to link almost any static description with a scene of action. Describe an elegant table, for instance, complete with crystal goblets, damask tablecloth, monogrammed napkins and sterling silver tableware; then let the maid pull a cloth from her apron and begin to polish one of the forks. Or describe a Superman kite lying beside a tree, then watch as a little girl grabs the string and begins to run. You will still be describing, but the nature of your description will have changed from static to active, thus quickening the story's pace.

Throughout this book we've discussed techniques for making descriptions come to life, including using active rather than passive prose, employing concrete, specific details, and describing our subjects in motion. We've also seen how description can create a sense of immediacy in both scene and summary. All the methods we've discussed can enliven your story's pace. Speeding up a story's action, in fact, is a natural outgrowth of writing vivid descriptions. The more effective our descriptions, the less likely our readers will be to notice time's passing, and the more likely they will be to keep turning pages. Accurate, detailed description, coupled with a lively prose style, is often enough to keep narrative tension alive.

Sometimes, however, we control pace best not by speeding up the action but by slowing it down. I learned this technique while working in the public schools. Fresh out of college, the only job I could get was teaching twenty-nine second graders, twenty-two of whom were boys. Young and fit though I was, I could not keep up with them, let alone control them. Noise and feral energy were such natural components of the second grade animal that my meek, domesticated gestures barely registered as movement. It was clear that I couldn't compete with the students on their own ground—by running after them or raising my voice. I'd have to get their attention in other ways. So in the midst of the fray—in the lunchroom, on the playground, at the blackboard or in the halls—I would suddenly pause, turn slowly on my heels, and, as if by magic, the sneakers of twenty-nine second graders would screech to a halt. Once I had their attention, I'd whisper my directions. The roar ceased. They cocked their little ears and leaned forward, silent with anticipation.

Swift, noisy activity does not always get our attention. Filmmakers, aware of this principle, use it to their advantage. Thus, in the clang and clamor of battle—cannons to the left of us, cavalry to the right, swords clashing, thunder rolling—one soldier leans down to recover a fallen flag. The moment seems to last forever. What's taking him so long? Slowly, slowly his arm bends, his hand begins its languorous ascent, the flag rippling in slow motion. The camera continues its deliberate tracking—up the length of his arm, across his square shoulder, his sinewy neck. Blue veins are pulsing—one beat, two.

At this point, we are clay in the filmmaker's hand. Through his skilled change of pace, he has grabbed our attention, and he'll keep it, at least for a while. In this suspended moment, this pause in the action, the filmmaker actually increases our hunger to know the outcome. He's free to move into the soldier's mind, perhaps into flashback or dream. He's free to dwell a while longer on the physical details of the scene—the soldier's frayed cap, his labored breathing. We will hold still for the details because the filmmaker has slowed the action.

Slow. Withhold. Delay. All techniques for increasing tension.

Perhaps the simplest, most obvious way to slow the pace of your story is to use short sentences, directives or fragments. You can also use short paragraphs, thereby creating white space, a visual pause for your reader's eye. The preceding paragraph takes up only one line, and its one word fragments require the reader to stop, start and stop again.

In poetry, also, short lines tend to slow the movement. For instance, the opening line to one of my poems—

When you left our new marriage for another woman's
bed

—would read quite differently were it broken into smaller bites:

When you left
our new
marriage for another
woman's bed

Breaking the long line not only changes the meaning of the poem by shifting the emphasis of certain words; it also forces the reader to slow down, both physically and psychologically.

Another easy, direct way to slow the pace of prose or poetry is to change the verb tense of the telling. Present tense, although it contributes to a feeling of immediacy, can actually prolong a scene. "She is sitting at the window" takes longer to write and to read than "She sat at the window." And even the shortened present-tense version—"She sits at the window"—although it takes just as long to read as the past tense version, gives the impression of prolonged action because it emphasizes the process rather than the completed event. Since a present-tense action is, by definition, an action *in process,* the reader expects to be led through the process, and will generally sit still as you describe each step. Writing in the present tense may also slow *you* down as you write, making you more conscious of describing precisely, specifically and in detail.

In general, it's best to be consistent with the verb tense of your story. But sometimes changing verb tense in midstream can be effective. Since switching from past tense to present tense usually slows the reader down, it's a good method for focusing attention on a dramatic action—say, a gun being cocked—or for achieving the feeling of suspension that occurs in dreams or reverie. A conscious switch in verb tense also serves a practical purpose: it alerts the reader to a change in focus, time period or psychological distance.

SPECIAL CHALLENGES OF FLASHBACKS

Flashback is one of the most common ways to modulate the pace of a story. Unfortunately, flashback often slows the pace *too* much, making our readers impatient to return to the main story. When this happens it's usually because we haven't established the tension effectively beforehand. Although flashback literally looks *back,* into the past, it should serve to push the narrative *forward.* What it's pushing forward may not be "what happens next." More often, flashback pushes the narrative forward by exploring the *why* and *how* of the main conflict the author has already set up.

Flashback is a suspension device, but you can't suspend something that isn't there to begin with. Before a flashback occurs, the main line of the story must be threaded, and threaded tightly. Let's say your main character is a timid, mouselike bookseller. After a few pages of description—of him, his bookstore, the bag lunch he's brought with him one rainy Thursday—you flash back to his childhood home. Painstakingly you describe the boy's beautiful but distracted mother and her succession of lovers, the leatherbound books that line the shelves of the boy's room, and the yellow chenille bedspread that leaves an imprint on his cheek.

Unfortunately, your reader probably doesn't care about the bookseller's childhood—at least, not yet—and she'll quickly become impatient with your flashback descriptions, however original, sensory and freshly rendered they are. The quality of your description isn't the problem; it's the *timing*. You've inserted a flashback too soon, before the main conflict has been established.

Try backing up a minute and reentering the opening scene: the bookseller in his shop on a rainy Thursday morning. Ask yourself where *that* scene is heading. Maybe a customer—say, a thin, dark-eyed woman in a brown raincoat—is browsing through a medical dictionary. Maybe the bookseller has noticed her before. After all, she comes in every rainy lunch hour, always wearing that same brown coat. He wants to talk to her, maybe even invite her to join him for lunch, but something stops him— what makes him think she would even talk to him, let alone join him for lunch? What on earth could she possibly see in him, and besides, what does he know about women? He's never even been on a date. All these thoughts are running through the bookseller's mind as he watches the woman. He takes a step toward her, hesitates, takes another step.

Now's your chance. You've established the tension, the uncertain *what* : Will he speak to the dark-eyed woman? By dwelling a while longer on the main story scene rather than moving too quickly into flashback, you've allowed yourself time and space to introduce a problem, maybe two. (The woman is reading a medical dictionary; maybe she's ill.)

At this point, having been introduced to the *what*, your reader is primed for the *why* and *how* that a flashback can provide: Why is the bookseller so frightened of women? How has he gotten this far without once having a date? Because the main line of the story has been threaded tightly, you are free to insert your flashback descriptions, which will now be not only original, sensory and freshly rendered, but also significant to the conflict.

Readers will gladly hold still for descriptions that deepen the essential mystery of a story. But they won't hold still forever. Overlong flashback descriptions are as deadly to a story as are badly timed flashbacks. There is no magic to knowing when a flashback is too long. Generally speaking, the longer the work, the longer the flashback it can support. A novel might sustain a flashback of several pages or more, but a poem may be too brief or tightly focused to allow even one flashback image. It's a question of balance: a flashback should not take up more time, space or energy than the main story. (An easy way to check for balance is to use a highlighter to mark all flashback sections. You'll quickly see how much space your flashbacks are consuming.)

If you find that a flashback is taking over your story, or that your flashback descriptions are more intriguing than the descriptions in your primary plot line, you'll need to reconsider your strategy. It may be that the real story lies within the flashback, and that the primary story was just a way for you to segue into the flashback. If this is the case, you may need to get rid of the introductory incident and restructure your story so the flashback is your main plot line.

If, however, you find you've simply gotten carried away with flashback description (this happens to me all the time), you'll need to either cut some of the flashback descriptions or expand the descriptions in your main story. Otherwise, the reader will lose his moorings. The main conflict should lie within the primary story. If we stray too far from the main conflict, the reader will become anxious to return to it. He'll start flipping pages, skipping over the descriptions you've labored so hard to craft.

The most helpful way I've found to keep my flashbacks under control is to employ the "accordion" principle I learned from Lynne Sharon Schwartz at the Bread Loaf Writers' Conference. (Although Schwartz applied the principle to the novel and short story, it works equally well for narrative nonfiction and narrative poetry.) Think of the structural frame of your story as an accordion. When the accordion is collapsed, it represents the framework of your main story; the edges of the accordion show where your telling begins and ends. The time line of your telling should be as whole and complete as the accordion is when its edges are pressed tightly together.

Once the time line of the main story is well delineated, you can open the accordion wide. Its pleats will remind you of the overall structure of your story, the main conflict that is unfolding, but the space between the pleats can be filled with descriptions, flashbacks, observations and all those other elements that make a story more than merely the sum of its plotted parts.

SCATTERING DESCRIPTIVE DETAILS
TO UNIFY THE PLOT

In an earlier chapter we discussed how beginning writers often clump descriptive details at the beginning of a story or when a character or setting is first mentioned. Often it's more effective to break these large clumps into smaller bits, sprinkling them throughout the story. This method not only helps you avoid overlong or static descriptions; it also provides continual proofs for your reader.

The notion of "sprinkling" details throughout a story should not be taken to mean that details can simply be dropped, willy-nilly, along the way. Like episodes in a novel, which must be placed so that they amplify the conflict, descriptive details must accumulate, gaining significance each time they are mentioned. Effectively releasing descriptive details a little at a time can strengthen your plot line. Each detail is like a crumb dropped for the reader, creating a trail to follow. In Flannery O'Connor's story "Everything That Rises Must Converge," the most memorable physical detail is the hat worn by Julian's mother. The hat is mentioned many times throughout the story, and each mention nudges the plot along. The first description of the hat, occurring in the third paragraph, is from Julian's point of view.

> It was a hideous hat. A purple velvet flap came down on one side of it and stood up on the other; the rest of it was green and looked like a cushion with the stuffing out. He decided it was less comical than jaunty and pathetic.

The next reference to the hat is not a description of the hat itself, but rather a description of an action involving the hat:

> She lifted the hat one more time and set it down slowly
> on top of her head.

On the next page, the hat is described again, but unlike the first description, this one is brief, only a phrase (which I've noted with italics) embedded seamlessly into a larger narrative passage:

> The door closed and he turned to find the dumpy fig-
> ure, *surmounted by the atrocious hat*, coming toward him.

As readers, we add this phrase to earlier descriptive details. The cumulative description gains momentum, and with each mention of the hat, the conflict between Julian and his mother grows. Although it's not yet clear if the hat will be the main focus of the conflict, it *is* clear it will play a significant role in the story.

After two more brief references to the hat, O'Connor progresses for several hat-free pages. Julian is accompanying his mother to her "reducing" class at the Y, and as they walk to the bus stop, they begin to argue. We learn that Julian hates his small Southern hometown, his mother's racial prejudices, her longing for a past when her grandfather was a wealthy land-owner and when "darkies" were "better off" as slaves. Most of all, he hates the way his mother controls him through her child-like helplessness. The next description of the hat demonstrates the anger silently raging inside him.

> He looked at her bleakly. She was holding herself very
> erect under the preposterous hat, wearing it like a ban-
> ner of her imaginary dignity. There was in him an evil
> urge to break her spirit.

The adjectives in O'Connor's descriptions have progressed from "jaunty and pathetic" to "atrocious" to "preposterous," mirroring the progression of Julian's disgust not only for the hat but for all it represents, the privileged past that his mother refuses to relinquish. The plot thickens as Julian and his mother take seats on a recently integrated bus, joined quickly by the "darkies" whose upward mobility Julian's mother has been railing against. For four or five pages O'Connor doesn't mention the hat; all descriptive attention is focused on the interaction among Julian, his mother and the blacks with whom they are seated.

The next description of the hat represents a turning point in the plot. O'Connor repeats the same description with which she opened the story; she even uses the same wording:

> . . . a hideous hat. A purple velvet flap came down on one side of it and stood up on the other; the rest of it was green and looked like a cushion with the stuffing out.

But this time the hat is on another head, the head of an imposing, strong-willed black woman. Julian notices the hat, but does not make the connection until several paragraphs later when his eyes, fixed on "the haughty face" of the woman and the "green and purple hat," widen in surprise and recognition:

> The vision of the two hats, identical, broke upon him with the radiance of a brilliant sunrise. His face was suddenly lit with joy. He could not believe that Fate had thrust upon his mother such a lesson.

As the plot moves toward its tragicomic climax, the hat is mentioned two more times. But the tide of the story has been reversed. The hat, no longer perched high and proud upon Julian's mother's head, lies defeated in her lap: everything that rises must converge. By breaking her description of the hat into several small pieces and scattering them throughout the story, O'Connor organizes the plot line, provides the concrete and sensory proofs that anchor us to the world of the story, and tightens the thread of tension between Julian and his mother and, finally, between the old world and the new.

WITHHOLDING DESCRIPTIVE DETAILS
TO CREATE TENSION

O'Connor's technique—of scattering descriptive passages throughout the story—relies more on repetition and variation than on the slow revelation of detail. We know what the hat looks like the first time it's mentioned; we don't have to wait for the visual image to be made clear. Sometimes, however, a writer consciously withholds descriptive details as a way of tightening a story's tension. This is writing as striptease, the opposite of "what you see is what you get." With the striptease method, what we get is precisely what we *don't* see, what we must wait patiently, or impatiently, to learn. Like the man in William Sansom's *The Loving Eye*, we wait at the story's window for any sign, however slight, to be revealed:

> One moment the window was empty, a dark square—and the next this strange new woman was standing against the sill.
>
> Her appearance was as sudden as if a blind had been snapped up.
>
> There she stood exactly in the centre of her little theatre of sashes and sill and darkness beyond. One expected her to bow.
>
> He backed away from his own window like a thief.

Looking out his apartment window, the man has been surprised, as the reader has, by the sudden appearance of a woman. But Sansom doesn't reveal what she looks like. He delays his description, making us all the more curious, and his use of short paragraphs increases the stop-and-start feeling of the moment. Although the woman appears as if onstage, the man backs away "like a thief." More delay. Even if the woman were to appear again, the man (who is our eye, the camera lens through which we view the scene) may not be there to describe it for us. The suspense mounts.

In the next paragraph, Sansom creates a kind of visual inter-ference, describing in detail the physical barriers rising between the man and woman:

> In between them a wild spring wind drove through the trough of back-gardens, raising sudden birds of white paper, waving the trees, whipping a storm of movement between all the rows of quiet shut windows. But that was outside. In, it was still.

Again, tension is tightened by the author's halt and delay. Although we feel the internal storm rising within the man, Sansom doesn't satisfy our curiosity. Not yet. Instead he shifts to an external storm, a "wild spring wind" that waves and whips through the landscape.

Although Sansom continues to withhold visual details of the woman, he nevertheless uses description to push the story for-ward. The man hears sounds from outside that "accuse his se-cret second"—a lumber cart, a blackbird, "the thrash of a beaten mat." The reader overhears the man's heart beating "loud as a clock, faster than the mat" as he crouches among the furniture, vowing not to look out the window again until he receives a sign:

> He thought: Not until that cart has called three times more, I won't move till then . . .

As readers, we won't move either. Not until Sansom gives us a sign, releasing the thread of tension he's pulled so tightly. We will hold still for his minute descriptions—of the gardens, a blackbird, even the taffeta swag on the window box—because the descriptions are not only sensory, concrete and exquisitely rendered but because they delay the inevitable moment when the woman, in all her complete and descriptive glory, will be revealed.

USING DESCRIPTION TO SUGGEST PSYCHOLOGICAL MOTION

Sansom's method—using description to delay the primary action of the story—serves an additional narrative purpose. His descriptions of the external landscape also mirror the internal landscape of the man's feelings; they "second the emotion." Since the passage is written from the limited omniscient viewpoint, we're allowed access into the man's head. We overhear his thoughts and even hear his heart beating, so when we encounter a description of a storm or a blackbird, we easily make the transition between the outer and inner worlds of the story.

When we are writing from the objective point of view, however, it's difficult to use description to mirror emotional states. After all, we have no access into our characters' minds; we can report only those external details an observer might perceive through his senses. Think of Hemingway, with his cold, objective eye. In most of his stories, his language is spare; he allows himself no emotional riffs, no detours of philosophical meditations. With Hemingway, what we see is what we get.

Or so it seems on the surface. Yet even Hemingway departs from "just the facts ma'am" when he wishes to suggest a character's mindscape. In "Hills Like White Elephants," arguably his most sparse, coolly reported story, the plot proceeds almost entirely through external dialogue and action. The two characters in the story—identified only as "the man" and "the girl" (except for one brief reference to the girl's name)—are not described at all in physical terms. Nor does Hemingway tell us what either one is thinking or feeling as they sit at a table talking. The main clues to the emotional world of the story, the psychological plot beneath the bare action, emerge in his descriptions of the neighboring hills. The first description occurs early in the story:

> The hills across the valley of the Ebro were long and white. On this side there was no shade and no trees and the station was between two lines of rails in the sun.

Then, after several lines of dialogue, Hemingway appears to move into the mind of the girl. He doesn't, of course; that would violate his objective point of view. But he suggests her emotional landscape through his next description of the hills, followed by the girl's statement.

> The girl was looking off at the line of hills. They were white in the sun and the country was brown and dry.
> "They look like white elephants," she said.

The colors and textures of the description—white, brown and dry—echo the aridity and sterility of the moment. Several pages of dialogue ensue, during which we come to understand that the man is trying to talk the girl into aborting their child-to-be. At this point, we are told:

> The girl stood up and walked to the end of the station. Across, on the other side, were fields of grain and trees along the banks of the Ebro. Far away, beyond the river, were mountains. The shadow of a cloud moved across the field of grain and she saw the river through the trees.

Notice how the description has changed. No longer is the scene brown and white and dry. It is green and fecund, ribboned by a distant river.

> "And we could have all this," she said.

Looking in one direction, the girl sees one scene; looking in the other direction, she sees quite a different scene. By now it's clear that the choice she makes—the internal, emotional choice of whether to bear the child or abort it—will mirror the external landscape that Hemingway so objectively reports. Although he remains removed from the scene, never entering the girl's mind, the author nevertheless uses description to suggest the girl's feelings, thus propelling the plot beyond merely "*what* happens next" to the more intriguing questions of *how* it will happen, and *why*.

EXERCISES

1. Read over one of your stories, using two different colored markers to highlight particular passages. With one color, mark the scenes; with the other color, mark the summaries. Is your story composed predominantly of scene or of summary?

If you've used mostly scenes, have you provided the reader with enough details to suggest the forces that have shaped your characters' inner lives and motives? Will your reader tire of dialogue, action and direct presentation of event? Will the scenic method become monotonous?

If you've used mostly summary, have you included enough concrete, sensory details to bring the reader into your fictional dream? Are there places where you could break away from summary to enter a scene?

2. Using the passage from *Go Tell It on the Mountain* as a model, insert a sentence or two of summary in the midst of a scene. Slip the summary information in swiftly; then move directly back into the scene.

3. At a dramatic point in a scene of brisk, even frenetic action, slow the pace. You can do this by using short, fragmented sentences or paragraphs, or by switching from past tense to present tense. Once the slow motion moment has been sustained long enough to rivet the reader's attention, return to the original swift pace.

4. In the middle of a summary section, insert a concrete image—a sight, sound, smell, taste or texture—that will create the illusion of scenic event. For instance, if you're summarizing the experiences that have led to a particular moment in your character's life, use sensory language to evoke one or more of these experiences. Let's say you've opened your story with a summary of the jobs Jane has held for the past twenty years. As you're summarizing, you might mention her "chlorine-soaked

summers as a lifeguard" or "the sizzle of grease" as she flipped burgers at the coffee shop. Don't expand the descriptions into full-fledged scenes. Give just enough detail to create the illusion of scene, then continue your summary.

5. If your story seems to lack suspense because the events unfold too straightforwardly, in chronological order, use scissors to cut your draft into discrete scenes. (A computer won't work for this activity. You need to be able to see all the sections at once and to physically rearrange them.) Once the separate scenes are laid out before you, reorder them. Rather than thinking chronologically, think in terms of mystery. Which scene would be most likely to grab the reader's attention? Which scene could follow the opening scene, revealing just enough to hold the reader's attention?

6. If your story includes a flashback description, look closely to see if you've inserted it too early in the story. Has your main story line been delineated, the conflict introduced? If not, try moving the flashback later in the story.

7. Using the hat passages from "Everything That Rises Must Converge" as examples, break a long description of an object, place or person into at least three sections. Plant these sections in different places in the story. Each time your subject is mentioned, vary the details so the description accumulates meaning as the story progresses.

8. After you've described at length a static subject, set the scene in motion by having a character interact with the subject, the way Miranda interacts with the wedding dress in this chapter's example.

9. Using objective narration like that in Hemingway's "Hills Like White Elephants," suggest a character's moods or thoughts strictly by the way you describe a scene, landscape or object within the character's view. Remember, as an objective narrator you can report only what you can witness externally; you cannot enter the character's mind.

10. Try the striptease method of description. Begin with an incomplete description of an object, person or scene, no more than a vague hint of what will later be revealed. (Using pronouns rather than specific nouns is one way to begin.) Depart

from the description for a few sentences. When you return, give one or two more hints, but do not reveal your subject completely. Delay your revelation by creating visual or other interferences, by switching briefly to another scene, or by the use of short, elliptical phrases that slow the reader's pace.

THE BIG PICTURE

W hen all is said and done . . .'' my grandmother would begin. The phrase was her coda, her theme song, a way to reclaim the dropped stitches and chipped dishes, to order the details that cluttered her days. "When all is said and done . . . what really matters is . . .''

You've completed the first or second draft of your story, essay or poem—maybe even the final one. Reading over what you've written, you're pleased with your descriptions. They're carefully worded, echoing both the sound and the sense of your subject. They're sensory and concrete, filled with specific details. You've brought your images to life through vivid prose, action-based description and metaphor. You've fleshed out your characters, created the illusion of time and space, and moved your plot along.

But you're still not sure how it all fits together. You're not yet ready to send your fictional dream out into the daylight. When the reader reaches the last line of your poem or the final paragraph of your essay, will he hear that inevitable "click" you want him to hear, the sound of a well-engineered lock slipping into place? Days after he finishes your story—or weeks, or even years, long after he's forgotten individual descriptions—what will remain in his memory?

When all is said and done, we want our descriptions to add up to something. No, not just add *up to*. We want to create something that's more than the sum of its parts. The painting, not just the brushstrokes. The song, not just the notes.

". . . What really matters is . . ."

What really matters, finally, is the big picture, the fictional dream that lingers after the details have vanished. The big picture is formed not only by our descriptions of characters, settings and events but also by forces that reside above and below our story's surface—atmosphere, mood, feeling, motif, theme, form, structure and tone. These terms are far from interchangeable. Each carries its own literary weight and could easily be the subject of an entire writing text. Theme is not the same as tone, atmosphere and motif aren't even distant cousins, and mood and form are worlds apart. But when we consider how each of these elements serves our writing, we begin to see how they are related. Each is, to some degree, an intangible force uniting the more tangible elements of our story—character, setting, plot and point of view. And each works behind the scenes to create that "something in the air" or "something underfoot" that the reader intuitively senses.

To understand how these intangible elements contribute to the big picture, we must go beyond the surface of the story, beyond even the most concrete, significant and effective descriptions of our subjects. In this chapter, we'll consider how description evokes the prevailing atmosphere of our story, poem or essay. Then we'll discuss how descriptive language shapes the tone of the writing. Finally, we'll show how description can suggest a story's theme, the overall idea that lives beneath the story line.

SOMETHING IN THE AIR: ATMOSPHERE AND MOOD

My husband believes the whole world should be placed on a dimmer switch. "Lighting is everything," he says, adjusting the shade beside my reading chair. He rips out fluorescent tubes by their ballasts and replaces them with golden incandescents or pink-tinted bulbs that warm our faces to a cherubic glow. Each night as we make our way to bed, we extinguish no fewer than twenty five light sources—wall sconces, chandeliers, table lamps, under-counter strip lights, down lights, up lights, votives, tapers, oil lamps—each with its own function, all working together to contribute to what my husband calls our home's "atmosphere."

My husband is wrong when he says lighting is everything. In terms of atmosphere, music is also important, so tonight Michael Feinstein is playing Gershwin, or Ella is crooning, or Jagger is thumping out "Brown Sugar" in the landing above our heads where my husband has positioned hidden speakers. He's camouflaged the wires too, threaded them behind walls— because beauty, he says, is in the eye of the beholder. And you can't behold beauty if you're staring at bare wires.

In literature, atmosphere is the element hidden behind the walls of our story. It's the overall mood or feeling we create through description, imagery and other language effects. Atmosphere is closely related to setting, but it goes beyond the bare wires of *when* and *where*. If someone were to ask me, "Where does the story of your life *take place*?" I'd probably provide the most obvious, verifiable answer: "In a townhouse in a southern city at the end of the twentieth century."

Those are the facts of my home's *setting*. But if I were asked to describe my home's atmosphere, facts would not suffice; I'd have to use words that evoked moods or feelings. I might begin with a label: *cozy*, perhaps, or *restful*. Maybe even *elegant* or *romantic* (on those evenings when the lighting in our living room is just right and a love song is playing).

An effective description, of course, must go beyond labels. Adjectives like *gloomy, forlorn, cheerful, inviting, sensual* or *foreboding* may be useful handles to help us focus our descriptions around a central mood. But they won't help the reader *experience* the atmosphere. "To establish a particular atmosphere, mood, or tone," says Jerome Stern in *Making Shapely Fiction*, "you must pay attention to your readers' short memory for sensation." Atmosphere, though in part intangible, must be evoked through tangible means.

We've already mentioned the importance of lighting and music; other elements of atmosphere include details of time, place, weather, sense impressions and special effects of language. The opening to Edgar Allen Poe's "The Fall of the House of Usher" encompasses all these elements:

> During the whole of a dull, dark, and soundless day in the autumn of the year, when the clouds hung oppressively low in the heavens, I had been passing alone, on horseback, through a singularly dreary tract of country, and at length found myself, as the shades of evening drew on, within view of the melancholy House of Usher.

This one sentence could well serve as a crash course in how to create atmosphere. First the bare wires of where and when are suggested (a country road; an autumn day in a time period when men still road on horseback to reach their destinations). Then lights and sound are added: the scene is dark and shadowy; a palpable silence reigns. It's not a peaceful quiet, the kind that might soothe a tired traveler. Rather, it's a disturbing silence described only in terms of what it *lacks*: "soundless." Other details add to the foreboding: clouds hanging low; a lone rider. And beneath it all a subliminal music plays. I imagine an oboe or a cello, its tones mournfully forlorn. Soon it's joined by a chorus of deep vowels whose tones are split by harsh consonants and stopped rhythms striking like gongs foretelling doom: dull, dark, soundless, day. Each phrase of the description, like each step of the rider's horse, draws us deeper toward the gloom that awaits us.

Nothing could be further from Poe's doom-filled landscape than the following passage, which demonstrates how another author uses lighting, music and language to evoke "something in the air." The where and when of the setting are straightforward, facts any writer might include: a garden on Long Island Sound; summer nights during the 1920s. But this isn't just any writer. It's F. Scott Fitzgerald, whose combination of lush imagery and musical language evokes an atmosphere that exudes sensuality.

> There was music from my neighbor's house through the summer nights. In his blue gardens men and girls came

and went like moths among the whisperings and the champagne and the stars . . .

. . . The last swimmers have come in from the beach now and are dressing upstairs; the cars from New York are parked five deep at the drive, and already the halls and salons and verandas are gaudy with primary colors and hair shorn in strange new ways and shawls beyond the dreams of Castile. The bar is in full swing and floating rounds of cocktails permeate the garden outside until the air is alive with chatter and laughter and casual innuendo and introductions forgotten on the spot and enthusiastic meetings between women who never knew each other's names.

The lights grow brighter as the earth lurches away from the sun and now the orchestra is playing yellow cocktail music and the opera of voices pitches a key higher. Laughter is easier, minute by minute, spilled with prodigality, tipped out at a cheerful word. The groups change more swiftly, swell with new arrivals, dissolve and form in the same breath—already there are wanderers, confident girls who weave here and there among the stouter and more stable, become for a sharp, joyous moment the center of a group and then excited with triumph glide on through the sea-change of faces and voices and color under the constantly changing light.

—from *The Great Gatsby*

In chapter five we discussed how every writer possesses a constellation of images, certain words and images that work together to form his personal vision. Each work of prose or poetry also contains a constellation of images that reflects an overall vision. In the Fitzgerald passage, visual images dot the description like individual stars in a night sky: garden, moths, blue, yellow, champagne, salons, sun, verandas, wanderers. At the most basic level, Fitzgerald's choice of images illustrates Aristotle's "proper and special name of a thing," each star in the constellation flickering with gaiety, mystery, and romance.

Each of his images, seen alone, shines a small light on the scene, but it is the larger pattern they form, the constellation of images, that illuminates the atmosphere.

In terms of lighting, Fitzgerald's colors are primary and bright; even the cocktail music is yellow. But as we said earlier, lighting isn't everything. Just as the atmosphere in my townhouse isn't complete without the music drifting down from hidden speakers, so the atmosphere of Gatsby's parties cannot be evoked solely through visual clues. Without the music of Fitzgerald's language playing in the background, the visual images cannot voice their tunes. Read the first sentences aloud and you'll almost hear the sibilant whispers of partygoers and moth wings. A few lines later, the whisperings strengthen and brighten to become the "chatter and laughter and casual innuendo" that finally explodes into an "opera of voices" pitched in an even brighter, more joyous key.

But as musically evocative as Fitzgerald's diction is, it's his luxurious syntax that choreographs the scene. Like the liquid movement of the partygoers, his sentences "swell with new arrivals, dissolve and form in the same breath." Fitzgerald's long, languid rhythms rise and fall seamlessly, then "with triumph glide on through the sea-change of faces and voices and color under the constantly changing light." His language is as opulent as the women's costumes and as free-flowing as the champagne, continuing breathlessly to the end of the passage.

As readers, we may eventually forget Fitzgerald's colorful and musical descriptions, but we probably won't forget the atmosphere of his fictional dream. Long after the last guest has departed and we've closed the covers on the novel, something— a fragrance, a snatch of song, a feeling—will remain in the summer air.

ATTITUDE AND TONE

Nothing has gotten me into more trouble—in my personal life or in my writing—than tone. "Don't use that tone of voice with me," warned my father before sending me to my room. I'd lie on my bed, plucking at the chenille spread and trying to figure out what I'd said to make him so angry. Looking back I see that it wasn't *what* I'd said but rather the way I'd said it—my inflection, the lift of my left eyebrow, the smug smirk. Although the words themselves were innocent enough, my tone was sarcastic, disrespectful or simply mean-spirited. It was *tone* that cinched my doom.

Years later, when I'd finally scraped together enough courage to send one of my stories out into the world, it was returned with a note from the editor. "Your story generated a lot of discussion. Your characters are well drawn, their actions believable, and the climax just right. But the tone of the story troubles us. It seems too playful for the subject matter—flippant, perhaps? We can't quite put our finger on the tonal problem, but in the end it was serious enough to keep us from publishing the story."

There it was again—the tone-beast, snarling my chances and sending me, defeated, to my room. This time, though, I couldn't blame it on body language. The problem lay in the inflection of my words as they appeared on the page. Had I been trying so hard to avoid sentimentalizing my subject that I ended up poking fun at it instead? I hadn't meant to make light of the narrator's situation, but as I reread the story I saw what the editor had seen, and I despaired.

Problems in tone are perhaps the most difficult literary problems to solve. It's one thing to change details of setting, characters or plot, or to revise a story's prose to make it more lucid, lyrical or rhythmic. But changing the tone of a story requires reconsidering each sentence, description and snatch of dialogue. In my case, revising the tone-plagued story meant that I had to interrogate every part of the story, looking for places where my tone—overly playful? too flippant?—had contaminated the fictional dream.

Although tone is not synonymous with attitude, our attitude shapes the tone of our descriptions. When we describe, we are revealing not only the qualities of the subject itself but also our attitude toward it. Tone is our personal comment—usually implied rather than stated—toward our subjects, characters and readers. And the most obvious way to reveal our attitude toward the subject we're describing is through our word choice.

How Diction Affects Tone

Since tone refers not to *what is said* but rather *how it is voiced*, tone is concerned less with denotation (the dictionary meanings of a word) than with connotation (what we've referred to previously as the overtones a word acquires over time). In chapter three we discussed how choosing words that call forth a significant image, attitude and emotion requires moving beyond mere accuracy. Let's say you're describing your neighbor's front yard, which is filled with plants and flowers. Depending on your attitude toward the yard, you could describe it as overgrown, out-of-control, natural, weedy, fertile, flourishing, chaotic, savage, unrestrained, junglelike or lush. Any of those adjectives would accurately *denote* the yard's qualities, but each word has a slightly different connotation.

To see how tone affects the vocabulary of your descriptions, choose one subject—an object, person or place—and write three separate descriptions of that subject, based on three different attitudes you might feel toward it. Do not change the basic facts about your subject. If the man you're describing is six feet tall and weighs one hundred thirty pounds, don't alter the physical details. Instead, alter the words you use to impart those qualities. For instance, he might be described as slender, skinny, thin, reedlike, Ichabod Crane-ish, lean, lanky, bony, scrawny, narrow or youthfully fit. Your descriptions could also include details about the character's actions, surroundings, and belongings—all the elements we discussed in the chapter on characterization.

When you're finished writing the three descriptions, ask a reader to respond with a word that best suits the tone of each passage, a word like one of these: admiring, solemn, condescending, awed, nostalgic, satiric, playful, sarcastic, bitter, hostile, admiring, apathetic, outraged, friendly, straightforward, evasive, lofty, elevated or strident. You may be surprised that the attitude you intended to reveal was not the tone your reader "heard" as he read your work. The tone of your descriptions can be altered by factors other than word choice, factors such as the *sound* of your words, the cadences of your language, or the psychic distance between you and your subject.

What the Dog Hears

Several years ago at the Bread Loaf Writers' Conference, Ellen Bryant Voigt described tone as "what the dog hears" or "what we hear through motel walls." The main point of her lecture was that tone resides predominantly in sound. Voigt is a poet for whom the music of words is as important as their meanings; her poems marry sound to sense. She is, in fact, a trained musician, so when she speaks of tone, I immediately think of music. Musical tone refers to the distinct pitch, volume, color or duration of a sound. We speak of sweet tones, muddy tones, clear or bell-like tones—even pear-shaped tones. (My college voice teacher taught me to visualize a ripe pear and to allow my sound to rise from that pear. Although the technique didn't help me win the music scholarship, it made for some interesting dreams.)

Singers vary the tone of a musical phrase by prolonging it, shortening it, pitching it higher or lower, making it louder (toning it up) or softer (toning it down), or changing its sound color (breathy, harsh, resonant, liquid). As writers we can control the tone of our descriptions not only through the words we choose but by the way we "sing" them. In chapter three we were introduced to Aristotle's principle of "a musical naming"—that is, how to choose individual words and phrases based on their sound qualities. And in our discussion of the senses in chapter four, we saw how to employ musical language to evoke the sounds of our fictional dreams. We can apply these same principles to control the *tone* of our descriptions.

Look back at the three descriptions you wrote earlier in the chapter, the ones that revealed three different attitudes toward the same subject. Notice the sound qualities of the words you used. Did you use soft, soothing consonants in one description and harsh, cacophonous consonants in another? Did you use deep-toned, solemn vowels in one description and high-pitched vowels in another? What about the lengths and rhythms of your phrases? Did one description gallop while the other minced, step by step, toward its end?

In the following descriptions the basic facts of the scene—a woman washing dishes while her children play outside—do not change. But the tones of the descriptions are miles apart:

> She watches through the kitchen window the comings and goings of her children as one by one the dinner dishes slide from her hands and into the steaming dishwater, one plate still holding the memory of potatoes and gravy.

> Saucers clatter. Cups clank. Platters rattle. She grabs a plate, scrubs its crusted skin. Dried potato. Gravy. Outside the window her kids scream and scatter.

Although some of the tonal difference between the passages is due to word choice, the sounds of the words and the rhythms of the sentences also shape the mood of the two descriptions.

We've seen how Poe uses sound and rhythm to evoke a sense of gloomy foreboding and how Fitzgerald "plays" his language to create the sensual gaiety of a summer party. As you review the descriptions in your stories or poems, looking for places where tone has gone astray, don't just *look* at the words, noting their denotations and connotations. *Listen* to their musical pitch, color and volume, and to the rhythms and durations of your phrases. Since tone resides not only in what you say but in how you say it, you can't ignore those messages even a dog can understand. Like muffled voices you hear through motel walls, the tones of your descriptions permeate your story's inner boundaries.

Tone and Psychic Distance

In chapter seven we introduced the principle of psychic distance—what John Gardner defines as "the distance that the reader feels between himself and the events in the story"—and discussed how shifts in psychic distance can erode the fictional dream. It's significant that Gardner refers to what a reader *feels* rather than what a reader intellectualizes. When we feel distanced from a story, as readers or as writers, it's hard to fully explain our reaction. Still, there are several ways to tease out why some stories or poems pull us close while others keep us at arm's length.

Besides altering our story's point of view (a subject we've dealt with earlier), the most obvious way to establish and control psychic distance is to alter the physical distance between the subjects we're describing and ourselves—or, if we're using a character-narrator, between the character and the subject being described. In *Rich in Love,* Josephine Humphreys uses physical distance to shape her descriptions while also revealing emotional changes in her narrator, a teenaged girl named Lucille.

Early on in the novel, Lucille is helping her father repair the roof on the family home. On the lawn below, Lucille's older sister, Rae, is lying on her back sunbathing. As Lucille watches, Rae's new husband approaches, and it soon becomes clear that Rae and Billy are preparing to move, as Lucille's father describes it, into "that honeymoon stage" that "looks possibly explosive." Lucille watches the scene at a psychic distance that mirrors her physical distance. At this point in the story, her new brother-in-law is simply a man, one whose motives for marrying her sister are, at this point, suspect. Lucille's description of the scene is almost clinical in its factual reporting:

> Billy's shoes looked like some kind of military boots, heavy-soled and old, stiff as wood. With one toe he nudged her side. Her arm was as fast as a sprung trap, grabbing the boot and twisting it as she rolled her body. Billy was off guard. Rae rolled into the grass with his foot in her hands, and he fell next to her.

Later in the book, Lucille realizes not only that Billy's motives toward her sister are pure but that he is exactly the kind of man she herself could love. As the physical distance between her and Billy shortens, the psychic distance shortens as well.

> I admit it had once crossed my mind that he had gotten
> Rae pregnant on purpose in order to marry her. But
> suddenly I could see that he was not that sort of person.
> I saw it only now because I had not been close to him
> before. Now with his face two feet from mine in the
> moonlight, I saw the planes of his cheeks, the wrinkle
> between his eyes, telling what kind of person he was:
> one that can lose himself to another.

If you want the reader to feel intimately related to your subject, try a close-up shot. Describe the character, object or scene
as if it were positioned directly in front of your eyes, close
enough to touch. Let the reader see the hand-etched signature
on the bottom of the wooden bowl or the white strip on the
divorcée's finger where a wedding ring once lay. Let him smell
the heaviness of the milking barn after a night of rain, hear the
squeak of the farmer's rubber boots. If you want to get even
closer, take the reader inside a character's body and let him
experience her world—the reeling nausea of Lydia's first morning sickness, the tenderness of her breasts, the metallic taste in
her mouth—from the inside out.

Then, when you need to establish distance, to remove the
reader from the scene as Shirley Jackson did in "The Lottery,"
pull back. Describe your object from a great distance. The
wooden bowl is no longer a hand-crafted, hand-signed original,
or if it is, you can't tell from where you're standing. The preg-
nant woman is no longer Lydia-of-the-tender-breasts; she's one
of dozens of other faceless women seated in the waiting room
of the county clinic.

As you vary the physical distance between your describer and
the subjects being described, you may find that your personal
connection with your subjects is altered. Physical closeness often presages emotional closeness. Consider how it is possible
that kind and loving men (like my father, who served in three
wars) are capable of dropping bombs on "enemy" villages. One
factor is their physical distance from their targets. The scene
changes dramatically when they face a villager eye to eye; no
longer is the enemy a tiny dot darting beneath the shadow of

their planes, or a blip on the radar screen. No, this "enemy" has black hair flecked with auburn and a scar over her left eyebrow; she's younger than the wives they left behind.

If you sense that your story calls for a closer, more sympathetic attitude toward the subjects you're describing, try positioning yourself closer to them. The angle of your position is as important as the distance between you and your subject. The psychic distance we feel when Lucille is on the roof, looking down on her sister and brother-in-law, is due in part to her position—a physically superior one. At this point in the story she is wary of Billy's motives, and her stance of judgment matches her bodily stance. But when she's standing eye to eye with him, she is on equal footing: one human being to another. Positioning ourselves, physically and psychologically, on the same plane with our subjects can help us avoid what Gardner refers to as "frigidity" in our writing, one of the "faults of soul" he warns against. Frigidity is coldhearted failure to respond on a deep, human level to the characters and events of our story.

Sometimes, however, our stories require us to view our subjects from an ironic distance. In the passage from *The Bonfire of the Vanities* we quoted in chapter six, Tom Wolfe describes his character's wife from a very unflattering angle. Actually, it's not the *wife* we meet but rather her broad backside looming huge in its flannel gown as she crawls to the edge of the bed—hardly the way most of us would wish to be publicly introduced. This description, like others in Wolfe's novel, are signals that the author is viewing his characters with irony.

If you find you're so personally involved with your subjects that you're unable to describe them effectively, it may be time for you to step back and view the big picture. This repositioning may provide a fresh perspective on your subject, suggesting possibilities for humor, irony or even pathos, qualities which may have been previously hidden from your view.

Temporal positioning is another technique for manipulating psychic distance in our writing. Setting a story in a time or place far removed from us can distance our reader psychologically from the story's events. Although some writers of fantasy or historical fiction manage to pull us close to the human drama, for the most part, the further our story is removed in space and time, the more psychic distance our readers will feel. "Once upon a time," begins James Thurber's *The Princess and the Tin Box*, "in a far country . . ."

Reading his first words, we escape to the never-never of fairy tales—to a time that never was and a place like nothing we've ever known. As the story continues, Thurber maintains his fairy-tale distance through simple diction and formal, balanced sentences—no pyrotechnics here. His rhythms are the time-worn rhythms of the campfire storyteller or the parent lulling a restless child to sleep:

> . . . there lived a king whose daughter was the prettiest princess in the world. Her eyes were like the cornflower, her hair was sweeter than the hyacinth, and her throat made the swan look dusty."

Although his language is simple and straightforward, his similes soar to hyperbole. This is no ordinary daughter. She's a princess! And not just any princess. This princess is so beautiful she puts even the most brilliant natural beauties—cornflower, hyacinth and swan—to shame. Because Thurber describes her in ideal, unrealistic terms, we sense that this is not a drama we will enter fully. It is, we begin to see, not a drama at all but a fable whose distant tone is sustained by the elements Thurber so skillfully employs: first, the faraway setting of time and place; then the carefully measured prose of the formal storyteller; and finally, the creation of characters who emerge not as living breathing entities but rather as props to support the fable. Thurber purposely manipulates psychic distance to keep us at arm's length from the story, which is precisely the proper distance a fable requires.

SOMETHING AFOOT: THEME, IDEA AND DESIGN

Talking about theme always makes me edgy. I never liked writing the "themes" my junior high school teachers assigned, those weekly compositions I'd plump and pad—how do you say five hundred words about nothing?—then recopy in standard black ink onto college-ruled sheets. When I entered high school, the notion of theme shape-shifted as I was forced to memorize the four basic themes of literature (man vs. man, man vs. nature, man vs. society, man vs. himself) and apply them to whatever novel or short story our English class was studying. An avid reader since kindergarten, after three years of deciphering theme I found myself unable to enter even the most compelling story without hearing the theme-beast huffing menacingly in my ear.

I escaped to college, hoping to fall back into the fictional dream. But the theme-beast was waiting for me at the classroom door. More ferocious than ever, he now sported horns, a tail and a thick leathery hide. "Using D.H. Lawrence's 'The Horse Dealer's Daughter,' " he hissed, "trace the theme of man's destiny as it relates to love. Cite passages to back up your thesis, but include only those elements of characterization, setting, plot and imagery that support your discussion of theme."

It took me many years to learn to live in harmony with the theme-beast, to understand that theme was a naturally occurring element of any successful story or poem, not just a concept English teachers had invented solely to frustrate me. I came to see how theme shaped the big picture, as did atmosphere and tone, those other literary beasts that had stalked my past. Reading back over my work, I was astounded to discover that even *my* stories and poems, the tales I'd spun at my desk and in my dreams, had themes. I hadn't meant for such a thing to happen; the themes had simply emerged, natural outgrowths of my descriptions of characters, settings and events.

In our earlier discussion we referred to atmosphere as the "something in the air" that contributes to the big picture. Theme could also be defined in those words, although I prefer to think of theme not as the feeling or mood that floats mysteriously around the edges of the story but rather as "something afoot," the hidden pattern that lies beneath a story's surface. Theme is the underside of the weaving, the design we may not see until we turn the story over.

We don't have to, of course. Like a beautifully woven shawl, a story or poem can be appreciated simply for its surface beauty and for the warmth it provides to our bodies and spirits. We don't have to turn the story over and admire the warp and woof, the underlying arrangement of color, line and pattern woven beneath its surface. But if we do, we may discover another design, one as fascinating as the surface design of character, setting and plot that first caught our eye.

The main theme or idea of a story may appear as an echo, like the musical theme that underscores a motion picture, its tune resurfacing now and again with slight variations. In William Faulkner's *As I Lay Dying,* one of the recurring musical themes is the song of Cash's saw as he builds his mother's coffin. At different points in the book, almost every character describes the sound of the saw, each in his own voice and with his own inimitable rhythms. Jewel describes the sound as "that godamn adze going One lick less. One lick less." Cora says simply, "It sounds like snoring." And Darl's description is heightened by Faulkner's placement of the words on the page:

> I go on to the house, followed by the
> Chuck. Chuck. Chuck.
> of the adze.

In chapter three we spoke of the importance of taking pains to describe the things of your story, of performing those menial tasks that convince the reader that characters, places, objects and events actually exist within the fictional world you're creating. Sometimes these tasks feel repetitive, for any successful piece of writing is a result of small cumulative strokes. It's not enough to say something once and be done with it, trusting the reader will remember the detail, attach meaning to it and be satisfied. So Faulkner doesn't stop with one description of the saw, or even with two or three. He weaves one description after another into the fabric of the story so that a pattern begins to emerge. The saw takes on a life of its own, moving from the realm of isolated image to the realm of motif.

Like a repeated scroll in an architectural design or a significant phrase in a musical composition, the noise of the saw contributes to the story's overall design. Sometimes pages go by
before Faulkner mentions the saw again; sometimes, whole
chapters. Between descriptions of the saw the story progresses,
and for a while we forget about the coffin Cash is building.
Then suddenly there it is again, the sound of the saw in the
background, reminding us that, yes, the coffin *will* get finished
and yes, the family *will* eventually bury Addie.

A motif often suggests the underlying idea of a story or poem.
In chapter nine we discussed O'Connor's use of the hat motif
in "Everything That Rises Must Converge." The hat was not
the theme of the story; rather, it was the recurring element that
not only moved the plot along but also suggested the theme of
reversal and loss. An image that appears and reappears in a
story or poem is like a colored thread in a weaving. It is not the
whole design, but it is an organizing element, and if we follow
its path we can begin to see how the larger design is formed.

Sometimes the motif is revealed through chapter titles or
other large organizational elements. The main ideas and
themes of E. Annie Proulx's novel *The Shipping News* are woven
chiefly through chapter titles that suggest mariner's knots
("Love Knot," "The Mooring Hitch," "Strangle Knot") and
by the descriptions that accompany each term. In the same way,
the theme of Terry Tempest Williams's *Refuge: An Unnatural
History of Family and Place* is shaped by section headings named
for birds ("Whistling Swan," "Red-Shafted Flicker") associated
with the Great Salt Lake.

A snake is the visual motif that slides in and out of a story by
Ervin D. Krause. "The Snake" is brief, no more than 2,600
words, but Krause's descriptions of the snake comprise about a
third of the story, and each description weaves the story's theme
a bit tighter. The narrator is an unnamed man plowing a field
with a tractor. The other character is his eleven-year-old nephew
(also unnamed) who is described as having blue eyes and
"finely spun blonde hair and a smooth and still effeminate
face"—in short, the picture of innocence.

When the snake first appears in the field's furrow, the man stops the tractor to avoid hitting the snake. After conceding that he'd never much liked snakes, and as a child had even killed them, he goes on to describe this particular snake as "clean and bright and very beautiful." When the snake refuses to move, the man gets off the tractor and follows the snake, intrigued by its beauty,

> . . . the brilliant colors on its tubular back, the colors clear and sharp and perfect, in orange and green and brown diamonds the size of a baby's fist down its back, and the diamonds were set one within the other and interlaced with glistening jet-black . . .

The man picks up the snake, caressing it with his hand, which "usually tanned and dark" looked "pale beside it." He speaks with reverence to the snake, swearing that "I couldn't kill you. You are much too beautiful." He is amazed at how strikingly the colors of the snake contrast with the black earth and his own pale skin. It's difficult not to notice the suggestion of Eden's paradise emerging in Krause's descriptions: newly turned soil, warm morning, pale hands, a beautiful snake with a forked tongue. Having rescued the snake, the man retreats into a blissful innocence, feeling "good and satisfied."

But as we all know, paradise never lasts, and when the snake's "sharp, burning colors" are described as standing out against the soil "like a target," we know the end is near. What surprises us, though, is that it is the smiling blue-eyed boy who bears the "fierce mark of brutality," stomping the snake to death. The man, astounded and angered by the boy's action, reprimands him: "This snake was very beautiful. Didn't you see how beautiful it was?"

Yes, the snake was beautiful. *Was.* What a difference the past tense verb makes. Eden is no more, as Krause's next description shows:

> The fire of the colors was gone; there was a contorted ugliness now; the colors of its back were dull and

gray-looking, torn and smashed in, and dirty from the boy's shoes. The beautifully-tapered head, so delicate and so cool, had been flattened as if in a vise, and the forked tongue splayed out of the twisted, torn mouth.

Because the ending of the story is so wrenching, an ending every reader should experience for himself, I won't divulge it except to say that the snake, though dead, will continue to shape the story's outcome. And the motif of the snake, sliding in and out of view, will eventually lead us to turn the story over and view its underlying theme: every person, however young or innocent, old or wise, is capable of evil that can forever reshape landscapes, turning even the palest hands a guilty red.

While we're writing our own stories, it's probably best not to focus on issues of theme and structure, at least in the early stages of the process. "One world at a time," said Thoreau, and most writers would agree. It takes enough concentration, energy and imagination simply to describe the world of the story without worrying about what the story looks like underneath. To keep the fictional dream alive, we must first train our eye on the people, places, objects and events of the story, describing what we see. If we proceed backwards, focusing first on the theme of the story or on other structural elements, we risk writing a story no one will want to read. Yes, the underside of the shawl might be intricately woven, but if no one picks it up, if no one throws it over her shoulders, what good is it? The surfaces of our weaving must be durable and beautiful; the story must come first.

THE BIG EAR

If we had a keen vision and feeling of all ordinary human life, it would be like hearing the grass grow and the squirrel's heart beat and we should die of that roar which lies on the other side of silence.

—George Eliot, *Middlemarch*

Throughout this book we've talked about paying attention to the world around us, being present in the moment and training our eyes to see the world in new ways. But attention is also accomplished through the ears; the French *attention* means "to listen." In the title story of Robin Hemley's collection *The Big Ear*, a twelve-year-old boy orders a listening device from a gag catalog (the boy is fond of gag items and employs them often on his unsuspecting victims). When the boy aims the Big Ear in the direction of an object or person, the sound from the object is amplified. Even situated far from his subject, the boy can eavesdrop on conversations and hear sounds a naked ear could never detect, such as the "dry rattle, then a crumbling sound" of dead leaves being stripped from a branch. The Big Ear can even penetrate windows and walls.

For a long time after I read Hemley's story, I couldn't stop thinking about the boy and his Big Ear. At first I just enjoyed being in his company, laughing at his brazen antics; what gall! But the more I listened in on the world his Big Ear was amplifying, the more sympathy I felt for the boy. (One mark of a successful comic story is when you find yourself laughing and crying at the same time.) At one point I wanted to climb into the pages of the book, kiss the boy's forehead the way his babysitter had, and murmur words of comfort. *Yes,* I would whisper, *sometimes we hear things we don't want to hear, things a child shouldn't hear, and it changes us for the rest of our lives.*

Later, when my reader self left me and my writer self appeared (and quick on her heels, my teacher self, God save us all), the Big Ear seemed to lift from the page and float in the space above my head. It was no longer simply a contraption a boy ordered from a catalog; it had been transported into symbol. As I told you earlier, I'm not overly fond of symbols. Too often they're merely grafted onto a story or poem, and the seams show. But when symbols grow naturally from the world of the real—in this case, the concrete and sensory world of which Hemley's story is made—I let them have their say.

Here's what this one said: Writers need to grow the Big Ear. We need it to hear the world around us, especially those small sounds that ordinarily get drowned out. With a Big Ear, we can penetrate the walls of our characters' homes, overhear what they're saying not only to their wives and daughters but to themselves. We can eavesdrop on secrets, the natural and manmade mysteries usually withheld from us.

Aimed in the right direction and focused to a concentrated point, the Big Ear can also silence the noise of the world—the verbal hysteria of radio and television, the babble of advertisers, even the numbing chatter of what the Chinese call the "monkey mind" inside each of us. If we can silence the chatter, clear our internal air waves, we will be more able to hear the voice of the poem, story or essay whispering its secret. As writers, we need to find ways to live within the silence, rather than always hurrying to fill it up with noise, music, words—even those written words we labor so hard to produce. As Nietzsche once wrote, "The author must keep his mouth shut when his work starts to speak."

Yet even when we're able to silence the white noise and train our attention on our subject—the physical world, or the world of the imagination—we may not receive a clear message. At one point in "The Big Ear," the boy thought he heard a man ask, "Are you going to salad control tonight?" As writers, sometimes all we'll be able to make out is a tone, a feeling, a mere approximation of sense. It may appear as static, a distant drone, a rumble or screech. When questioned about her creative process, Flannery O'Connor answered that no, she never heard voices, only "something that might be a continuing muttering snarl like cats courting under the house."

Occasionally, however, the voice will come through loud and clear. Too clear. Our main character begins speaking in a voice that turns the whole story on its head, canceling out everything that's gone before and sending us back, emptied, to the writing desk. Or our theme, our message, what we thought we knew without a doubt, begins to whisper its secret. It's what we most feared: Truth, with a capital "T." Mother Truth having her say—surrounded by all the little truths, her lowercase children, biting and scratching and tugging at our sleeves. We had thought we'd slide through this one, an easy in and out, no one gets hurt, then suddenly the story is dusting for prints and they're ours. Description has tricked us into telling the truth not only about our world but about ourselves.

The Big Ear is a necessary tool for anyone attempting to describe the physical world or the world of the imagination. It helps concentrate our attention, block out distractions and provide access to the mysteries hidden beneath the surface. But these gifts are not granted free and clear. In exchange, we must pay the price of increased awareness. Like the boy in "The Big Ear," we may overhear what we could have happily done without, something that changes forever the way we navigate our world.

In giving our attention to the thing itself—the sight or smell or taste or sound or texture—we may forget to say what we originally thought we wanted, or needed, to say, some thought or purpose that probably calcified years ago. We become so involved in bringing forth the qualities of the thing itself that we are thrown headlong into the present moment. The roar, the squeak, the corduroy, the itch of it so fully consumes us that we can't stop to think of what it all means—or what our inner censors have warned us not to say. We no longer have to struggle to force breath into our description. Suddenly it gasps and sputters. It begins to breathe on its own.

EXERCISES

1. As an experiment in varying the rhythms and duration of your sentences (or your poetry lines), try writing "grammatical rhymes" modeled on another writer's words. In a grammatical rhyme, you imitate the rhythmic and syntactic structures of a piece while using your own words. Don't worry about reproducing the sense of the passage; pay attention only to the structure of the lines. Here's a brief passage from Richard Selzer's essay "Four Appointments With the Discus Thrower," followed by my grammatical rhyme, my imitation of Selzer's syntactic structures:

In the evening, I go once more to that ward to make my rounds. The head nurse reports to me that Room 542 is deceased. She has discovered this quite by accident, she says. No, there had been no sound. Nothing. It's a blessing, she says.

In my dream, I stumble yet again over the weeds to get to him. The doggy moon barks to me that my boy is gone. "I have sniffed it through my nose," it says. "Yes, there will be no boy. Never. That's the end," it barks.

2. A simpler variation of exercise one is to type (or write out, in longhand) a passage of prose you admire for its style. One August, mired in my own syntactic rut, I typed several chapters of *War and Peace*. After stretching my muscles in this way, I was limbered up enough to try some cadences of my own.

3. Write a brief physical description of someone you know. In the first version, use lots of deep vowel tones (long *o*, long *u*) and liquid or resonant consonants (*r, l, w, y, m, n, ng, z*). Then rewrite the description changing the deep vowels to light vowels (short *i*, short *a*). Finally, rewrite it using harsh consonants (*k*, hard *g*, hard *c, t, p*) or sibilants (*s, sh, ch*). Notice how the tone of the description changes depending on the sound qualities of your language.

4. In chapter two we suggested wearing headphones as you walk the same route in your neighborhood several times, varying the style of music on each trip to help you visualize the scene in different ways. This same exercise works to musically "color" the scene and help you vary the tone of your description. For instance, if you walk past the schoolyard while listening to Louis Gottschalk's "Cakewalk," you'll get quite a different feeling than you'll get while listening to "Pomp and Circumstance"; one composition is comical, almost slapstick in its energy, while the other is dignified and layered with sentimental associations. The tones of your two descriptions will also be vastly different from each other, affected by the musical score playing beneath the scene.

5. Write an opening paragraph that evokes the atmosphere of a particular scene. Begin with the basics of setting—the where and when. Then add lighting, sound effects, weather and any sensory detail that will contribute to the mood you want the reader to experience. Refer to the passage from "The Fall of the House of Usher" as an example.

6. Sometimes the weather in our story or poem cooperates *too* fully with the story's events, resulting in a hackneyed description. The wedding morning (of course it's June) blooms sunny and mild; the day of the funeral is cold and gray. Try describing an event with weather details that work *against* the mood or tone most readers would expect.

7. If one of the characters in your story is one-dimensional (purely evil, for instance, or too good to be true), change the physical distance or angle from which you're describing him. Move in for a close-up on your villain, showing us an endearing personal trait, or describe your hero from far away or from a physical stance that reveals his all-too-human proportions.

8. In chapter nine I suggested that you break a long description into several smaller sections and then "sprinkle" these sections throughout the story, the way O'Connor sprinkled the hat image throughout "Everything That Rises Must Converge." Try the same technique with a sound image—like the sound of the saw in Faulkner's *As I Lay Dying* or the sound of motorcycles in Mary Hood's "How Far She Went." Start by writing a long description of a sound that is important to your story—ocean waves, a baby's cry, footsteps rustling leaves. Then break the description into three or more short passages. Plant these passages into different parts of the story so that the sound image becomes an echo, the recurring musical theme that plays beneath the story line.

END NOTES,
TOWARD A BEGINNING

This book began with a description of apples in a glass bowl on my table. Those apples are long gone. Some were devoured straight from the bowl. The less perfect ones were stuffed with raisins and stewed. Others were sliced, dusted with sugar and flour and nutmeg, dotted with butter, and folded beneath a fluted crust. A few never made it to mouth or oven. While I wasn't looking, their bodies turned soft and heavily fragrant, bruising from the inside out. I carried them to the garden and laid them on the compost heap.

Now as I prepare to send the book on its way, I reread my words, recalling those two or three descriptions that were delivered into my hand polished and whole, the ones I consumed in one greedy sitting. I remember the flawed ones, too, the sentences that stewed forever in their own juices, and the lumpy, sour paragraphs I peeled and sliced, sweetened and seasoned, baked and fried and dried and pureed—how many ways can you spell *apple?*

I'd expected that when the time came to release the words I'd feel proud but sad, reluctant but relieved, the way I always feel sending a story out into the world, the way I felt walking my niece to the bus stop for her first day of school. "Go on," I said, shooing her toward the bus. "You're a big girl. Up the steps, now."

And yes, I feel all those things, just as I'd expected. What surprises me is not my feelings toward the words I'm sending off but rather my eagerness to return to the compost bin. The descriptions I tossed aside, the words that never made it into the book, have decayed sweetly, storing up heat. Having been returned to the Eden of their beginnings (seed, core, juice, skin), they wait patiently to be resurrected.

When asked which of his many poems was his favorite, William Stafford replied, "I would exchange everything I've written for the next one." Writing is not about endings. Writing is about how nothing is ever lost—not even the clichés we excise with tweezers or the mixed metaphors that arrive, like feuding guests, at the same party, and must be shown to the door. The words I tossed into the compost bin—the description of my second-grade teacher Miss Ranney, who wore a silky blonde bun skewered with chopsticks and whose stocking seams were always straight; the joke about the farmer and the cow; the chapter that refused to roll over and die no matter how hard I tried to kill it—wait to be reborn in a new story or poem. In the beginning was the word. Some things never change.

ABOUT THE AUTHOR

Rebecca McClanahan has published three books of poetry, most recently *The Intersection of X and Y* (Copper Beech Press), as well as a book of lectures and readings, *One Word Deep* (Ashland Poetry Press). She also co-edited a book of poetry by children, *I Dream So Wildly* (Briarpatch Press). Her work has been anthologized in *Pushcart Prize XVIII* and *The Best American Poetry 1998*, and has appeared in numerous periodicals, including *Boulevard, The Georgia Review, The Gettysburg Review* and *The Kenyon Review*. She has received a PEN/Syndicated Fiction Award, the J. Howard and Barbara M.J. Wood prize from *Poetry*, the Carter prize for nonfiction from *Shenandoah* and a Governor's Award for Excellence in Education. She has taught writing for over twenty-five years.

SELECTED BIBLIOGRAPHY

Throughout this book, I've quoted numerous passages of description from novels, short stories, essays and poems that are readily available in most libraries and bookstores. Because I've cited those sources within the text, I've chosen not to include them here. Instead, I've limited the bibliography to writing texts I've referred to and to additional sources that I feel will deepen your exploration into descriptive writing. These sources are organized according to the predominant concerns of *Word Painting*—eye, word, and story.

EYE

Observation, concentration and the creative processes of writers and other artists

Marvin Bell, *Old Snow Just Melting.* University of Michigan Press, 1983.

Olivia Bertagnolli and Jeff Rackham, eds., *Creativity and the Writing Process,* John Wiley & Sons, 1982.

Dorothea Brande, *Becoming a Writer.* Putnam, 1981 (reprinted from 1934).

Annie Dillard, *The Writing Life.* HarperPerennial, 1989.

Betty Edwards, *Drawing on the Right Side of the Brain.* J.P. Tarcher, 1979.

Reginald Gibbons, ed., *The Poet's Work: 29 Masters of 20th Century Poetry on the Origins and Practice of Their Art.* Houghton Mifflin, 1979.

Anne Lamott, *Bird by Bird.* Pantheon, 1994.

Rollo May, *The Courage to Create.* W.W. Norton, 1975.

Flannery O'Connor, *The Habit of Being,* edited by Sally Fitzgerald. Farrar, Straus & Giroux, 1979.

Tillie Olsen, *Silences.* Delacorte Press/Seymour Lawrence, 1978.

Peggy Whitman Prenshaw, ed., *Conversations with Eudora Welty*, Washington Square, 1984.

Rainer Maria Rilke, *Letters on Cezanne*. Fromm, 1985; and *Letters to a Young Poet*, Norton, 1934.

William Stafford, *You Must Revise Your Life*. University of Michigan Press, 1986.

Janet Sternburg, ed., *The Writer on Her Work*. Norton, 1980.

Anne Truitt, *Prospect: The Journal of an Artist*. Scribner, 1996.

Alberta T. Turner, ed., *Fifty Contemporary Poets: The Creative Process*. Longman, 1977

Eudora Welty, *One Writer's Beginnings*. Harvard, 1983.

WORD

Shaping the description

Phillip Dacey and David Jauss, eds., *Strong Measures: An Anthology of Contemporary American Poetry in Traditional Forms*. Harper & Row, 1986.

Richard Hugo, *The Triggering Town: Lectures on Poetry and Writing*. W.W. Norton, 1979.

X.J. Kennedy, *An Introduction to Poetry*. Little, Brown and Company, 1966.

James J. Kilpatrick, *The Writer's Art*. Andrews, McMeel & Parker Inc., 1984.

Michael Montgomery and John Stratton, *The Writer's Hotline Handbook: A Guide to Good Usage and Effective Writing*. New American Library, 1981.

Karl Shapiro and Robert Beum, *A Prosody Handbook*. Harper & Row, 1965.

William C. Strunk and E.B. White, *The Elements of Style*, 3rd ed. Macmillan, 1979.

Alberta Turner, *To Make a Poem*. Longman, 1982.

J.E.C. Welldon, translator, *The Rhetoric of Aristotle*. MacMillan and Co., 1886.

William Zinsser, *On Writing Well: An Informal Guide to Writing Nonfiction*, 5th ed. HarperCollins, 1994.

STORY

Writing texts and sources on narrative technique

Carol Bly, *The Passionate, Accurate Story: Making Your Heart's Truth Into Literature*. Milkweed Editions, 1990.

Janet Burroway, *Writing Fiction: A Guide to Narrative Craft*, 3rd ed. HarperCollins, 1992.

E.M. Forster, *Aspects of the Novel*. Harcourt, Brace, Jovanovich, 1956.

John Gardner, *The Art of Fiction: Notes on Craft for Young Writers*. Vintage, 1985.

Philip Gerard, *Creative Nonfiction: Researching and Crafting Stories of Real Life*. Story Press, 1996.

Robin Hemley, *Turning Life Into Fiction*. Story Press, 1994.

Rust Hills, *Writing in General and the Short Story in Particular*. Houghton Mifflin, 1977, rev. 1987.

Milan Kundera, *The Art of the Novel*. Harper & Row, 1986.

Phillip Lopate, *The Art of the Personal Essay: An Anthology From the Classical Era to the Present*. Anchor Books, Doubleday, 1994.

Eve Shelnutt, *The Writing Room: Keys to the Craft of Fiction and Poetry*. Longstreet, 1989.

Gay Talese and Barbara Lounsberry, *Writing Creative Nonfiction: The Literature of Reality*. HarperCollins, 1996.

INDEX